the Queen's Tale

The Summer Country Trilogy
BOOK TWO

Cover artwork "Awen" by Jen Delyth ~ celticartstudio.com
Layout & Design by ZDP Digital Media ~ linkedin.com/in/zacparker

© 2021 Mary Angelon Young. All rights reserved

SAORSA PRESS
PO Box 4100
Chino Valley, Arizona
86323 USA

Contents

Prelude 1

CAMELOT

A Wounded King 27
The Queen's Burden 33

CAERLEON

Return to Cymry 47
The King's Command 53
A Knight's Dilemma 67
Interference Arrives 79
A Lover's Tryst 91
Imbolc 101
The Rending of Veils 111
Words of the Wise 121

BETRAYAL

Return to Camelot 133
The Knights of Lothian 139

Intrigue and Infamy 145
The Chains that Bind 161
Trials and Tribulations 173

AVALON

Refuge 183
Avalon 191
Summer Idyll 201
The Seneschal's Advice 215
Into the Mists 227
Beckery 241
On Toward Camelot 251

CAMELOT

Desperate Hours 261
Truth and Consequence 265
A Healing by the Pool 277
The Hand of Fate 285

EXILE

Caradog and Tegau 303
The Mending of Hearts 317
Caledonia 333

EILEAN ARAINN

A New Life 345

GLASTONBURY
(Ynis Witrin)

Epilogue 361

Prelude

"And what of you, Lancelot?" Gwenhyfar's smile was kind and inviting as she leaned forward with interest, her eyes gleaming in the dim light of the sconces "Tell us your story."

With a lingering glance at the queen, Lancelot reached to stir the coals then took the goblet from Arthur's outstretched hand. Moments slid into timelessness while he gazed into the fire that sizzled and popped. The winter storm that had kept them inside all day still wailed and moaned outside the stone keep. Bright flames licked dark air, making shadows play upon the faces of the king and queen, who sat close to the hearth, warm in their furs. Lifting his cup with a nod, Arthur encouraged his knight to speak and he stirred, as if coming back from some place far away.

"My mother was born on the Isle of Avalon," Lancelot began softly, "Elaine was her name. She was descended from the Old Ones who populated the earth, before the great flood came and drowned the ancient lands of the world. It was their ancestors who placed the standing stones and built the great burial mounds and citadels of stone across these islands, long after that cataclysm, thousands of years ago.

"In those days the tribes of Briton and Alba knew the Old Ones as supernatural beings, whose knowledge was kept alive through the healers and bards and the keepers of wisdom. So it is with my grandmother, Lacine, where my story really begins. In the language of Erin, she called the Old Ones the Aes Sídhe—the shining beings that dwell in fire, water, earth and air, who once took form and lived among the standing stones and the holy mounds. It is known to all that Avalon and the Tor is such a place of magic and power—a portal to the Otherworld."

"When Lacine was only a maid, a druid bard named Dagdan arrived in Avalon at the time of Beltane. They met at the sacred fire on that fateful night, when the two ran from the blaze hand-in-hand to lie among the heather, mingle their kisses and fall in love. Dagdan renounced his druid vows to take Lacine away to the land of his people on the west coast of Erin. There my mother, Elaine, was born to them, and she grew strong running wild on the green hills of the Connemarra Mountains."

"But their peace was not to last, for Lacine was the younger sister of Nimuë, who had ruled in Avalon as the Lady of the Lake longer than anyone could remember. Elaine was only seven years old when Nimuë arrived at their mountain croft, an unexpected and unwelcome visitor. A fierce argument erupted, in which Nimuë insisted that

Elaine must come to know her true nature and learn the ways of Avalon. Finally Lacine relented, and when the Lady of the Lake left with Elaine, my grandmother and Dagdan wept tears of loss and grief, but they could not stop the juggernaut of fate."

He paused a moment, and Arthur poured more of the sweet golden wine of Bretonnia, first for his queen, Gwenhyfar, and then for Lancelot.

"In Avalon, Elaine grew in poise and beauty and knowledge. When she was coming into the blossom of young womanhood, she often wandered the woods and marshes beyond the shallow lake that surrounded Avalon and the Tor.

"One day, as she picked the bluebells that grew thick as the scattered stars of the Milky Way, she encountered a darkly handsome young soldier. He came from the Roman fort, some miles northwest of the Tor, and a child was soon conceived in their woodland trysts. Like her mother before her, Elaine left Avalon. But instead of going west, like Lacine, she traveled east to live across the sea with my father, Ban of Benoic, in the land called Bretonnia."

Lancelot glanced from the king to the queen and saw that their faces were keen and flushed. The night was long, and they basked in the peace that had fallen upon them after the last battle at Badon. The Saxons invaders had been driven away, a certain peace had been made with those Saxons who had settled the land. Now Arthur and his warriors and the people of Briton enjoyed the comforts of plenitude, in an idyll of calm and serenity after a long and terrible war.

The queen appraised the man before her, for he was beautiful to look upon, with thick, waving brown hair that fell to his shoulders and dark eyes that shone like light on polished silver. Her heart went out to him, for Lancelot, despite his talent for leading the men who would give their lives for him upon the battlefield, remained enigmatic and almost solitary. She watched as Lancelot reached to toss a log once again upon the glowing embers, then he settled back as the blaze roared up to wash their faces in gold. When she spoke, Gwenhyfar's voice carried power, yet it was husky and soft as water purling upon sand.

"Lancelot, your eloquence as a storyteller is a gift. We must hear the entire tale." She settled back beside Arthur and lifted the goblet to her lips as the knight continued.

That year, a boy was born in the autumn, at the time of Samhain. He was given an unusual name—Lancelot. The babe's father had been schooled in the Roman way and dreamt of his son becoming a great warrior. Ben was jealous and possessive, and did not allow Elaine to speak of Avalon or her heritage. But in solitary moments, when Ban was nowhere about, Elaine hugged the boy to her breast and whispered.

"Your father is a Celt by blood, but he was trained in the Roman way and wishes you to follow his path. Never forget that you have the blood of the Old Ones in your veins, and your true name is Laëllon."

When he asked for more, his mother was unwilling to explain. "When the time is right, then you will find out the truth of your origins."

As he grew, Laëllon came to know that Elaine was plagued by a great unhappiness. Though he did not know its cause, he sensed that she missed her faraway home. When he was six years old, she died of a sudden ague, and the child heard her handmaidens whisper of a broken heart. Wondering what that could mean, the boy grieved for his mother, crying into his nursemaid's arms.

Some weeks later, a stranger on horseback appeared on a chill and foggy night, just before the evening meal would be served. Ban took pity on the stranger, for she was damp and cold from the misty rain that fell. When Ban asked who she was and from whence she had come, her response was curious.

"My name is Viviane, and I am a here on a quest from a land across the sea."

Ban was suspicious, but reluctantly he gave the guest a room in which to sleep, according to the laws of hospitality of his time and place. When young Lancelot joined them for dinner, Ban saw that the boy and the lady made friends right away. As the evening wore on, the father became agitated, seeing how it was—as if no one was there but the two of them.

When Ban was called away by his chief steward to attend to pressing business, they sat close together by the fire. The boy listened raptly as the lady told him that she was his kinswoman—the sister of his mother's mother—and regaled him with tales of a magical place called Avalon, the Isle of Apples, in a land across the western water.

The next morning when Ban returned, the lady was gone and his boy along with her. Ban raged and sent his servants in a frenzy to search the countryside. They galloped out with lances high and swords at their sides. But there was magic involved, and they returned crestfallen to be harshly rebuked by their master.

In the darkest hour before dawn, Viviane had left with the boy by wagon and traveled swiftly to the mysterious standing stones on the western coast of Bretonnia. There, Viviane bade him to step into a stone circle, and instantly Lancelot was lifted up, swirled about, turned like a leaf in a whirlwind, until he fell to the ground and discovered Viviane holding him in her lap. How it was that there were attendants waiting for them with a wagon at the great sarcen stones, which Viviane called the Elders, he did not know. All he knew was that they were going to Avalon, the magical place of his mother's childhood. Once there, he discovered that Viviane was known as Nimuë, the Lady of the Lake. As he learned and grew, he came to know himself as Laëllon, a boy who ran free upon the Tor, who loved the peaceful orchards, the music and rituals and temples of the Apple Isle.

The years passed until one day, after he had turned ten years, the lady once again changed his life. Her brow was smooth and her eyes were soft as she delivered news that shattered his world.

"It will soon be time for you to leave, Laëllon."

When he begged to stay, her counsel was gentle and firm as she asserted that he must fulfill his destiny. He plied her with questions and all reasons why he should not go, but she remained intractable in her enigmatic way.

"You will see. Your grandmother, Lacine, will teach you now. All will be well, Laëllon."

Within a few weeks they left the gates of Avalon and made their way carefully in a currach across the shallow lake that changed with the tides, then trodding over marshes and traveling by horseback for some days over the moors and a range of low hills. Finally they were back, once again, to Elders, the great stones standing upon a wide plain.

Now he could see that these stones were far more imposing and grand than those in Bretonnia, where—long ago, so it seemed—Laëllon had been spirited away by Nimuë. In awe, he followed her into the great sarcens.

Leaving their horses with her attendant, she meandered through the stones, weaving this way and that, touching one and then another. To Laëllon's eyes, each stone became a living being that awakened to the Lady's touch. When Nimuë found the stone she sought, she murmured in an unknown language that was sweet to his ear.

In a flash of swirling light, he found himself with the Lady of the Lake, standing on grass as green as the emeralds of ancient Babylonia, which she kept in secret and had once shown to him in the temple on Avalon. He stood with mouth agape, gazing in wonder at the soft silver light that shone in the tremulous air.

"Where are we?"

"These are the Connemarra Mountains," Nimuë replied. "We are in Erin, on the sea of Atlan."

Before them was a mountain croft, built of stone with a low thatched roof. A thin wisp of smoke rose from its one chimney, and sheep grazed upon the flanks of verdant hills. As they walked toward the house, a woman with silver hair came forward to greet them. Clutching Nimuë's hand,

Laëllon gazed somberly at her familiar face and the tears of joy and sorrow that glinted in her brown eyes. When the Lady of the Lake spoke, her words were gentle and tender.

"This is your kinswoman, your mother's mother, and my sister, Lacine. She will guard and guide you well."

Laëllon clung to Nimuë as she said goodbye, for he had come to love the Lady of the Lake. Nimuë held him close to her heart and whispered in his ear.

"I know you have lost your mother but four years past, and now you feel that you are losing me and Avalon as well. I too am loath to let you go, Laëllon, but destiny will not be denied. Do not fear, for we will find our way back together again. When you have a great need of me, call me with this talisman," she pressed a small carved bird into his hand, "and I will come."

Ranging across the mountainsides at his grandmother's side, Lancelot grew intimate with sun and sea and with the primordial powers of nature. Lacine was wise and kind and full of strange earthly magic and mysterious skills of the healing arts. In her care Laëllon thrived and developed many unusual qualities. He had a way with beasts and birds, with children and babes, and with the very old. His grandmother encouraged his skill with the harp, and under her guidance his singing voice became as sure and sweet as he was strong and agile.

In the summer of his fourteenth year, his grandfather took him to the harvest festival in the largest village of the region. There Laëllon met the renowned chieftan, Finbar, who filled the boy with tales of warriors and great deeds, and sparked a wanderlust in him. When Finbar asked permission of Dagdan to train the boy, Laëllon begged to go. Though Dagdan objected, speaking of Lacine, Finbar shot a piercing look at the boy, answering gruffly.

"We leave on the morrow for our encampment, in the north of Erin. There is no time for goodbyes."

Remembering the many partings he had endured in his young life, Laëllon resolved that he would return to Connemarra when he was grown into a man. Then he would clasp his grandmother in his arms and whirl her around, and so he begged Dagdan to let him go.

Reluctant, Dagdan returned home to Lacine, who wept and grieved for the loss of her grandson. Once again, the great goddess who ruled their fate had taken a child from her arms. In her heart, she knew full well what he did not—that they would not meet again in this world.

Swept up in the excitement of the adventure, Laëllon soon became absorbed his new life. The word spread among the young warriors that Laëllon not only bested them but eclipsed his master in swordplay and footwork, jousting, knives, wrestling and throwing his opponents in hand-to-hand combat. He was naturally adept with words, played the lyre and sang as well as he wielded a sword. As Nimuë had instructed, he kept secret the faery blood that ran in his veins, which gave him the inborn gift for healing with his hands—when any of the men threw a shoulder or wrenched their backs, Laëllon could restore the bones and muscles to their rightful place.

Finbar was jealous of his talented protégée. He was ruthless with his ward, demanding total obedience, inflicting unjust criticism, and exacting harsh disciplines. Unaware of Laëllon's origins, Finbar would laugh and hide his gibes within a double-edged compliment.

"Are you a warrior or an old woman, peddling potions and herbs? Mayhap you be better trained as a bard! Come now, sir poet," he taunted, giving the boy's shoulder a hard push, "give us a wee limerick."

Finbar was not the only one who was eaten by envy; one of the boys, Mabon, had been an apprentice to the swordmaster for a year before Laëllon came. Mabon took great pleasure in gloating and jeering when the master criticized his best apprentice. One day, when Laëllon was mocked thus by his teacher, Mabon induced the other boys to laugh and poke fun at him until Laëllon was so ashamed that he fell silent and turned away.

Gwenhyfar had followed the story closely, discerning the meaning between the words Lancelot spoke. Now she burst out in praise, "Indeed, you are poet, healer, and warrior, Lancelot—Arthur's first knight whom none can best!"

Arthur also beamed in appreciation and chuckled, "And champion of my queen. We all benefit from your gifts, Lancelot—carry on with the tale, brother. Your eloquence serves you well. What happened next?"

"And then I met Myrrdin." Lancelot shook his head in amazement, eyes shining with the memory.

At sixteen, young Laëllon and several of the boys had accompanied Finbar on a quest—the mystic voyage of an immrama. They sailed with their companions, crossing the narrow sea from the eastern shores of Erin toward the coast of Alba, the land of the Picts, which lay north of Briton. They landed first upon a small island called Eilean Arainn.

The island was rich in many resources, abundant with game and places where grain was cultivated by the tribes that lived there in low, round stone huts with thatched roofs. Finbar's young warriors wandered about, exploring the primordial hills, the mysterious standing stones, and the contours where land met sea. There were druids living in many places on the isle, especially near the standing stones in a place called Machrie Moor, where a village thrived and people grew oats and raised sheep and cattle.

At Machrie Moor, one of the druids attracted Laëllon's attention. He was a man apart from all others, swathed in power and mystery, and his name was Myrrdin Emrys. An accomplished bard, some said the tall druid was a master magician and a master of men as well. His impenetrable silences communicated more than words, and his knowing glance stirred the young warrior in strange ways. In that magnetic attraction, Laëllon recognized his fate; indeed, the very presence of the man answered a deep call of Laëllon's heart, and he began to spend his days in the company of this rare person.

It was the enchanting quality of Myrrdin's songs that revealed what Laëllon suspected: here was another man with the blood of the Old Ones running in his veins. Laëllon carefully broached the subject one day when they were alone.

Myrrdin's response was cryptic. "Those whose blood is of the Old Ones are drawn together."

Trying again, Laëllon ventured. "Master, do you know of a place called Avalon?"

"Yes, I know Avalon, the place you learned as a boy."

Stunned for a moment, Laëllon then eagerly plied the master with questions, but Myrrdin would not explain how he came about such knowledge. After a span of silence, the master spoke in a hoarse and whispery voice.

"Aye, in Myrrdin the old blood runs faint but true."

Laëllon smiled with satisfaction. "True it is, but faint it is not!"

Myrrdin turned away to hide the smile that flickered behind his dark, silver-streaked beard, and he stroked its three long braids with a contemplative brow, his lips pursed. After this, the two men—one very young and one whose age was known to no man—became close companions. The day came when Finbar arrived at their fire near the standing stones, where Myrrdin Emrys was encamped with the young warrior.

"Get your things ready to sail on the morrow," Finbar ordered, glaring at Laëllon, who lifted his chin and stared down at the older man.

"I will not be going with you. We are parting ways, sir."

"I think not, boy. Your grandfather gave you to my guardianship—you are my apprentice." He scowled and set Mabon and another young warrior to advance upon Lancelot. Swords were drawn and clashed, their breath heaved and sweat flew as they parried and thrust, until first blood was drawn—Mabon stood holding his arm, his face blotched with emotion as dark red as the blood that dripped from his fingers.

"Enough!" Myrrdin stepped out tall and forbidding from the shadow of a large ash tree where he had watched, leaning against its trunk. Finbar cast a brooding glance at the dark druid who gazed at him with calm and inscrutable eyes. He tossed a handful of carved pebbles in one hand while with the other he held a long black rowan staff that he pointed at Finbar and said again, softly. "Enough." A menacing presence oozed from the druid, and, seeing the fearsome look that flashed in those cold dark eyes, Finbar called off his lads. They readily sheathed their swords, for they knew that none of them could dissuade Laëllon. It would have been a fight to the death for one of them. With a snarl on his lips, Finbar glared at the druid, but even so he and his apprentices left in haste. Chest still heaving, Laëllon's sword arm relaxed as he watched them scurry away without a backward glance.

Captivated by Myrrdin and ready for adventure, Laëllon followed him to a remote cave by the sea. When they arrived, the druid dropped his bags and sat down, asking Laëllon to gather wood and build a fire. When the fire was crackling and bright, the druid began to sing in a language unknown to the young man. He sang for hours that stretched into days, past dawn and high noon and twilight times. He sang for weeks, stopping only for a few hours' sleep and the necessities that kept him alive.

During this timeless interlude, he took only spring water mixed with wild honey collected by Laëllon in a shallow horn bowl from the wildwoods nearby. As the days passed and the tides came and went, Laëllon learned many of Myrrdin's conjuring songs and sang in complex harmonies with him. Exactly why they were fasting and singing, Myrrdin did not say—nor did Laëllon ask, as he had learned to flow with the enigmatic ways of the druid. He simply did as instructed, and in this way they fell into an easy rhythm that occurred mostly in silence.

Most of the time it rained and gusted outside, while they sat before a small fire in the shelter of the cave, huddled in their woolen cloaks and the sheepskin blankets of their bedrolls. Then, after many days of fasting and singing, they began to search the windy shore for clams that proliferated in the tidal pools. They cracked the shells open easily with their dirks and gulped the slick, salty morsels. When Myrrdin sucked the meat down his throat, he grunted with satisfaction.

Though he could not say exactly what was happening during the weeks that turned into months, Laëllon sensed vast currents of power flowing around them. He sensed that Myrrdin communed with the terrestrial sphere of the earth, the planets circling the sun, and the greater cosmos as well. One rare clear night, the moon was in her phase that the druid called "the horns of the goddess," as he pointed toward the radiant crescent that sailed luminous in the night sky.

"Do you see yon star beside the moon?"

The young man nodded.

"She is the goddess whom the Romans call Venus and the Greeks before them knew as Aphrodite. She has been known by many names in many lands. She is not a star, but a planet—a terrestrial sphere like our own—and she circles around the sun, just as we do now, even as we sit here."

Laëllon stared in wonder at the bright light that shone beside the sliver of moon.

"Those who carry the blood of the Old Ones remember this knowledge—of planets, galaxies, stars and much more. Where and how they learned it is lost now in the mists of time."

The young man peered at the sage with inquisitive innocence. "How old are you, master?"

"Hmnh," Myrrdin grunted. "Older than you can imagine," he muttered with a flicker of a smile. "Older than I should be! Some say I should have died long ago," he chuckled, "but the goddess keeps me alive. She has her reasons."

When asked for more, Myrrdin began to rifle through his bag.

"My time for fasting is done. You have earned a fortune in the coin of the spirit, by keeping watch with me. It will soon be time for me to go."

The young face fell, and his eyes dropped to the ground at the thought of being parted from the wise man. When he found the courage to look up at the druid, he saw that Myrrdin watched him appraisingly. Laëllon straightened his shoulders, becoming uneasy under the druid's weighty gaze.

"Do you want to come with me, then?" Seeing the joy that spread across the young man's features, Myrrdin nodded once, a hint of a smile curving his lips.

"Alright then, let us be gone from this place on the morrow. It has served us well."

The next day after they had broken fast with a few wild oats mixed with hot water and honey, the druid put his reed pipe and conch horn away in the woven bag, along with his wooden bowl and small bronze cooking pot. Laëllon scrambled to pack his own few belongings in his bag, and, throwing it over his shoulder, he strapped on his sword, sheathed his dirk, and checked his two small hidden knives. Lifting his bedroll to his back, he watched as Myrrdin sheathed his dirk in a scabbard and clasped it about his waist, donned his heavy woolen cloak and hoisted the bag and bedroll to his shoulder where his lyre also hung from its strap.

Taking his walking staff in hand, Myrrdin glanced around at the cave while the young man whisked the ground with length of gorse brush. There was no sign of their habitation but a pit of cold ash, and, with a nod from the druid, they were on their way. The two travelers set out northeast over moors and rocky hills, skirting the forbidding, mist-swathed mountain called Goatfell. Finally they came to a dùn—little more than a fortified hill called Lochranza—on the northern shore of the island. There they cajoled a currach from an old fisherman in exchange for a small gold coin, and in this dubious vessel of lashed hides and supple withy branches they sailed for the mainland that lay to the northeast of Eilean Arainn.

Not long after they set foot on Alba, they traveled over land until they reached a vast valley with burial mounds and a circle of ancient standing stones. Many people lived in this valley around a great dùn, which Myrrdin called Dunadd. As they arrived it was clear that everyone knew Laëllon's companion, as he was greeted with an intriguing combination of joy, respect, and what appeared to be fear.

They camped near the stone circle, and, as they settled in, Myrrdin pointed toward the massive rock escarpment to the south.

"That is where the Gaels of Dalriata are coming from Erin—to the village here at Dunadd," he explained. "There is a king's stone atop yon crag, where they stand and proclaim themselves to be king of this land. Indeed, they have a hard fight ahead of them, as some of the tribes—especially the painted people of Alba—do not take so kindly to the Gaels ruling here."

With one hand resting upon a stone, Myrrdin fell silent and looked far away, as if he peered into a distant past.

"You know something of the stones and their magic, do you not?" Myrrdin looked down at the stick in his hands, which he sharpened with swift, short strokes of his dirk.

Laëllon frowned, trying to remember.

"Nothing but a vague memory. It was when the Lady of the Lake came to take me as a lad from Bretonnia to Avalon. And then again, when she took me to Erin. It was many years ago, sir, but I remember that she touched one of those tall stones, and in a flash we were standing on the Tor at Avalon.

"She did it again when we left Avalon and came back to the big sarcen stones, the Elders, she called them, on the great plains near Sorviodunum." He added, "They are the biggest standing stones I have seen."

Myrrdin made a humming sound deep in his throat, then muttered, half to himself. "Nimuë knows well the old ways."

Perplexed but fascinated, Laëllon startled at the sound of the Nimuë's secret name, but he waited, a question written upon his face. After a while the druid stirred, pulled gently upon his braided beard.

"Yes, I know the Lady of the Lake. She is known to me as Nimuë, but she called herself Viviane when she came to retrieve you from the Roman Gaulois."

He paused to look toward the Tor, ignoring the surprise on Laëllon's face.

"The Old Ones erected these stones, in a long-forgotten age. They had immense power and purpose in their season of time, many epochs past."

Laëllon remained still, hardly breathing for fear the druid would stop speaking. He waited patiently as Myrrdin scratched his beard, considering his next words.

"We terrestrial creatures have fallen asleep, Laëllon. Some say we have fallen from grace. But either way, in these times, our minds have grown weak, and human beings no longer comprehend the great stone circles. We do not perceive their magic."

Though Laëllon urged him on with questions, he would say no more. The next day they left, walking south along the shore toward a place called Earra Ghàidheal, where the druid sang songs and performed magic tricks at a wayfaring inn to earn them some sturdy horses. Slowly they made their way south on these beasts, passing by Luguvalium and traveling into the land of the Cymry, crossing mountains and rivers and going around the Severn Sea until at last they came upon a pleasant land that Myrddin called the Summer Country, at the northern edge of Dumnonia. It was a place of beauty, with rolling hills, many rivers, and lush forests.

One afternoon before dark they were camped by a rocky ledge at the curve of a streamlet that meandered through level marshes into the expanse of a shallow tidal lake. Laëllon had lit a small fire, and they sat together in a peaceful silence as the young man looked wistfully at small hills that rose like islands out of the lake. His eyes focused upon one in particular, which stood much higher than the others, rising up to a green point in the distance.

Toward the sea to the west, the sky was awash in the amber gold of the sun's last light. After a time, Myrrdin gestured toward the hill.

"You are drawn to yonder Tor, are you not?"

Laëllon replied, "Yes, it has been in our sights all day. Somehow I feel I know it well."

"You do. Avalon resides within the mists of yon shallow lake, at the foot of the Tor. Nimuë took you to live there as a child."

Laëllon looked at the sage, eyebrows raised in surprise.

"This morning," he turned toward the strange hill, "when the Tor first came into sight, my heart told me it was Avalon, the home of my childhood." He swallowed hard to calm the flutter of excitement in his belly. "I did not know if I would ever see it again."

The druid flashed him a lingering, sideways glance. "You will know it again. It is your fate that draws you there."

Laëllon admitted, "Tis my kinswoman Nimuë that I miss. She took me to her heart after my mother died. I loved Avalon as well, and my heart is glad to return there."

"Aye," Myrrdin muttered, "tis the sweetest place in this world." The druid poked at the fire with a stick, then scratched his beard with one hand.

"There is no place on earth like Avalon, though it has changed over time. Now its inhabitants are a mix of people—descendants of the Old Ones, like Nimuë, as well as the many Celtic tribes and even Picts from Alba and Gaels from Erin. But it is Nimuë, the Lady of the Lake, who is the spirit of Avalon."

The druid's odd chuckle caused Laëllon to look sharply at him.

"Some say," Myrrdin continued, "she is the lover of a druid, a scoundrel with whom she disappears for long stretches of time."

This was confessed with a smile of such irresistible bright mystery that Laëllon's mouth hung agape, his eyes riveted upon Myrrdin.

"But for now," the druid continued with a wry air, "be aware that west of here is a hill fort, a stronghold left behind by the Romans. In the years ahead it will be called Camelot. You will live there, soon enough."

Laëllon peered to the west, then looked again at the rising hill of the Tor, his face alight with curiosity and excitement. Twilight would soon arrive, and he could see a thick blanket of mist spreading across the lake and rising up the green flanks of the hill, causing the smaller islands to stand out in the deepening shadows of day's end.

Seeing that a brooding silence had fallen over Myrrdin, he waited, pondering the druid's words and knowing in his depths that they rang true. He thought of Nimuë, who he kept close to his heart, and he remembered her last words to him, uttered so long ago as she pressed the carved bird into his hand. He felt into the inner pocket of his tunic, touching the small talisman that was safely wrapped in a cloth and tucked away there. He marveled that the druid had hinted that he knew her well. Surely Myrrdin himself was the lover of whom he spoke.

Laëllon stretched his hands over the crackling fire to absorb its warmth, until after some moments had passed the druid began to speak again.

"Tomorrow we will pass near the Tor, but we will not stop. Avalon is not our destination now—though you will return there one day. We are traveling toward the sea, to the southwestern coast of Briton. When we arrive there, once again you will be Lancelot, son of Ban of Benoic, and not Laëllon of Avalon."

Myrrdin looked up at the sky, where one or two stars twinkled dimly between mountains of purple cloud.

"This land of Briton is in a vast transition," he mused, his mood taking on a poignant cast. "It has stretched its soul to embrace so many different people—invaders, people in exile, misplaced wanderers seeking a fair home. Some have come from as far away as ancient Troy, in the land of Greece, long ago. Yes, this sacred land has embraced all—their religions, gods, goddesses, their stories, their wisdom, their blood and tears.

"In our time, the oldest dwellers in this land are the Cymry, those who came in remote times from Erin to merge with the inhabitants of this isle. Yes, the Cymry and the fierce Pictish people of Alba in the north—their roots run deep."

He sighed. "But Avalon is older than all. Some say the inhabitants of Avalon came from the descendants of

Atlantis, a civilization of the most remote era, which was destroyed in a cataclysm that brought on the Great Flood. A Greek wise man named Plato wrote of this, hundreds of years ago."

The young man listened, marveling and leaning forward to absorb Myrrdin's words. The druid picked up a twig from the pile of dry firewood and sucked it between his teeth. Darkness had overtaken both shadow and light, and the night swarmed with life around them.

"Yes, the Romans sought to conquer this rich and fertile land, and now the Saxons and Angles—the warring tribes of Germania—and Jutes want to claim it. But the power of the Old Ones is still alive here. Briton, Cymru, Alba will survive, pure as their mystic origins. This is our purpose in coming here. When we arrive at our destination in Dumnonia, you will meet the one who will lead us into the future. The coming king."

Laëllon straightened his back to ask a question, but Myrrdin held his hand up, palm out, commanding him to stay quiet. He paused to toss the stick into the fire, then spoke.

"In time, you will understand all. For now, never forget that you are close kin to Nimuë, and Avalon is a part of your soul. The ancient blood will always beat a rhythm in your veins, Laëllon, and it will prove to be your strength and grace in times of need."

Myrrdin lay his head back upon his bedroll and with an arm behind his head gazed up at the sky.

"Yes, all will become clear in time, Laëllon. Though for now you are Lancelot, son of Ban, the time will come when you will be called Lancelot du Lac. Soon you will hear me called by the name Merlin, in the Roman fashion." The fire popped and crackled at a wind that rose, whipping the first of the raindrops into the fire to sizzle on the coals.

"It will rain soon," he said, crawling deeper under the rock overhang and gesturing for Laëllon to come closer. "Now, it is time to rest. Tomorrow we leave before dawn. We still have many leagues to go."

Lancelot paused and looked from the king to the queen. He raised his cup and smiled, bringing the story to a close.

"And so it was that, in three days' time, we arrived at the southernmost edge of Dumnonia and came to the castle of Tintagel, which is perched upon the high cliffs where land meets sea. It was there I encountered the one I would follow into the heat of battle and even to into the jaws of death—the young Pendragon, son of Yraine."

Arthur's face shone with pleasure, and he reached out a hand to seize with affection the shoulder of his knight.

"You know the rest of the story," Lancelot laughed, placing his hand warmly upon the king's outstretched arm.

"At the time when we met, Arthur, it had been less than a year since you wrested the sword Excalibur from the stone, sealing your fate and setting the destiny of Briton in motion.

"A year after that, you married Gwenhyfar," he inclined his head tenderly toward the lady, "sovereign queen of the Cymry. How many battles we have fought together! I have been at your side, my Lord and Lady, from that day forward. And that," he gently slapped his hands upon his knees, "is where I must bid you good evening, for the night has grown late and the candles burn low."

Setting his cup down upon the table, Lancelot rose and bent low before his king and queen. His sun-browned face was brightened by the warmth in his smile as, picking up his cloak, he strode from the room.

"His story is marvelous, indeed," Gwenhyfar sighed, turning to look at Arthur as the door closed quietly, "and he is a skilled storyteller. How little we actually know of anyone."

"Yes, I too am pleased to finally hear the full tale of his past." Arthur reached for his queen, drawing her close into the circle of his arms. "I knew he had met Merlin along the way, but I did not know how. It is wondrous to hear of him, and how he guided Lancelot and I together. In truth, Lancelot is a rare man. And truly a brother to me. Yet I must admit," he laughed softly, drawing one finger along her cheek, "I am glad it is he who sleeps alone on this night, while I have the pleasure of my queen's loving arms. Come, Gwenhyfar, let us go to bed while the coals still burn bright."

Camelot
528 C.E.

A Wounded King

Arthur lay in a swath of summer sunlight like a wounded lion, his long, muscled flanks bronzed by the sun. His body in repose was a beautiful thing to behold. Golden hair fell about his shoulders in a thick, tangled mane that glimmered with light. His face was a finely chiseled poem that she longed to write upon the flesh of her beating heart. Gwenhyfar gazed at the powerful hawk-like profile and wide smooth brow. What if he had died from the wound? She shivered at the thought. They were blessed by Nimuë, the Lady of the Lake, who had appeared mysteriously out of a thick fog to heal him after the battle.

Arthur groaned in his sleep as Gwenhyfar rose and walked to the table to prepare a potion of comfrey, boneset, and feverfew. Nimuë had given her a strange-smelling powder to add, and Gwenhyfar wondered what essence of Avalon it might contain. But no matter, it was magic from the Blessed Isle, and it would heal her husband. She measured the exact amounts into a flagon and fed the brazier with small sticks to encourage the flame, then moved back to his side.

Sitting on the edge of the bed, she soothed his brow, grateful that it was cool to her touch. Thanks to the goddess, the fever had finally broken and he was at rest now. It had been four days of desperate prayers and constant vigilance. She wondered, did he roam now in the realm of Caer Siddi with Arianrhod herself?

A faint sound at the door drew her attention. "Come in," she called softly, knowing it would be Laëllon, Arthur's most trusted companion. The door creaked as it opened and a tall, lithe knight dressed in a simple tunic and cloak entered the room, bringing with him a calm and steady demeanor. Just as his king was fair, Lancelot was dark, slender and graceful as a swan, yet he was strong, powerful, even dangerous—not a swan, she thought, but a panther to his king's lion. She had seen these amazing beasts, traveling in cages or leashed, with the dark-skinned people who came from the lands of the far south, across the sea from Rome, to trade spices, cloth, and other goods with tin mined in the green land of Briton.

The knight's face was composed and somber as he swiftly crossed the room to kneel at the king's side. "Has he spoken yet?" he asked, turning toward her where she sat, one hand resting on the hand of the king.

"No. He has not come back from his journey to the Otherworld." She spoke softly, her gaze focused on the king's sleeping face. "He is deep in Annwyn—the Goddess heals him there as we speak."

Deep blue eyes the color of a twilight sky met his eyes of dark brown with a steady, trusting gaze. Returning her faint smile, he felt his heart contract with longing. He quelled the impulse to take her into his arms to comfort her.

She had been at the king's side for almost a week, hardly sleeping, not allowing her serving women to take over the task of caring for Arthur, as they kept the secret of his injury between themselves, for his sake.

"You have not rested for days, Gwenhyfar. Let me serve him for a while. There is a long recuperation ahead, you must rest and renew your strength."

He encouraged her with his eyes, asking if not pleading. When she hesitated, he said softly, "You know well that I love him as much as you."

She knew the truth of what he said, though she was loathe to leave the sleeping man—nay, more than a man. For her, Arthur was greater than a battle leader or even the Pendragon. He was her husband, her consort, whom she had made the high king of Briton.

"You are wise, as always." She smiled, but her face was pale, and the lines about her eyes seemed deeper than before. "I will go to rest, but call me if he stirs." She pointed to the brazier and added, "The potion must simmer for one hour. Will you watch it and, when it is ready, soak a cloth and dress his wound?"

"Of course, I will take care of all that he needs. Please, now go, and rest," he urged with a glance and nod toward the brazier.

"Very well then," she sighed in acceptance. "I will be close by, in my rooms."

As she rose to leave, he took her hand and pressed it gently to his lips. Pausing, she looked in his eyes and lingered, then pulled away to leave. At the sound of the door closing, Lancelot turned toward the king.

"Twelve years we have fought together, Arthur Pendragon, with you and your knights the scourge of the Saxons. And yet try as I might, I could not save you from this wound."

He took the large, bronzed hand and held it between his own. "At least the gods allowed me to find you in time, before you bled to death—and thanks be to Nimuë for that blessing."

The battle had been unexpected but brutal. Perhaps they had been lulled by the peace that reigned these years after the celebrated success of Arthur's warriors and knights at the battle of Mount Badon. It had been a turning point in their mission to unify Briton and wrestle the power over their land away from Saxon invaders.

Now a band of Saxon warriors ravaged villages in a beeline from Cynnit in the east. Arthur had ridden out with his knights to meet them head on, west of the sarcen stones of Sorviodunum. They had routed the Saxons once again, but the unexpected skirmish had brought a close brush with death for Arthur and for Lancelot as well, though he had not suffered a wounding. With Nimuë's help, he had managed to get Arthur back to Camelot, but barely alive. They had worked hard to keep his injury a secret over the weeks, telling the knights and the court that Arthur was away at Avalon, keeping tryst with Myrrdin.

Lancelot spoke as if, by some uncanny knowledge, he knew the king was listening. "Rest easy, Arthur. Gwenhyfar and I have kept the secret of your wound, except for the Lady of the Lake, who came when I called to her in desperation." He bowed his head and muttered a prayer to the gods of his youth, to Ceridwen and Cernunnos, the great Goddess and the horned God of the Celts, and to Aeron, God of war, then muttered, "Your secret is safe, my king."

In these days of vigil, as the king's life flickered like a candle in the wind and he hovered between this life and the one that comes after, the Lady of the Lake was the only talisman they had to stay the relentless power of death. The thought of losing the king caused an unbearable grief to well up within Lancelot, and he knew it was so for his queen as well.

Now the worst of it was over, and the Lady Nimuë had disappeared as mysteriously as she had come, making her way by currach back across the foggy stretch of shallow lake to Avalon. Keeping such intimate company with death caused Lancelot to reflect upon his own mortality and the aching call of his inner search. He pondered, what does it mean to live a life that is unfulfilled in its deepest yearning? There was only one word that defined his longing—Gwenhyfar.

Standing at the brazier, Lancelot poured a spoonful of the potion into a bowl and picked up a clean linen cloth from the table where several were folded, ready for use. Walking to the bed, he sat down and carefully pulled the coverlet away from the king's wound to dab gently at the weltering gash that had been carefully cleaned and sewn together with catgut string. Inwardly he winced, and he thought again of Gwenhyfar and what she must be suffering. Looking up, he was greeted by a pair of bright blue eyes that gazed at him with surprising clarity.

"Lancelot," the king whispered, lifting his head slightly. He raised two fingers of his hand up from the coverlet as if in greeting.

"It is well you have sent the queen to rest." Arthur closed his eyes as his head sank back onto the pillow, exhausted from the effort of speaking. His next words were faint, and Lancelot leaned close to hear them.

"I trust you to care for her well…"

The king's face went slack as his spirit retreated to the remote place where he had been, wandering in that far away land. Lancelot dabbed gently at the wound, replaced the coverlet, then moved to the brazier to stir the coals. Turning back to the bedside, he sat down beside Arthur and waited.

The Queen's Burden

A small meal and flagon of wine awaited Gwenhyfar in her apartment. Sitting on a low couch beside the table, she picked up a salty flatbread and tasted it, looking out the window at the rolling green landscape and bright blue sky. Enormous white clouds piled high behind the southern hills. It was midsummer, and yet it remained cool in Camelot, with daily storms that came in sudden downpours then moved away inland, leaving heavy fogs to rise from the always misty waters of Ynis Witrin, the Glass Isle, where Avalon hummed at the foot of the sacred hill.

She looked southeast, toward the lake and the Tor that rose from it, some three leagues away, then noticed a ceramic vase filled with wildflowers that graced a nearby table. She smiled, knowing that the sunny day had called her young cousin, Bloedwyn, out around the water to gather bluebells. The girl was true to her name, Gwenhyfar thought as she drank in the bright colors—yellow, dark pink, and a celestial shade of blue. She said a prayer for Arthur, knowing in her heart that he would be healed, but he would never be the same.

The king had always been protected, or so it seemed, by the amazing charisma of his person. For so many years Arthur had fought countless battles, charging into the thick of the fight and walking away unscathed. Even at Mount Badon he had escaped whole and well. Finally, he had been struck down.

Though he was well loved, there were some who would be glad to hear he was not as strong as he was, including his nephew Gawain. It was of utmost importance that his enemies never discover his weakness, lest they contrive a way to break him down, or send rumours of the king's fallibility throughout the land to threaten his sovereignty. He had saved them from the Saxon demons for now, but Briton was not yet secure under his kingship.

Though it was healing slowly, the wound in his groin was angry and deep. She worried that he might have difficulty with walking, and this would send a message loud and clear—the king has been compromised. Oh, but Lancelot was excellent with his hands and could give a therapy like none other. It was the deeper question of the wound that troubled her.

Her smile was wistful as she remembered her husband, golden hair falling about his face as he leaned over to steal a kiss as she sat at her loom. He had a rare vitality that animated his virile nature, which, combined with his expansive and gregarious personality, made their lovemaking passionate and joyous. Even with his frequent liaisons and children born of other women, he always came back, calling her, "Heart's joy, light of my life." She understood well that a man like Arthur would never contain himself for one woman alone. Even so, their years together had been rich and deep; with him, she had known pleasures undreamt of.

The sage Myrrdin had taught her much about the star knowledge of the Greeks, the more ancient Egyptians, and the Sumerians before them. With Myrrdin, she learned that Arthur was born under the stars of the Water Bearer, called Aquarius by the Romans. This sign imbued him with an inspired vision, a greatness and vast capacity for defending and uplifting the goodness of human nature. But the star on the horizon at his birth was in the constellation of Leo—and never was there one more regal, brave and courageous and fiery, more lion-hearted than her king.

Gwenhyfar herself was ruled by Venus, born under the star pattern of balance—the cosmic scales. She sought harmony and balance and beauty in all things. The sign on the horizon at her birth was Scorpio, along with the moon, which had given her a deep connection to the mysteries of death and birth and a fluid, sensual nature. Even more so, it gave her keen insight and the power to lead others. It also gave her a natural chemistry of the stars with Lancelot.

She sighed inwardly, thinking of how her gift for leading, even for ruling, was the dominant thread that ran through her life—not the role of mothering. That she had never borne the king a child that lived long, unlike his mistresses or even those women with whom he shared a romp in the hay on festival nights, was a constant, vague pain that dampened the joy of her days.

Her thoughts roved to the Lady Garwen, who had a son with Arthur before his marriage to Gwenhyfar. She was grateful for Garwen's friendship at court, and her thoughts dwelled a moment upon Rowland. He was twelve years old now, a fine lad. Lancelot also had a son, Galahad, who was twelve as well. Galahad, the birth son of the Lady Elaine of Pelles and Lancelot, lived far away, growing up with his foster parents in Bretonnia.

Tears spilled over her eyes to run down the curves of her cheeks. Along with the pleasure, there had been pain—great losses and grief, her two babes that died, countless trials over the years, so many battles in service to their shared vision to bring Britannia together under the Pendragon sigil. In truth, with Gwenhyfar at his side, Arthur was the only one with the power and charisma to unite all the petty kings, who ruled within their own regions, to drive away the Saxon invaders, to keep her people and her land safe from the wild tribes of the north, the ferocious Picts.

And now this terrible wound. She forced her mind away from dwelling on the changes such a wounding might bring, and her thoughts drifted back to Lancelot, who sat now with the king and kept the vigil at his side. Thanks to the Goddess for her champion, who had brought the king back from the battlefield and had the presence of mind to swiftly call Nimuë to come to his side.

She pondered the enigma of Lancelot and the life he had lived, which had formed such a rare character as his. She had been careful to avoid Lancelot at the Beltane fires each spring over the years, sensing that, if she had gone with him, it would wreak devastation upon them, the pull to his arms was so great. This discipline had stayed with her, even when Arthur disappeared with one lovely woman after another.

Gwenhyfar had no interest in the many other men who flirted with her, made advances at Beltane and took liberties when Arthur's head was turned. No, the only man who moved her heart was Lancelot, and the magnetism between them had never gone away. Instead of lovers, they had become dearest friends and allies.

Arthur, Gwenhyfar, and their first knight had become inseparable over time. She remembered how, years ago, Lancelot had revealed the truth of his origins to them, as the three sat together in deep companionship one winter night beside a roaring fire. They had shared many flagons of a sweet golden wine that had been delivered by boat that very day—a gift from vassals of Bretonnia—and listened to Laëllon tell his story.

Her thoughts skittered over a kaleidoscope of memories: how they had discovered the born storyteller in the self-contained, mysterious Lancelot, who often appeared remote and inward. How he had spoken with the flourish and natural elaboration of a poet, talking for hours, sharing secrets unknown to the other knights of the Round Table—much less the royal court.

She remembered well how their amazement had unfolded along with the story of his birth in Bretonnia, his journey with Nimuë through the standing stones, his childhood years on Avalon. With verbal dexterity he had embroidered the tale of being spirited away to Erin to live with his grandmother, Lacine, then as a lad of fourteen leaving on a immrama, a voyage of no return, landing on Eilean Arainn and meeting Myrrdin there.

Gwenhyfar thought of the many years of battles, fought by Arthur and his knights, and the multitude of sorrows, spawned from the pits of hell, when men are driven to conquer and dominate, to fight each other for supremacy. Long before the Saxons had arrived, the people of Cymru had defended their lands and protected their ancient right to rule. Her own people had to drive away not only the Picts from the north but the Gaels from Erin—their own ancestors.

Like, her foremothers—the queens of Powys, Gwynned, Dyfed, Gwent, and all the regions of Cymru—she could ride and hunt as well as any man. She was happy to don leather breeks beneath a cloak and buckle a short sword around her hips, but she was essentially peace-loving. Her thoughts ranged back to her childhood, before her marriage to Arthur. She had grown up knowing that she would be queen someday, in the lineage of her mother, Tarian. Queen of Dyfed, Gwent, and Gwynedd, Tarian's consort king was Gogrvan, called Leodegrance in the Roman style of address. They ruled in the southernmost parts of Cymru, in its outlying fertile lands along the Severn Sea and the River Afon. Caerleon was their citadel, where Tarian's mother and her mother before her had ruled at the Round Table with their consort kings.

Gwenhyfar was sixteen years when the powerful druid-priest Emrys Myrrdin brought a tall golden-haired young man and introduced him to her mother and father. His Roman name was Artorius Aurelius, for he was the son of Uther, brother of Ambrosius Aurelius, slayer of Vortigern, the leader of the Britons who had betrayed them to Hengist and his Saxon invaders. Uther had inherited the right to rule from his brother Ambrosius, who became king after Vortigern, then passed it on to his son, Arthur.

When she first met Arthur, his story was already a legend that had spread wide and far, reaching Cymru and the court of Queen Tarian and King Gogvran before the young man himself arrived. Truly Uther had passed a glorious legacy on to his son, along with his name—Pendragon. It was both name and iconic sigil. Before his brother Ambrosius died, Uther saw a passing comet that he perceived in the shape of a great dragon. This was the sign Myrrdin Emrys interpreted as the beginning of Uther's reign as king. The druid then dubbed Uther "the Pendragon," saying that the comet foretold the coming of Uther's son—a powerful warrior and leader of the people who would unify the Britons, drive away their enemies, and insure the safekeeping of their land.

From the beginning Gwenhyfar had called him Arthur, in the Roman style. Gwenhyfar's bride gift to the young battle leader was her mother's massive oaken Round Table along with two hundred cattle and five hundred silver denarii. The Round Table was the most valuable of these, for its power to imbue wisdom and strength to whoever sat around it. Once the marriage was sealed, it was the Round Table that played a vital role as Arthur pursued their aim to bring the tribes together and drive away the Saxon invaders.

Gwenhyfar was taken completely by Arthur, set aflame by the vision of the young war lord from the rolling hills of Dumnonia, across the narrow inlet of the Severn Sea. She believed that, together, they could unite the clans and small kingdoms of Cymru and free her people from the Saxon blight. Indeed, all of Briton would benefit from her union with the shining young man with a mythical past. Had he not pulled the magical sword, Excalibur, from the stone, fulfilling Myrddin's prophecy and setting in motion his destiny toward a great kingship to come? And Gwenhyfar would become Queen of the Summer Country, ruling in the south as well as in the Cymry lands to the north.

Arthur's charisma was unique. Indeed, the young battle leader's warriors were fiercely loyal to him. He and his knights ranged between his birthplace, the castle Tintagel in Cornovia on the southern sea, to Dumnonia and the River Exe to the southeast, to Caerleon in the Cymry lands in the north. In the middle of this triangle was the old Roman hill fort called Camelot, which Arthur had made his headquarters. Camelot was central because it was close to Ynis Witrin, the "Isle of Glass," place of the ancient powers of Avalon and the mystic Tor.

The first time Gwenhyfar came to Camelot and the Summer Country with Arthur, she was enchanted by Ynis Witrin, and with Avalon and the Tor. As a child, Gwenhyfar had heard stories of Avalon and the great hill—a place of ancient magic that rose above the shining silver waters of a shallow lake. The Tor was a magnet, a place where many streams of influence converged; its powerful magic had drawn not only the descendants of the Old Ones but also druids and Celtic tribes, as well as the Christians and Romans.

The Roman conquerors had followed on the heels of a Christian saint, Joseph of Arimathea, who five hundred years before had come with a small group of disciples dedicated to their great prophet, a man named Jesus. The followers of Jesus had stayed, and now a small enclave of monks lived at Ynis Witrin, having forged a delicate harmony with the powers of nearby Avalon.

As her thoughts drifted, Gwenhyfar moved to the table to pour a cup of water and lift it to her lips. Although they were often in Camelot, from which Arthur and his knights could keep the peace Dumnonia, after their marriage it was Caerleon that became Arthur's major stronghold. It was in Caerleon that Arthur held court, gathering with his knights at the Round Table. She remembered well the gift of her mother's Round Table, given freely with pride and joy to the beautiful young warrior who became her husband and king of the land—who now lay feverish in his bed not far from her apartment. Gwenhyfar thought of the Round Table, how it carried the potencies of Arianrhod and her realm of Annwyn, of Ceridwen and Brighid and all the great goddesses of her tradition. It was these great celestial beings—harbingers of the Old Ones—who brought wisdom to all who sat in council there, guiding them in nobility, chivalry, and generosity.

She had been trained in the ancient way of her people, when women ruled as queens who bore a sacred geasa—a spiritual obligation—to serve as the goddess on earth. Born and raised to be sovereign of her lands, Gwenhyfar had never thought to conquer and subjugate but to lead, to guide, to serve her people that they might thrive and live in peace. She sighed as she pondered the years of war and bloodshed. Some women of her ancestral line had been warrior queens who charged into the grist and blood of battle, but most were peace loving, as Tarian and her mother had been. As embodiments of the goddess in all her expressions, the Cymry queens of Dyfed guided their people to sit in a circle together at the Round Table, where they weighed the affairs of the people and took each other's council. Now, the invading Romans and Saxons and other warring tribes had brought a different spirit to her land.

Gwenhyfar picked up a woven blanket and moved to the couch. She sensed herself standing at an invisible crossroad. It seemed the very air was redolent with the smell of change, and somehow of something else—danger. Perhaps it was Arthur's terrible wound and sickness, and her own deep exhaustion and grief, that had carved deep into her heart, churning up memories of how all this had come to be. She bit her lip as she reflected that the deluge of memories signaled another turn of fate's wheel—Ceridwen stirring her cauldron, for surely they were poised upon the brink of change.

Closing her eyes, her thoughts returned to the enigmatic Laëllon. She gave thanks to the goddess for his steady presence. She could lean upon him, and now more than ever, since the travail of Arthur' wounding. Though Lancelot was an accomplished warrior—the greatest of all, as many said—she had always known he was different from other men, including his king. Lancelot's heart and soul were ruled by a deeper song of life. Laëllon was her champion because his heart beat to the same rhythms as hers. They shared a kinship with ocean tides, the rhythms and elemental spirits of nature, with the poetry of life and the mystic cosmos itself.

She remembered how Lancelot had embellished his tale that wintry night by the fire, relaxed with the king and queen over cups of wine, and how she had listened with all her senses piqued. So many threads were woven together in the tapestries of their lives; as she mused upon the meaning of it all, she hoped that someday a bard would write everything down, so that the great deeds of their lives would be sung for generations yet to come.

At the center of it all was Myrrdin Emrys. Some said the druid holy man was a sorcerer; some said he was a devil and others said he was a god, immortal and invincible. Gwenhyfar was not sure of the truth, but she knew Myrrdin as the peerless and indefatigable guide of their lives. His wisdom—in truth, his vision—had always proven to chart the best course of action, and she trusted him without reserve. But where was he now, when they needed him most, with Arthur wounded and everything so uncertain?

No one knew. He had a way of disappearing suddenly and reappearing in his own time and season. Perhaps he was with the Lady Nimuë in Avalon, although Nimuë had only shrugged and kept silent when Gwenhyfar asked about the mage and his whereabouts. Throughout the time that Nimuë worked to heal Arthur, the druid did not appear. The man lived by unfathomable powers and signs, and now he had been gone for the better part of two years.

Myrrdin was a puzzle she would never solve. Gwenhyfar sighed as she plumped a small goose down pillow and placed it under her head. Pulling a light woolen shawl around her shoulders and closing her eyes, she took a deep breath and relaxed. When Lancelot was with the king, she did not have to worry—all would be handled well. Soon her breath came deep and even, and she slept well for the first time in many days.

Caerleon
528–529 C.E.

Return to Cymry

The tufted grass was winter green in the light of a November sun that lay across the land in great swaths of radiance. The sea churned, dark sapphire against a pale blue sky, and seagulls rode the currents of air and cried in plaintive calls. Back once again in her homeland, glad to be with her own people in Caerleon, Gwenhyfar basked in the pristine air of a rare day. Soaking in the sun's rays, she watched the rhythm of the waves that washed, foamy and white, on the beach below. It had been Arthur' wish to move his court during the summer to Caerleon, and she had gladly packed for the trip north. Now she felt a deep satisfaction to be back in Cymru, close to the sea and in the land of her blood, among her own people.

"Lady, lady!"

Gwenhyfar turned, her reverie broken by the sound of a serving maid's voice, and she shielded her eyes against the light so she could see the girl who hustled up a worn footpath with a red woolen cape in hand.

"It's too cold out here, lady, you'll need your cloak,"

Bloedwyn chided sweetly. "The sun may be out, the grass is green, but it is well past Samhain!"

Gwenhyfar smiled and reached out to take the heavy woolen garment, then put an arm around her cousin.

"Thank you, Bloedwyn. You take good care of me, my dear cousin."

The young woman, still a girl in many ways, smiled in return. "You are the jewel of our lives, my lady! A queen as kindly and wise and beautiful as you is a rare advent in this world, as my grandmother and mother often say. And I know it to be true for myself, by the Eyes of the Goddess, the beautiful Blodeuwedd herself! Every one of our people loves you, my queen! And now that the Pendragon is recovering well..."

Gwenhyfar stopped the chattering with a brisk toss of her head. "Bloedwyn! You are not to speak of such things!" She reached out to grasp the girl's arms in her hand and shook her slightly. "Not even here, where no one can hear! The king's life and sovereignty depend upon our loyalty and discretion."

Crestfallen, Bloedwyn hung her head. "Oh my lady, I regret my hasty words. It is my worst fault—why do I not think before I speak? You have instructed me well, and I suppose I thought, here, we could speak freely."

"We cannot speak freely anywhere, Bloedwyn," Gwenhyfar admonished gently. "A man of power like Arthur, whose destiny is great, has many enemies who would bring him down. His close ones are pledged to shield and defend him."

She lifted the girl's chin and looked into her eyes.

"Little one, I love you well and have since you were a babe in arms. I know your good qualities, your loyalty and love and courage, and for this and many other reasons I have taken you into my service. Do not cry, it is good you made such a blunder now, so we can set it right with no consequences, and you may fortify your intention for the times ahead. Now, dry your eyes."

Dabbing at her cheeks with the edge of her cloak, Bloedwyn took a deep breath, then asked, "Will you stay here for while, my lady? Or may I escort you back to the fort? Before I left, Sir Gawain came looking for you, with a message from the Pendragon. The king would like to speak with you, when you have returned from your walk."

Gwenhyfar looked out at the ocean longingly, then turned toward the path leading down the cliff's escarpment and across the grassy meadow. "Then it is time to go," she sighed, her heart thumping hard with dread. A message from Gawain could never come to any good! He had not been her ally for a long time—not since five years ago in Camelot, when Gawain had approached Gwenhyfar in secret, professed his desire, and begged for a secret liaison. He had never forgiven her for the rebuff when she said no and, later, for choosing Lancelot as her champion.

She had not told Arthur about Gawain, but she suspected that he knew. The eldest son of Arthur' sister, Morgause, Gawain was arrogant, hot-tempered, hard to manage—even for one as skilled as the king in leading his men. Arthur never showed prejudice among his knights, and Gawain chafed at this, as he was the king's closest kin at court.

The king had an uncanny way of working with the various factions among his knights, juggling the reins of power yet always keeping them close and inspiring their fidelity, even as they disagreed or jockeyed for position amongst each other. Anyway, she resolved, Arthur would choose whoever was close at hand to deliver such an order to her maidservant.

She pushed a heavy strand of hair away from her face as she strode across the plush meadow grass. Her mind was uneasy, and she fretted with the thought that since the Pendragon was wounded, many things had begun to change. Arthur had pushed her, nay, in fact he forced her to depend more on Lancelot—to spend time in his company and seek his counsel in all things.

Arthur had long ago invited Lancelot to move into the king's apartments in Caerleon, where he had been given rooms next to Arthur and Gwenhyfar. In the past months, Arthur often invited Lancelot to play games with Gwenhyfar, while the king watched. This was not easy for the queen and her champion, as the natural magnetism between them began to grow. Arthur had to notice their easy laughter, the way their eyes lingered when their fingers touched over a chess piece, and how one of the two would then look away. At these times their faces were flushed and discomfited, often sparking the abrupt end of an unfinished game.

Even so, the camaraderie between the king, his queen, and their first knight revealed a deeper bond between the three. Seeing this blossom, the knights had become more fractious than ever, especially Gawain. She could see the envy and suspicion written upon their faces as they watched warily, their eyes not missing any nuance or interaction. Like wolves, she thought, circling for a kill. And it was not Arthur they hunted, but Lancelot and Gwenhyfar.

Ah well. Their destiny was already swirling in Ceridwen's cauldron. Yes, she would go to see the king, and she knew her husband would speak of that which she dreaded most of all—the wound that would not heal despite her tender ministrations and Laëllon's best efforts of therapy.

Stepping in the wooden doorway, Gwenhyfar hung her cloak on a peg beside the door in her quarters, then walked into the room with Bloedwyn close behind. She sat down at the dressing table and picked up the wooden comb, handing it to the girl.

"Would you, my dear?" While Bloedwyn combed and re-braided the queen's heavy black hair, Gwenhyfar took out a pot of ointment and gently massaged a dollop into the smooth fair skin of her face. The smells of meadowsweet and calendula—the yellow flowers brought from the south by the Romans, which grew well in their northern clime—blended with bog myrtle to waft around her, and the scent lifted her spirit. When her toilet was finished, she sighed and reached for a shawl of thick wool, which she wrapped around her shoulders and pinned with a brooch, a finely wrought golden stag. With a smile at Bloedwyn and an affectionate pinch of her cheek, the queen walked out the door, heading toward Arthur's quarters.

The King's Command

"Does your champion not please you?" Arthur looked directly into her eyes, and it was blue on blue in that gaze between husband and wife, but her hair was dark as midnight and his was fair as sunshine on a field of wheat. She hesitated, ill at ease.

"I, I…. Yes, of course he pleases me. Laëllon is loyal, courageous—a gifted warrior of integrity. The best of champions," she said, seeking his eyes with her own, "and he is not you, Arthur."

"Gwenhyfar, you are beautiful, healthy, still young enough to bear a living child. We have no legitimate heir. There is no Pendragon to come after me, as I came after Uther."

He sighed. "Lancelot is the obvious choice to father our child, and it is your right as queen to have your champion as consort in the old way, the way of your ancestors. It is your right to take him as your lover. Your foremothers did this—even your own mother had lovers and champions over the years, and all kinds of dalliance at the Beltane fires!

And Leodegran bore it without a complaint. God knows he had an excess of women of his own!"

She stared at him, incredulous. "Arthur," she protested, "I do not deny what you say, but this is madness. Times are changing. The old ways are fast disappearing as the Christians influence our people. I fear you are turning the wheel of fate, and it will bring destruction down on us all."

Waving her aside, he plunged ahead.

"I have had many women over the years, known to you, as are my children by them. Your kindness to Lady Garwen and her son Rowland is well known in Camelot. But you, Gwenhyfar, have been occupied with standing beside me in the war against the Saxons, ruling your people—and bearing my children, may their souls wander happily in the Otherworld with the Goddess herself! For some reason, you and I are not blessed with the joy of children.

Her face creased in a frown. "Yes, your children by other women have grown healthy and flourished over these years while our babes withered and died," she murmured. "It is a pity that Rowland cannot be named tanaiste, for he grows stronger and more pleasing with each passing day."

Arthur snorted. "Garwen is not high born. Even though she is connected to Avalon, she was a serving wench before you lifted her up. Her son would never be accepted as heir to the Pendragon throne."

She bowed her head in agreement, looking down to finger a heavy gold ring on her left hand, which Arthur had given to her at the time of their handfasting. It was made of intricate interwoven strands that formed a pattern—an oval love knot signifying eternal love.

"Mordred is high born," she countered, looking up.

He snorted. "Mordred! Even Lancelot cannot make a man of Mordred."

Her blue eyes flashed, reflecting silver in the light. He stared at her, his face sculpted by unspoken anger and sorrow as he pulled at his beard with one large hand.

"I hardly have to tell you, Gwenhyfar—you know very well that Mordred was conceived before I knew the truth of my parentage. By the Goddess, I was a youth of fourteen years!"

His voice grew heavy with the poignant and bitter truth. "The spawn of my half-sister and me, born in the confusion of a young stag who would someday be king, maddened by whatever herbs she put in my ale at a Beltane fire. Aye, Morgause knew well enough, and tricked me into it.

"Nay, Mordred will not be king—though the evil of his conception was not his fault. He may become a skilled warrior, but there is a darkness in Mordred that chills my heart, even though my blood runs in his veins. I know you have seen this as well."

She gazed out the window with a heavy heart. It was true that Arthur had sons and daughters by others but not with her. His eldest, Mordred, was training under Lancelot's skilled instruction and now, at sixteen years, was soon to take up arms with the other knights. The ignoble facts surrounding his birth plagued the boy—she had seen his cloaked glances, the envy and hatred in his brooding face.

"Listen to me," Arthur counseled. "You are still fertile, Gwynhyfar—your blood flows red with the flux of the moon. Our hope for a true heir is not lost! It is one thing to have children with other women, even those of noble birth, but the continuation of the Pendragon line depends upon a legitimate heir, whose veins flow with royal blood, who the people will acknowledge and follow. For the sake of all the gods, it is the future of Briton that is at stake!"

Her heart sank as the king's argument gained power and momentum. She stirred to speak, but he would not be stopped. His large hands came down to cover hers, and she was stilled by the power of that touch. Stunned for a moment, she rallied, speaking with the fury of a growing certainty.

"You speak like a Roman! Yet you speak of the old ways…Arthur, it is our way to wait for the tanaiste to prove himself, as you did before we married. Your worthy successor would need to marry a maiden of royal blood—like Rhana, the daughter of my mother's sister—to become king. And we do not know that I will have a child by Lancelot. You and I have lost two babes already, and I fear that there will be no more children born from this body."

Seeing the closed look on his face, she drew a breath and fortified herself for yet another argument.

"You sound like the Caesars of Rome, who tried to conquer our world by force! They've changed us far too much. Is this what it comes down to? You are willing to risk everything for a son to inherit your power? Nay, Arthur, you should wait until the time is right, then name one of the young knights as your successor—Lancelot's son Galahad, when he is older and comes to court, or the sons of Cai or Bors, or some other…"

She paused, knowing full well that he was trenchant, his shoulders squared and set. Changing tact, she softened.

"Arthur, it hurts me to see you like this. This wound has caused you to lose hold of yourself."

He slapped his hand upon the table and stood to pace impatiently across the room and back. As if she had said nothing at all, he continued, augmenting his position like the battle commander he was.

"The wound, as you remind me, has brought me to my senses! I cheated death of its due with that wound. Tis a miracle that I live still. I have seen my own end, Gwenhyfar. The spectre of death has breathed upon me."

He stopped to stare at her, then turned to pace again. "Now, hear me out. It is too late to make a child of my own loins with you Gwenhyfar, and if it cannot be a child born of you and me, then I will make the child you bear with Lancelot my heir. He will be called Gwydion, named for your ancestors, in the way of your people, but he will bear my sigil...Gwydion Pendragon."

"What? Gwydion, the god of illusion and enchantments?" Her half-smile was wry and bitter with disbelief. "Like the enchantment that was wrought to accomplish your birth, thanks to Myrrdin? You pursue a dangerous irony, my lord. Are we not still paying a price for that, in some way? Both good and ill effects have long been set in motion by these causes. What is the teaching of the Christians—the sins of the fathers visit the sons?"

Her words seemed to penetrate through the haze of his obsession. He stopped pacing, sat down beside her, and reached out to take her hand. Seeing that she now had his attention, she argued.

"Listen to me. Myrrdin has disappeared from our

world—we don't have him to cast a glamour on the knights to hide our actions. The knights will never stand for this. They will destroy us. They are already jealous and suspicious of Lancelot and me. Their substance is being eaten away by the worm of envy. They do not share the same love for you, Arthur, as me or Laëllon. This is especially true of Gawain. Surely you realize the truth of this?"

She shook her head, her brow furrowed as she argued her point. "Arthur, you must be aware that Gawain is interested in power only. But even worse, many of them have been influenced by Christian ideas of sin and all that goes with it! They do not hold to the old way of the Celts, of Cymru—of the queen's consort, the sovereignty of queens, much less the queen as the Goddess, her very body the land itself! They do not hold the relationship of champion to the queen as a sacred trust. They will revolt. Gawain himself, who has been jealous of Lancelot for years, will try kill your first knight. They will kill me. There will never be a child. Surely you know the truth of this?"

Releasing her hands and unfolding his long legs, he stood and walked to the window, which looked out upon a garden and the tilting yard, where some of the men were practicing their skill at swords. They could hear the clang and ring of the metal as they lunged and parried. For a moment he watched the swordplay, then he looked back at her from the corner of his eye. "Is that the reason you would say no? You are afraid you'll be murdered or put to death by the knights?"

Gwenhyfar sat heavily on the couch and stared at the flagstone floor. Arthur turned and walked to a long wooden table that flanked the couch. Spreading his hands flat upon the polished wood, he leaned over to look into her eyes. His breath was warm and spiced with wine on her cheek.

"I see the way you look at him, Gwenhyfar," he breathed. "I have borne it for these past ten years. It was the least I could do, as you have always been so tolerant, so... generous. I feared you would take him as a lover long ago. He is your champion. It is your right, and especially now, when your husband can no longer fulfill his duty as a man!"

The ragged edge of his voice pierced her heart as he turned away quickly and walked back to the window. Stunned but glad that the bone of truth was finally bared, she sat in silence, absorbing her husband's words, his damaged pride, the complex weave of his emotions. She rose and walked to the window. Standing cautiously behind him, she moved closer to wrap her arms around his waist, pulling him to her.

"I am not bound by the old way any more than I am bound by the new way of the Christians. It is my right as queen to choose who will grace my bed, and I have always chosen you, Arthur... I chose you still, wounded or not wounded."

He turned and clasped her to his chest, his strong arms enfolding her. She yielded easily to the strength of him, the sheer power of him flooding her body with warmth as it always had. His hands moved with sensuous grace down her back to circle her waist in a caress that melted her heart. They stood thus for some moments, and she dared not move until he released her and turned back to the window. She stayed close with one arm around him, hoping to sustain the moment of intimacy, but his eyes narrowed as he looked out upon the distant green fields beyond the tiltyard.

"Yes, you love me," he whispered. "And, you love him. I know it, Gwenhyfar, with all my heart."

She dropped her arm and stood looking out the window, her face impassive and distant. The moments grew thick with all that went unsaid, until, after a time, he relented, taking her hands in his.

"Come. Let us sit down together and talk some more. Let us be of one mind and heart about this, as we always have been," he soothed, leading her back to the couch.

There was a clay pitcher of wine and another of water on the table, as well as dried cherries and firm, juicy red apples, walnuts from the recent harvest and a platter of still-warm fish cakes. The wood of the table was smooth from years of use, polished to a sheen that reflected the bowl of late autumn flowers that sat in the middle. As tempting as it was, the food went untouched.

Taking her hands again between his own, he spoke with quiet persuasion. "Gwenhyfar, do you think I don't know that without you I would not have become king? That is the simple truth. It was my marriage with you, Cymry queen, royal daughter of Tarian, which legitimized my quest to bring the tribes and small kingdoms together against our enemies. Our people remember and know this.

"It is my union with the goddess in her many forms that makes me their king. You, Gwenhyfar, are Ceridwen herself! You carry the charm of Blodeuwedd—even the Romans call you Venus because of your beauty! You are Aphrodite, Arianrhod, Brighid! You are the land herself. All is embodied in you, Gwenhyfar, your body, your flesh and blood form. The people understand that you have bestowed your sovereignty upon me. You know the truth of this!"

She could not argue with what he said, for he spoke the truth. He had been a great warlord, a battle general, the scion emerged from the union of divergent peoples—part Roman and part Celt, all Briton. The stars of a high destiny shone upon him, the foretold son of Uther Pendragon and Ygraine, whose ancestry disappeared into the mists of Avalon. But it was his marriage to Gwenhyfar that had made him a king. His words touched the queen in her, and seeing this, he plied his argument.

"I am what I am. My mother had the blood of the Old Ones in her, and though I did not know her until just before she died, when I was almost a man full grown, I loved her as a warm and wonderful woman. You are quite like her, Gwenhyfar—noble, regal, with hair hanging to your knees and eyes the color of the twilight sky."

He reached out to trace her cheek gently with his fingertips, eyes roving over her face as if he absorbed the vision of her to store in memory. She gazed steadily at him, listening intently, taking him in as well. Then he shook his head.

"Yes, I have had Merlin's wisdom to guide me, and a good deal of his magic! Without Merlin, nothing would have been possible. As you say, even my own birth would not have been accomplished." He laughed with light irony at his reference to the dubious magic that Merlin had worked to insure the birth of Uther Pendragon's son.

"Even so, without you, the magic would not have taken root and flourished among the people—whether in battle, at Camelot in the south, in council at the Round Table here in Caerleon, in the tilting yard, or in any part of our lives together.

"The northern tribes of Gwynedd, Powys, Gwent, Dyfed—these people, who live by the gods of their ancestors—would never have followed me without your sovereignty and the authority of your Round Table, the gift of your mother and your mother's mother and hers before her. That is why our meeting was arranged, the reason why Merlin did not oppose the marriage—because it sealed a bond between our different peoples."

Gwenhyfar sat half-turned on the couch to face him, with her hand resting upon his shoulder. Had Merlin truly supported their marriage? She had her doubts. Years ago Merlin had said their happiness was not certain, their destiny together was unclear.

But she had loved Arthur obsessively, even worshipped him as a god. His life was her life, his mission was her mission—to rid her people and her land of the marauding Saxons and all the others who threatened to swallow up not only Dumnonia and Demetia, indeed all of Cymru, and eventually the rest of the isle of Briton. Like the Romans before them, the Saxons would take even the wilds of Alba if they could fight the fierce tribes of the north. If they were successful, the way of life of her people—their gods and goddesses, their ancient rituals, their matrilineal succession of queens and their consorts, their customs and language and rites—all this would come to an end.

She watched the nuances of feeling that flickered over his ruddy skin, his breath coming and going, the way the light played upon his golden hair, the blue depths of his eyes and the beauty of his broad brow. A gold circlet, inset with amethysts, rested upon his forehead. She breathed gently, not wanting to disturb the current of his thoughts, knowing that it was time to listen to the deeper message of his heart.

"You and I came from different worlds, different people, Gwenhyfar. We have merged well, despite my sisters' doubts and interference. Morgause has been nothing but trouble to me, to us both, even while Morgan, difficult as she can be, has been our friend and ally in many ways. But that is another story."

Gwenhyfar's eyes flickered in surprise at this news—Morgan had influenced this turn of events? He stared at the floor, heaving a sigh before the next words.

"I cannot simply ignore what has happened to my body. I can still fight on the battlefield, yes, but it eats at my gorm that I cannot love you as I once did."

Her heart ached for him. She took a deep breath and slowly released it, choosing her words with care.

"Arthur, my king and my love, I took one look at you that day when you arrived in my mother's court, and I knew we had a destiny to fulfill together. I was young, but I was happy that it was you who had come to bring forth the queen I would become. My darling, you know very well the truth of what I say, how deep our love has grown over the years and all that we have shared, living, loving, working, struggling, the battles, the laughter," she paused, "the loss and the tears."

They fell silent, awash in memories and unable to speak further. They sat in a similitude of peace until a knock came at the door.

"Ah, our champion is here." Arthur's smile was bittersweet as he squeezed her hand then rose from the couch and walked to the door. Swinging it wide, he greeted Lancelot with open arms. "Come in, brother. Come in."

Lancelot smiled at Arthur and then uncertainly at Gwenhyfar when he saw the shadows in her eyes and the furrow on her brow. Arthur poured wine for all three, offered fish cakes to Lancelot, and enjoined him to sit on the couch beside Gwenhyfar while he pulled up a low stool and sat facing them.

"You are wondering why my queen is subdued. It is because she is uncertain about her future. She does not trust that I will defend and protect you both when she does as I ask and takes you as her lover, to make a tanaiste for the Pendragon line."

"Arthur!" Gwenhyfar objected, blue eyes flashing fire. "How could you?" She turned away, willed her breath to slow, forced herself to quell the fury that surged within.

Lancelot did not move. He sat still beside the queen, meeting the king's gaze evenly, one eyebrow raised in question. Gwenhyfar looked out the window, her face flushed with feeling. Moments ticked by until Arthur reached out a hand in supplication.

"Forgive me. I have insulted you both and myself as well, and it is most unfair to my queen to begin in this way. I speak with hard words because this is difficult for me—and yet it is necessary. I do not question your loyalty, either of you, who are my most ardent supporters, my first knight and my lady queen. Because of you, I am king here."

He turned away, rubbing his face with his hands,

suddenly haggard. Seeing the burden upon him, the way he had lost his bearings, Gwenhyfar knew the king was not healed in more ways than one—his body was strong again, but his soul had taken a brutal blow. Relenting, she leaned forward and reached toward him one more time.

"Arthur, you don't have to do this. You are not yet yourself after the long recovery. I love you, more than my own life, as does Lancelot. We have endured much together, we three. We have shared the cup of bloodshed, of terror and death and loss. We were called to make great sacrifices for our people. So many enemies we have faced and overcome."

Despite the truth behind her words, the steel in Arthur's blue eyes told her that his resolve had hardened again. She glanced at the darker of the two men, who sat still as a stone. Her voice became low and somber, and she spoke each word with great, slow care.

"Arthur, I warn you again, as I did before. You are willfully stirring the cauldron of Ceridwen. Nay, you are unleashing all the powers of Morrigan. This will not come to good for any of us. I beg you to reconsider, before we cannot turn back."

With the graceful dignity they knew so well, Gwenhyfar stood and walked to the door. Her eyes lingered for a moment on her husband and then, with a glance at his knight, she was gone.

A Knight's Dilemma

The air seemed vacant without Gwenhyfar, as if a lacuna was opened by her departure. The two men sat blankly. Lancelot was the first to move. With a deep inhale he stirred to reach a hand toward the king.

"This wound troubles you, Arthur. It eats at you, heart and soul. We will find another way to solve the problem, to fight this new enemy that strikes at you from within."

The king hunched his broad shoulders and fingered the wine cup in his broad hands. He glanced sideways at Lancelot.

"You always have a way of knowing the nuance and core of situations, of going straight to the point. It's true that the wound, and its lasting effects on me, troubles me deeply. But Lancelot, there is more at stake than my problems. Everything we have fought for hangs in the balance. I must ask this of you. I have my reasons—there are many."

Leaning forward, Lancelot placed his hand on Arthur's shoulder. As if carefully threading his way through an inner labyrinth, he spoke.

"It is true that I love her. I would die for my queen, Arthur, just as I would die for you. You are my king. We are brothers, beyond blood, before and beyond this life. My fidelity belongs to you, before all others. I will do whatever you ask of me. But I beseech you, be careful what you set in motion. It could bring harm to Gwenhyfar."

"It is never my intention to hurt Gwenhyfar," Arthur snapped. His shoulders twitched as if he would shake off the hand that rested there. The air snapped with tension, then the moment passed. Arthur's shoulders relaxed as he sighed.

"I am accused of being too influenced by Rome. True, I have Roman blood, but I am glad they are finally gone from our land and Briton is free to be who and what she is! I am not a son of Rome but a Celt of this land, of the Old Ones, whose blood ran in my mother's veins, as it does in yours. And like you and Gwenhyfar, my heart is rooted in the ancient ways, even though I am accused of favoring Roman ways."

As always, Arthur's passion moved Lancelot's heart, and he watched intently as the king rose and paced the room.

"I am no Christian, who quells and shivers in fear of hell at the thought of sin—that what is natural between a man and a woman is evil. Nay, it goes against the man in me—the Pendragon in me!—to see Gwenhyfar's light grow dim since I have struggled with this wound." His pacing ceased as sat heavily in his chair. Lancelot, it has been more than a year since we have lain together as man and woman." Arthur stared at Lancelot, his face creased with pain.

"No!" He cried in sudden passion, pounding a fist against his thigh. "I would have her full of light and life, and fulfilled. Gwenhyfar is the land itself. She is the deep pool of Llyn Dinas that reflects the northern hills of Dinas Emrys, as much as she is the sarcen stones of Sorviodunum and the waves that crash on the shores of Demetia, Cornovia, and Dumnonia alike. She is the power in the crops that causes the seed to ripen, she is the tender light of dawn upon these fields, the clouds and rain and mists."

Listening quietly, Lancelot's brow grew knotted with worry as he watched Arthur. It seemed that the king was carried by a fierce wave that lifted him up as easily as it crashed him down on rocky shores. Arthur shook his head, passing a hand across his eyes. It seemed his passion was sated for the moment, for his voice became sober and quiet as he continued.

"It goes against her nature to have a cold bed. It has been almost twenty moons since we lay together as man and woman, for I cannot, Lancelot. I cannot!" Arthur stared in agony at his knight. "Yes, my queen is strong and courageous, but I see how her face grows pale and strained. Her bright nature is going dark and quiet; I see her grappling with the reality of the wound I bear, with her king unable to love her as a man who loves a woman should…"

His eyes bored into Lancelot's as he admitted, his tone grave, "All the court watches, wondering why as she grieves and slowly diminishes. As much as I depend upon the other knights, they have weaknesses that make it impossible to trust them as I trust you. If they should find out that I am impotent…"

His voice faltered and he covered his face with his hands. "Gawain, my nephew by blood and prince of the north, would be the first to challenge my right to kingship."

Lancelot pulled back his hand and sat pondering, knowing the truth of Arthur's words. Deeply sobered by what he had seen and heard, Lancelot looked silently out the window, his eyes following the movement of a flock of birds soaring across mounting gray cloudbanks.

"As long as Gwenhyfar is strong, the land and the people thrive," Arthur drove his point home with all of his awesome magnetic power. His voice became almost quiet with the focused power of his will.

"You, Lancelot, will bring her back to life. Gwenhyfar will have a child, and I will have my heir—and the line of Pendragon will live on. And for the truth of all that, I will entrust her to you, Lancelot, only because I cannot bear the thought that Gawain, who has lusted for her for so long, would have her. Or any of the others who leer in her direction at Beltane each year, even those who avow themselves Christians."

Deeply moved, Lancelot's somber eyes were drawn back to Arthur's. face. He swirled the wine in his cup and finally spoke. "Nor can I, brother, bear the thought of the queen in Gawain's hands. I understand all that you say. But you must also listen to Gwenhyfar. She is wise, Arthur. She sees in ways we do not see."

He tossed back the last sip of wine then leveled his gaze at the king. "You know well that she has stood beside you without a word of recrimination, caring for Lady Garwen and her son even as you bedded and bore children by other women, and when you brought Mordred into the court and trained him as a knight.

"Unlike you, she never took a lover of her own at the Beltane or Imbolc fires, as she celebrated the old rites with her people. Her words are true. You can seek a tanaiste in the old way. There are worthy lads who will come of age in the years ahead who can be groomed, who could marry into Gwenhyfar's royal line. Could it be that you are pushing her away? In your anger and grief and pride over the wound you have endured. Think about it, my brother."

Arthur grunted in resignation. "I can always count on you to speak the truth, Lancelot." He glanced at the graceful dark-haired man sitting next to him. "But it's also true that Gwenhyfar loves you, and you love her as well. It is hard to bear, knowing that I can no longer fulfill her bed."

He held Lancelot in his gaze with lustrous eyes. Leaning in close, he whispered, "Listen to me! Gwenhyfar is a passionate, sensuous woman, full of love and desire. Make no mistake—she truly is a goddess! And she is still young. Yes, I am pushing you to act, with my knowledge. It would drive me insane to watch you and Gwenhyfar, unable to stay apart, finally drawn together in clandestine meetings and trysts. This way, I will know and be part of your joining—and I will have my tanaiste, a son who I can raise and guide and form by my own vision and will.

"If you are her champion in all ways, at my command, becoming her lover as well in the old rites at Beltane, the knights will accept it. Perhaps they do not need to know," Arthur equivocated, "and if they find out, then I will convince them to accept."

Lancelot's eyes sharpened as he watched Arthur. Could he really believe the other knights would not know? It was madness. Fear moved in his belly, flashing a warning signal.

Arthur picked up the pitcher of wine then moved to fill their goblets. Lancelot sat silent, but his frown deepened with the knowledge that there was truth in much of what the king said. He had looked longingly at Gwenhyfar when she presided at the Beltane fires, when he saw Arthur slip away with one woman or another—usually someone the king had courted for weeks with sideways glances and smiles, little courtesies at court or over a meal, offering a special cake or piece of sweetmeat with fire burning in his eyes.

How many times had Gwenhyfar watched these flirtations, or known when Arthur asked one of the women to sing a ballad for him, that this was the foreplay of a tryst or a tumble at the Beltane fires to come? Often Arthur simply disappeared for days at a time, leaving Gwenhyfar alone or at the mercy of court gossip.

When Gwenhyfar took refuge in her horses, riding out on hunting parties with her ladies and favored knights, Lancelot and his squire followed to guard her. And then there was the birthing of Arthur's bastard children, and the recognition that the child was the king's, brought to court to be dandled on his knee. Others were given special privileges, fostered and educated by noble families of the land.

Especially Mordred, who had been born before Arthur was wed to Gwenhyfar, raised by his mother—the king's older half-sister, Morgause, the queen of Lothian in the north. It was a difficult situation indeed, as Arthur had bedded Morgause when he was hardly more than a boy himself. Raised as foster son to Sir Ector, along with Ector's son, Cai, Arthur was unaware of his blood ties when—as a very young man—Morgause had seduced him around a Beltane fire. When he realized what had happened, it was too late. When he became high king, he exiled Morgause to the cold northern kingdom of Orkney with her powerful husband, King Lot.

Morgause had taken Mordred to her bosom and raised him in Orkney with her other sons, Gawain, Gareth, Agravaine, and Gaheris. Some years before Arthur had brought these young warriors south and initiated them as knights of the Round Table. Better to keep your enemies close so you can watch what they are up to, Arthur had said, though his move had raised eyebrows among those who knew well the deep, unnatural hatred that Morgause harboured for her half brother, the Pendragon.

Now, whenever the king moved to Caerleon or any other location where Arthur established his court, Mordred begged to go. The boy's attachment to his father—equal to his cunning and contempt for Gwenhyfar—was evident to many at court, and particularly to Lancelot. Indeed, Mordred was a thorn in Gwenhyfar's side, always sneaking about, stirring up trouble wherever he could.

Gwenhyfar had had other dangers to contend with. Lancelot remembered one night when she had walked away from the Beltane fire, eyes brimming with tears. He had accompanied her back to her quarters and said goodnight. Or the year when she had been abducted by Meleagant and taken away to his castle. Arthur had ordered Lancelot to the rescue, and he thundered down the road on his horse to being back the queen.

The fight with Meleagant and his men for Gwenhyfar's honor was short and to the point. No match for Lancelot's rage, three lay dead and Meleagant was held with a knife at his throat, soon to be dispatched to the Otherworld himself. When Lancelot discovered Gwenhyfar disheveled and pale, locked in a tower room, she had fallen into his arms. Deeply shaken, her spirit remained strong, but it had taken every shred of inner fortitude he had not to lay with her then, and he knew it was the same for her.

Afterward they had traveled together, talking softly, with surreptitious looks of longing that lingered between them. They set a slow pace on their horses, relishing the interlude of freedom to be alone in each other's company. As twilight fell on the third night, there was a moment when, knowing full well each other's longing, they hung suspended in the pull of love that vibrated on the taut wire of connection between them.

Finally, Gwenhyfar had said simply, "Arthur could not bear it, Laëllon, if we act upon our love." Then both had turned away and said goodnight, retiring to opposite sides of the fire, which Lancelot kept burning at a high blaze through the long, wakeful night.

They had returned to Camelot the next day, emerging from a dense fog with Gwenhyfar riding a gray palfry, claimed from Meleagant's stable, beside Lancelot's huge black gelding. Gawain, Gaheris, Peredur, Agravain, and the others watched with grim faces, hands resting on their swords, eyes shadowed, as the queen and her champion approached and she ran joyously into Arthur's waiting arms. With these memories flashing like wildfire through his mind, Lancelot looked at the king in disbelief.

"Arthur, surely you must admit that the knights will not accept. Since she was abducted by Meleagant—and you sent me to her rescue—they have suspected Gwenhyfar and me, though nothing happened between us. They dishonor her. If they were not your vassals, and you our liege lord, I would have fought them for her honor long ago.

"The knights of your Round Table may be Celts of Dumnonia and Demetia, but they have grown accustomed to the ways of Rome. They have been influenced by the Christian monks and their teachings. Except for Gawain and the sons of Orkney, who are ruled only by their quest for power."

Arthur stared out the window, cup in hand. When he did not respond, Lancelot's argument grew more intense.

"Arthur, how can you think they will not know if Gwenhyfar and I become lovers? They watch everything I do. They will find out, and you will not be able to turn them to your purpose by inciting the ancient laws! They do not see Beltane and Imbolc as holy rites. They will not see Gwenhyfar as a queen with the right to bed her champion; they will see adultery—worst of all, between the king's first knight, his closest friend, and the queen—and they will seek to kill us both. They will say it is to avenge and protect your honor, or they will accuse us of treason, but in truth they would kill us for jealousy and their own lust for power."

He shook his head in agitation and stood, pacing back and forth to the window, raking a hand through his hair.

"Arthur, I will not deny my love for her. It is true that I love her. I have always loved her. But I love you as much, and I would not dishonor you. My love for Gwenhyfar is not separate from my love for you.

"Let me continue as I am." He turned and smiled faintly at Arthur, warm brown eyes revealing the irony in his words. "I accept my fate, even gladly, Arthur." He laughed. "I am a solitary knight of your Round Table, grateful to be so favored by my king, a wanderer who yearns for the unattainable, a puzzle to the other knights, who do not understand my past—or the blood that runs in my veins, as you do."

Arthur watched Lancelot with knitted brow. Passing a bronzed hand over his face, he looked askance at Lancelot.

"Your arguments always carry weight, but in this case the risk is worth the cure. It sorrows me that you have never known true love, Lancelot, even though you have bedded many, besides your relationship with Elaine of Pelles—Galahad is the proof of that—and your brief affair with Elaine of Astolat, who was so troubled. As long as I am king and you are my knight, you shall go to Gwenhyfar's bed, as I command you." He paused, as if to allow his command to sink in.

"I have a plan." His fleeting grin was conspiratorial, and he lowered his voice as if he might be overheard. "I will send Gawain and his brothers away with a task, a quest of some kind, then you and Gwenhyfar will tryst. You will bring her to my chambers, and there we three will be united through an ancient rite, and you will come together as man and woman. And you will give me the next Pendragon."

The smile turned grim as he cautioned. "But make no mistake about this, brother—she will always be my wife. Though I demand this of you, at the same time I dread it, I resist it with all my heart! I am caught like a salmon speared against a rock. Even so, I stand firm in my resolve."

"I want you to woo her, and soon. Do not wait. Her protests will not last. Woo her, and then you will give me an heir. Like her mother, Tarian, it is in her blood to take a lover. I know my wife very well—she loves you already. It is her destiny, brother. I can bear this, Lancelot, because you are a part of me. How many times have you saved me on the battlefield?

"Imbolc is coming, when we worship the fire and sow the seeds of the coming season. It is the perfect time to conceive a child. And if not then, by Beltane, in only a few months, you will go to her bed, and you will love her well, that night and from that time onward, as the goddess demands, until you give me a son. A Pendragon."

Lancelot listened, his eyes shadowed with doubts. When at last Arthur was silent, the knight rose, walked to the window, and stood pondering. A heavy brooding fell over the men, and Arthur poured another cup of wine for them both.

"Come, Lancelot, let us drink," Arthur enjoined, waiting for Lancelot to sit down. They remained in silence, listening to the wind that rose outside. After awhile, Lancelot said, "A storm is coming."

"Hmm," Arthur responded, looking toward the window and the hangings that billowed in the wind.

"Myrrdin warned me that something like this would happen," Lancelot mused. "I didn't understand him at the time, but now it comes clear in my mind."

"What do you mean?" Arthur watched him carefully. "What did Myrrdin say to you?"

Rubbing his brow, Lancelot pushed back thick brown hair from his forehead.

"The day that you and Gwenhyfar married, he said your fate was uncertain—do you remember? But you and Gwenhyfar were unfazed by his gloomy prophecies. Your joy could not be dimmed. Later, after many cups of mead had been drunk, he stared into the fire as he mumbled, 'Gwenhyfar's fate is entwined with both of you. She will be torn between you someday. All three of you will suffer.' When I asked what he meant, he only shook his head and refused to say more."

Arthur looked away. Moisture gathered in the corner of his eye and glinted in the afternoon light. The air pulsed between them, and after awhile Lancelot stood to go, putting a hand on the king's shoulder.

"I ask you to dwell on what Gwenhyfar has said to you this day. I wish Myrrdin were here to advise us in this, Arthur. We have not seen Nimuë either, not since she came to save your life. I sense that there have been changes at Avalon this past year. I will leave you now, my lord. But I will be nearby, if you should call."

Interference Arrives

"Stop!" Gawain shouted, reining in his roan stallion, Gringalet, as he trotted through a chill winter morning past the tilting yard and across the lawns outside the king's stronghold in Caerleon. Coming to a halt alongside Agravaine and Gaheris on their mounts, he dismounted and walked briskly to the castle toward a fracas outside the large wooden door that led to the king's private quarters.

"What is this," Gawain demanded imperiously, pushing his way through the other knights and eyeing the terrified lad held at knife point by Farquar, the king's page. His breath frosted the air as he snapped, "Who are you and what do you want with the king?"

The boy, not more than fifteen, stammered. "I am only a m-messenger, sire. P-please, allow me to deliver an urgent message from Ynis Witrin entrusted to my hands."

In his shaking hands he held out a vellum wrapped in buckskin and tied with leather thongs, which Gawain snatched away.

"Come, Gawain, he is a peaceful messenger. The war is over, sir!" Lancelot attempted a smile as he stepped up to interject from the yard where he had been at swordplay with Mordred. With a gesture to Farquar, the knife was lowered and the lad released. Dropping his hand from his own sword, Gawain stepped back, his face flushing a dark red that was only a few shades short of his hair. His black eyes flashed with anger at Lancelot.

Ignoring Gawain's temper and the scowling faces of his brothers, Agravaine and Gaheris, Lancelot faced the boy with soothing words. "Do not be afraid—we will not hurt you. What is your name, lad?"

"Ebe is my n-name," the boy replied hastily. "I was sent here by the monks at Ynis Witrin, with a message from Father Donnan for the king. Please, grant the peace to deliver it into the lord's hands."

"Sir Gawain will take it to the king," Lancelot assured him, holding out his hand to quiet the boy. "But I do find it curious that you are not wearing the colors of the church on the Glass Isle. You would have received a more pleasant greeting from Farquar had you been dressed in purple and yellow. Has Father Donnan changed the protocol?"

"No sire, not at all. I had to get away unseen, and there was no time to dress properly. Father Donnan urgently wanted me to deliver this," he gulped, "but clearly I have been prevented from fulfilling his command. As soon as I raised my hand to knock upon the king's door, this one assailed me."

"I was only doing my job," Farquar rejoined. He eyed the messenger, who was close to his own age. "Protecting the Pendragon."

Mordred stepped up to watch as Lancelot extended a reconciling hand to Gawain, but the towering burly knight shrugged him away with a brooding glance toward Agravaine and Gareth. With the rolled buckskin in hand, he walked to the door and knocked, then waited impatiently until Bloedwyn answered. She looked curiously at the knot of people gathered there.

"How may I help you?" The girl's question was hesitant, and she looked from Gawain to Lancelot, then back again.

"I am here to see Arthur." Gawain shouldered his way brusquely past her to the inner corridor. Instantly he was bounding up the stone steps that led to the king's quarters, leaving Bloedwyn gasping at his rude breach of protocol. She turned and followed him as he disappeared up the stairs.

"Well, Farquar, see to it that Ebe has food to eat and a place to rest." Lancelot placed his hands on the shoulders of the two young men. "No doubt the king will have a message to send back to Father Donnan this afternoon."

While the other knights led the horses away, Lancelot and Mordred went back to the tilting yard, Lancelot glancing over his shoulder once with a shadowed line between his brows.

A loud pounding on the door roused Arthur from the maps he studied at a trestle table. Rising to answer, he swung the door open to reveal the mottled face of his nephew, Gawain. Even Arthur had to lift his head slightly to look eye-to-eye with the imposing man who stood before him.

"Gawain! Come in, come in. There must be some necessity, or you would not be standing there looking like you are soon to explode." Arthur's smile was grim as he gestured to a nearby couch covered with furs and tapestries.

"A glass of wine?" Arthur offered, moving to his chair of ornate wood, carved in dragons of intricate Pictish design and draped with thick furs. Gawain declined both the wine and the seat, choosing to sit on a hassock opposite to Arthur.

"Here is a message from Ynis Witrin for you. I intercepted it outside, where Farquar held the messenger at bay with the blade of his knife at his throat."

Arthur raised his eyebrows but reached for the buckskin without comment, seeing that Gawain's brow was knit with emotion.

"I was on my way to see you, nonetheless. There is something important I must say to you, Uncle."

The king's icy gaze met the snapping black of Gawain's and locked there until the elder of the two instructed, "Go on."

"Arthur, it concerns me and many of the other knights that you do not have a legitimate heir. The queen lost two of your children, for unknown reasons, and you have no successor. Though my half-brother is your son, Mordred was ill-conceived. Despite my mother's royal blood that runs in his veins, he carries the stigma of incest. He is unfit to rule for other reasons apparent to all."

Gawain stared, his mouth downturned. "Arthur, it is time for you to name me, your closest kin in this court, as your tanaiste."

The words hovered between them like a rip in fabric, as if they had the power to rend the air itself. Arthur said nothing but held his nephew's eyes with his own.

"I am a king by right. I was born to rule in Lothian. My father is aging, as are you. As the eldest son of King Lot, I will inherit his kingdom when he dies. With me as king in both the north and the south, our lands will be united and further the cause of Briton." Gawain shifted on his seat and forged ahead, speaking rapidly with force.

"You have not been the same since that unexpected battle over a year ago," Gawain snapped with an offhand shrug. "You disappeared then for three moons, your queen and Lancelot took over, saying you had gone to Avalon with Merlin for a secret purpose. It was hard to believe then and hard to believe now. You can be sure there was much dissatisfaction and grumbling among the knights and warriors, who did not care for the queen and her champion ruling over us. To honor you, I kept the peace among them."

He paused and watched for Arthur's reaction. Encouraged by the king's silence, Gawain continued, intent on his course.

"It has been eighteen moons since then. Even your loyal seneschal Cai cannot make excuses for you. There are rumours that you were wounded. Perhaps you have grown soft this past year, melded with your comforts and cossets."

Ignoring the fury that grew dark on Arthur's face, Gawain pressed further. "Listen to me, Uncle. Lancelot is not the one to rule. He has always been an outsider. No one really knows the truth of his past, except that he comes from Bretonnia across the sea and has ties to Avalon. He is not trusted or liked by anyone, except you and Gwenhyfar—and the followers of Avalon."

At that moment a light knock came at the door. Arthur snapped out, "Yes?" The door was opened by Bloedwyn, who bowed then spoke hesitantly.

"Queen Gwenhyfar asked me to announce that she will be here momentarily to take the midday meal with you, my lord, as you requested."

"Very well, Bloedwyn," he replied. "Tell the queen that Gawain will be leaving soon." The maid withdrew, closing the door with care upon the knife edge of tension that reverberated between the two men.

Arthur pursed his lips and considered the knight with narrowed eyes, taking the measure of the man before him—a man as dangerous as a wounded wolf. Gathering power about himself like a cloak, Arthur placed the buckskin message on a low table, then straightened to lean forward in the king's seat toward Gawain.

"You worry too much for me, nephew." He parried with a half-smile, but the irony of his words rang hollow.

"My decisions and my actions are always guided by what is needed to secure Briton." The king's words were clipped and terse. Shifting his weight to cross one long leg over the other, Arthur tilted his head to stare at the younger man until finally Gawain looked away uneasily, straightening his shoulders.

"Son of my sister Morgause, I love you still, though you have made it clear that you covet my throne. There is no question of your royal blood." Arthur's voice fell low and deadly with sheathed power.

"Yes, you will inherit your father's throne, and that is as it should be. When that happens, we will see how Dumnonia and Cymru and Lothian will be allies—as well as the other regions of Alba and Briton. For now, the Romans no longer occupy our land, the Saxons have been driven away, the Gaels of Erin are at bay, and the small kingdoms and chieftans are united under the Pendragon banner. These victories, achieved by my reign, have left us free to pursue the glorious destiny of Briton. Let us continue, go forward as kinsmen and allies with noble purpose and high minds."

Arthur's tone turned to one of unquestionable command as he leaned forward in his seat and spoke in a low, dread tone. "But, know this, nephew. I am not wounded, and I do not intend to cede the power of Pendragon to you or anyone but the son of my own blood. I am thirty-six years of age, fit of mind and body. The power of the ancient gods runs in my veins. My queen is not barren, she is young and healthy, and a legitimate tanaiste of our royal blood is in our future."

Quick to rebuttal, Gawain argued. "You are not stupid, Arthur. You turn a blind eye to your queen and Lancelot ..."

"Enough!" Arthur silenced him with a fierce gesture and eyes of fire and ice. "I will hear no more of this. You tread on the edge of treason, Gawain. The chieftains and princes of this land are loyal to me. You will do well to follow their example! Blood kin or no, I demand your fealty, your integrity, and your honorable vow of service to your sovereign king, to the sigil of Pendragon. And you can give 'the other knights' of whom you speak this message."

The wrath of the Pendragon had struck like lightning, and Gawain was surprised to be so shaken by it, but he sat rigid and locked into Arthur's glare, his face sculpted in a grim scowl. Rising from his seat, Arthur gestured to Gawain. The large man rose uneasily and walked toward the door behind the king, wiping beads of sweat from his bow. When they reached the portal, Arthur stopped and gripped the younger man's shoulder with powerful fingers that dug to the bone and pushed him against the cold stones of the wall, pinning him there.

Lowering his voice to a whisper, Arthur's eyes fixed on Gawain's as he spoke between clenched teeth. "Mark my words, Gawain. Beware of treason. I am, and I remain, the Pendragon. And never again speak of my queen in that way...do you understand?"

Releasing his grip, Arthur smiled, regaining his usual decorum. His voice became warm, as if cajoling a beloved brother.

"Overweaning ambition never comes to good, Gawain. Be satisfied with the power I give to you. There will be more to come your way."

Arthur opened the door to find Gwenhyfar standing there with Bloedwyn.

"My queen! The beauty of your countenance is a balm to my heart, as always." He bowed from the shoulders and reached out a hand to usher her into the room. "Sir Gawain was just leaving, and our midday meal will be served soon. Please," he enjoined.

Gawain's bow was stiff and marred by the anger on his face as he offered a tense, "My lady," with one fist pressed to his heart. "A good repast to you both."

Without a glance toward his swiftly departing nephew, Arthur led Gwenhyfar into the room toward the table where the meal would soon be served. Escorting her to her seat, Arthur sat down, heaved a breath and passed his hand over his forehead, smoothing back his fair hair.

"My lord," Gwenhyfar inquired cautiously, "Gawain seemed quite agitated, and you are clearly disturbed."

"Aye, we had words—unpleasant ones at that. It seems my nephew wants to be named tanaiste to the Pendragon throne, because I have no legitimate heir. He suspects that I was wounded at the battle last year. It's exactly as I said to you and Lancelot, when we spoke after Samhain."

She listened, saying nothing. Arthur picked up the buckskin, untied the leather thongs and unrolled the skin. He read in silence, then stood and walked to the window that overlooked an orchard and flower garden in the back of the stronghold, a place he visited when he needed to contemplate an important decision.

Food was delivered and laid out on the table by servants who quietly withdrew. The knights had killed a wild boar the day before, and the cooks had roasted it with salt from the sea and dressed it with apples and tender winter sorrel from the nearby woods. Gwenhyfar filled two bowls with meat and greens then added a flat rye bread from the platter.

"Come and eat with me, Arthur."

Returning to the table, he sat beside her on the bench. They ate in silence, then he poured two cups of wine and handed one to her.

"All things are connected, Gwenhyfar. Just as Gawain threatens and makes demands, on the same day I have received a sign from the gods! Gawain and his brothers and some of the other knights will ride out tomorrow on a quest. They go to Ynis Witrin, to deliver Father Donnan and the Christians from peril, which only now I have received news of."

She looked at him quizzically.

"They have been attacked by a renegade band of warriors, led by Gorlon, the young kinsman of my mother's first husband, Gorlois. They have fomented a petty rebellion with the ambitious sons of a few peace-loving Saxons who have lived near Tintagel for years."

Gwenhyfar listened as he explained that the rebels had forced their way into the church, demanding shelter, food, and silver—while denouncing the Pendragon rule. The monks and Father Donnan, known to be friends of Arthur and Camelot, were held captive along with several families of the area, all Christians.

"Father Donnan hardly had the time to send his messenger before they were besieged, locked behind the church walls."

Gwenhyfar frowned. "Young warriors of the south who joined forces with Saxons? It is unfortunate indeed, after all these years, that they would seek retribution for the death of Gorlois, your mother's first husband. Now, when there is peace at last."

"Yes," Arthur shrugged, "but blood feuds last for many generations. These fledglings seek revenge for their great grandsire's betrayal by Uther—and his subsequent death. They took the monks' settlement by surprise, in the hours before dawn. They killed our knights, Lefflyg and Ulfin, who guard the place, and then overthrew the warriors who road straightaway from Camelot at the signal of alarm—Gordon, Rory, and the others who came to the rescue—and now hold them prisoners in the church. I am sending Gawain, Agravaine, Gaheris, Bors, Gareth, and a host of warriors to set this right. I only hope they arrive before there are any more deaths."

He glanced at Gwenhyfar. "Do you see? The goddess arranges everything. In three days we celebrate at the sacred fire of Imbolc, when we pray for the rebirth of spring, to make all things fertile—when we plant the unseen seeds that will fructify in the coming year. It is the time when marriages are made or broken."

Gwenhyfar recoiled with a sharp breath, but Arthur reached out a reassuring hand to her.

"Do not worry, Gwenhyfar. Our marriage stands firm, but it will be remade to include Lancelot. At Imbolc I will join you with Lancelot, and he will act on my behalf. With the knights away, there will be freedom for you and Lancelot to come together. Conceiving a child at Imbolc is auspicious—we do not have to wait until Beltane. The sooner you conceive, the better it is for all."

She stared at him, dismay in her eyes.

"So, you have not changed your mind but carry on with your scheme, and now you elaborate it without my agreement. Tell me, Arthur, how can you know that this is the will of the goddess? You are set on proceeding without Myrddin's guidance." Her voice rasped with the effort. "Would that he or Nimuë were here to read the signs for us."

When he did not respond, she stated flatly. "You refused to listen when I warned that this will unleash the powers of Morrigan upon us. She will have her way. There will be consequences, and we do not know what those will be. The irony is that we risk everything, when the midwives and healers have told me that I cannot have more children!" Her words were cast in sorrow, and she watched the king with troubled eyes.

"I cannot believe this is what you want."

"It is not what I want," he conceded, "but it is what I need."

She bowed her head in resignation. "So be it."

A Lover's Tryst

The next morning long before sunrise, with lances held high and swords secure in their scabbards, six knights of the Round Table set out into the dark mists on a mission to Ynis Witrin with a band of the Pendragon's warriors led by Sir Gawain. They expected to be gone for two weeks, as they would stay on at the monastery after the rebels were routed, killed, or driven away to help restore order and peace. Those taken captive would be brought to Camelot, imprisoned and, most likely, punished by death. At the king's order, Lancelot stayed behind with the young knights in training, including Mordred, who grumbled at the decision, while Gawain clearly relished the chance to lead without Lancelot's influence at play.

Caerleon was busy preparing for the ceremonies at Imbolc, when people would come from all over Dyfed and Gwent and as far away as Powys and Gwynned to observe the ancient rite with their Cymru queen and her consort, the Pendragon. The castle stronghold was a beehive of activity, with the careful cleaning of all the rooms, while rugs were taken outside and beaten, floors were scoured, then freshly woven reed mats were placed upon them.

Countless casks of wine and ale were brought from the cellar stores, along with sturdy winter vegetables—carrots, turnips, parsnips, radishes—that had been stored in sand since the harvest in the cool depths of the root cellar. Cabbages were brought from the winter garden with baskets of wild greens from the woods and cress gathered from nearby streams. Three lambs were slaughtered, and Lancelot had come in from a hunt with a stag hanging over his saddle. They would have lamb cooked slowly on the spit over low fires and venison stewed in huge pots with vegetables aplenty. The cook and his helpers were busy roasting meats and simmering pots over kitchen fires, while the bakers turned out countless honey cakes.

The day before Imbolc, the king and his seneschal Cai went out at mid-morning to hunt grouse and partridge with Bedevere, Peredur, and a few of the men. The cooks would bake these, stuffed with wild onion and spiced nuts, to add to the feast the next day. With a carefree smile, Arthur waved goodbye to Lancelot.

"Guard the queen well, Sir Lancelot, as you always do," he called. "We will be back at nightfall."

Lancelot watched the party depart then turned toward the castle and made his way to the queen's quarters.

Bloedwyn answered the door and, seeing that it was Lancelot, bid him enter even as she called to the queen, who was sitting at her loom in the inner chamber of her apartment. She looked up from her work as Lancelot entered.

"Is there anything you require of me, my lady?" Bloedwyn asked.

"Yes. Please tell Dafydd that I will need my horse one hour before sunset—I will go for a ride at that time. Have my riding britches and boots ready for me, would you?" The queen moved from the bench at her loom to sit upon a low couch covered in a tapestry and draped with rich furs. "I will be accompanied by Lady Garwen, Lady Carys, and Ghleanna. Would you let them know as well? You may leave us now, Bloedwyn, and I do not wish to be disturbed. I would speak in private with Sir Lancelot."

"Yes, my lady." Bloedwyn bowed her head and left, leaving the queen and her champion alone in a surcharged atmosphere that shimmered between them as they gazed intently at one another. She beckoned him to sit.

"Lady," Lancelot greeted her with a formal bow before he sat down at her side.

"Sir Lancelot," she responded, indicating with one graceful hand a seat on the couch beside her. Then, more softly, "Laëllon."

He settled beside her and waited, not touching her but looking steadily looking into her eyes, dark blue pools as clear and forthright as the words she spoke.

"We have not spoken of this for a long time," she began. "Not since you rescued me from Meleagant, and we made the journey back to Camelot."

Lancelot bowed his head in acknowledgement.

"We have stayed apart for the king's sake, because of the jealousies among the knights, and for the sake of our mission to unify Briton. And now, this strange turn of fate. Arthur commands us to conceive a child, after all these years of discipline, of guarding our words and thoughts and glances. Years of faithful care and loyal concern not to betray the king's trust."

"And we have never betrayed him..." Lancelot glanced down at his hands, then looked back to the queen.

"Not even at Beltane, or at Imbolc," she whispered, "when the king went with others, and you and I longed for one another. Isn't it so?"

Searching his eyes, an anguished sound broke through her body, releasing tears that came as sudden and cleansing as a summer storm. He reached out to enfold her in his arms and they passed the next moments with Gwenhyfar leaning into his strong warmth. Then, wiping her eyes with trembling fingers, she pulled away and breathed deeply, restraining her emotions by force of will before she spoke again.

"I have warned Arthur twice," her voice was weighed with the gravity of her meaning, "as you heard in the autumn past when he called us together and told us of his plan for a tanaiste, and again two days ago when the messenger arrived from Ynis Witrin. Arthur tempts the Goddess of fate to interfere in our lives. Morrigan is ruthless and wild when She comes to call. We can only hope and pray that She is pleased and gratified by our deeds!"

The conviction in her words turned lambent with passion.

"But in truth, Laëllon, my blood and bones tell me that the king is not the ultimate architect of this dilemma.

Currents of fate are stirring in Ceridwen's cauldron, and these are drawing you and I together like the sea tides to yonder shore. You have always been my champion." Her eyes searched his with urgent need. "God help me for the yearnings of my heart! I will hold back from you no more."

Clasping her hands in his, he lifted them, turning them up to kiss the palms.

"Gwenhyfar! It may be that Arthur has set in motion the patterns of many lifetimes. But, my queen, know with all your heart that I joyously and fully accept this cup, whether it is sweet or bitter."

Clasping her to him with fierce tenderness, Lancelot whispered against her cheek. "And truly, at the root of all things, this cup is sweet, my beloved."

She clung to him as he stroked her hair with a tremulous hand. "Tomorrow is Imbolc, the time of new beginnings. Arthur plans to marry me to the two of you. What is your will, cariad, your deepest wish, in all this?"

That one word, darling, spoken with reverence, released the bonds that held her in check, and her words rushed out like a flock of birds startled from the heather.

"I wish that we might have the freedom to come together as we are, Laëllon and Gwenhyfar, in sacred love and delight, not under these strictures and foreboding rituals and political tensions—and under the watchful eyes of Arthur Pendragon and his knights!"

Pushing him back gently to look in his eyes, she was fervent, her face flushed and her eyes shone.

"For so long Arthur has been as a god to me. Over the years my view has wizened, just as time and experience have changed us all. I know Arthur first and foremost as my husband, who I love without reserve. He is also Pendragon, and I am loyal to him and to his command." She shook her head in disbelief. "Yet I fear what he has planned for us, tomorrow night after the Imbolc fire, and the consequences it may bring." She hesitated to say what came next. "The truth is that Arthur is not free of jealousy or the darkness of pride."

Turning one of her hands within his own, he gently stroked the palm, his fingers moving up her wrist to touch the soft flesh of her inner arm beneath the silken robe. When he looked up to meet her eyes, the raw longing in his gaze enflamed her, raked the tender flesh of her heart. Heat flowed from his body in a wave that flooded her in its wake and she swooned against him. He moved swiftly to circle her waist with one arm and, pulling her close, pressed his lips against hers.

The kiss was almost chaste at first, constrained by the many concerns that jostled for supremacy in their minds. Then his tongue found hers and the barriers held in place for so long were shattered by a current of sweetness, equal parts fire and water, and they were swept away in a river of desire. All decorum and formality fled like wraiths before the flame of love that incinerated their cares and left them soaring beyond reason. A primal sound, almost a whimper, came from Gwenhyfar's throat as she clutched at his leather jerkin, grasping him hard against her, seeking his mouth again for a lingering kiss.

"Laëllon!" Her breath was hot and pure upon his cheek. "By the goddess, we have been chaste all these years, and how I have yearned for you!"

Caught in a paroxysm of desire, Gwenhyfar rubbed her body against his, as if she would burnish them both to a golden shine. Reclining back upon the couch, she pulled him down to lie with her. Eyes blazing, he followed eagerly, molding his body to hers as his hands roved hot over the fabric of her gown, winnowing its folds until they reached the hidden treasure he sought. In a deft flick of his wrist, he exposed the white mounds of her breasts with a cry of delight and, finding her nipples rosy and dulcet, he sucked their sweetness, one and then the other, until they were hard as cherry pits.

"Do not stop," she cried, half prayer, half command. "I am glad for your touch! Laëllon, let us not wait for whatever plan Arthur has devised—come to me now!"

"Gwenhyfar! My soul is parched for you, cariad..." Reveling in the curves of her body, his hands moved urgently to her thighs, pulling the silk up over alabaster flesh. All restraint was breached as he confessed, "Surely I will die of this desire, yet I surrender myself to you."

Leaning back, breath catching in his throat, his eyes burned as he looked upon her naked breast. The pulse beneath the delicate skin of her throat was beating wildly.

"My queen, I am yours to command! Do with me as you will," he urged. "Let our destiny be fulfilled."

The sun had moved across the sky to hover in the west when Lancelot emerged cautiously from the queen's chambers. He glanced down the hallway, checking to see if he was alone. After the conflagration of their joining and the long afternoon idyll in each others' arms, he had put himself back together well, his dark green woolen cape covering leather jerkin and pants, sword in its scabbard. But his cheeks were flushed, his eyes glowed dark and silvery as a moonlit night, and his mouth was soft. Glancing to the right down the hall, he could not see Mordred, the illegitimate son of the king, who hid lurking by the servants' stairs at the far end of the hall. Closing Gwenhyfar's door firmly behind him, Lancelot made his way in the opposite direction to trod with sure-footed gait down the stone stairs to the gardens.

With narrowed eyes Mordred watched. Disdain, envy, revenge and a score of dark emotions stamped the features of his young face in a mask of ill design. Throwing his woolen cape across one shoulder, he moved silently down the stairs, slipped past the busy kitchens and out the servants' entrance unnoticed. He headed for the stables and soon galloped away toward the south.

Before sunset the king, his seneschal and their party came cantering down the road, their horses laden with birds that hung by their feet from their saddles. Seeing Mordred sitting under an oak tree with his horse tethered nearby, Arthur reined in.

"Mordred, what are you doing here? I thought you decided to return to Caerleon this morning."

"My king!" Mordred stood hastily and bowed. "I am waiting for you. It is urgent that we speak."

Arthur looked to Cai and, with a reluctant shrug, gestured that his seneschal should continue on.

"I will come along soon, Cai. Will you attend to my birds as well?" He smiled and untied three birds from his saddle and handed them over to Cai, who handled them efficiently, while Bedevere and Peredur exchanged a glance.

"Of course, my lord. I will see you tonight, after supper," Cai replied evenly.

With a click of his tongue, his horse started forward, and the rest of the party followed, secretly downcast that their joyous day of camaraderie with the Pendragon had been cut short by the ever-troublesome bastard son.

Imbolc

All day the stronghold had prepared for the celebration that night, on the eve of Imbolc. The cleaning, sweeping, and scrubbing were finished, the final touches of embellishments were complete; long branches of pussy willow covered in fuzzy white buds were placed in burnished clay pots throughout the halls, and wreaths of evergreen hung about the doors and mantles. Every corner and nook in the castle and on the grounds—from stables and tilting yard and kitchen to private apartments—was freshened, rejuvenated, brought to life in honor of the Goddess. Even the Romans among them, who called this day the first of February, looked forward with high anticipation to Imbolc.

In the great hall, a long oaken table was laden with sacred oblations for the Imbolc fire that night. According to the oldest customs, Ariana, the high priestess, had filled three baskets with carefully cleaned seeds of mistletoe, hawthorn and rowan; these would be offered into the fire for the pleasure of the Keeper of Hearths. Baskets of acorns gathered from the oldest oaks were also prepared for the ritual, along with several flagons of oil and more precious distilled essences in small vials.

Three bulls and three lambs were ritually slaughtered, reminders of more ancient times when the sacrifice was of human bodies. The blood of the animals was collected by Hadyn, the chief druid, and the meat of their carcasses prepared for roasting upon spits for the predawn feast. With these precious gifts, they would invoke the goddess for her blessing—for the spring planting, for the fertility of the beasts that kept them alive with meat, milk, and eggs, for the birth of many babes in the next year, for the fecundity of all nature and human relationships.

Imbolc arrived each year in the late winter, when it was often overcast or raining. This year an auspicious orange and gold sunset signified the time to light the fire. Over the past two days a huge crowd had gathered, coming from Gwent, Morganwwyg, from Dyfed in the West and as far north as Powys to join the celebration. Most were Gwenhyfar's subjects of Cymry, but many others were from the Summer Country in the south, Celts from further north or from Alba, Irlandis, as well as Britons from the east, Romans, and Saxons who had mixed into the native culture. Some were dressed in rags with matted hair, while others were arrayed with fine furs, wolf and fox and bear, gold or silver torcs adorning necks and arms, long hair and beards braided with strips of colored cloth and set with silver beads. Some bore the blue marks of woad upon their faces in curling designs that showed their allegiance to the tribes of the north. Many families dragged their old, infirm, or wounded on litters while most walked on foot, the children running and shouting among them with high anticipation of the feast to come. The warriors road proud and erect astride their horses, swords laid across their thighs, axes tucked under wide leather belts.

The burgeoning, lively encampment sprawled across fields and into the surrounding forests of Caerleon. As sunset drew near the milling crowd jostled and strained to see Hadyn and Ariana prepare to initiate the rites. The queen and king sat in seats of honor, their chairs placed near the fire to preside over the festivities. Eager to worship their goddess—the benign and loving Brighid—a hush fell over the crowd as Hadyn stepped forward with a burning brand that he thrust into the mound of dry wood.

Flames burst forth from budding green branches heaped upon a thick underpinning of logs doused with the fat of sacrificed animals. As the Imbolc flames leapt up into dusky air, Ariana and Hadyn intoned hymns in the language of their ancestors to call forth the spirit of the goddess and praise the sun as they circled the growing conflagration three times, moving sunwise. After the inception of the rite was complete, they stepped to the dais where the king and queen sat and bowed low from the waist. Ariana's voice rang out across the masses.

"Hail to our goddess of the land, our sovereign queen Gwenhyfar and her consort, the majestic Pendragon, who has rid us of the Saxon blight, freed our people and our land, who have brought abundance and plenty to our fields and gardens and peace to our hearthfires!

"Gwenhyfar, noble queen and priestess, pre-eminent Sovereignty! We ask you to fulfill the geasa of your mothers and grandmothers. Come to the holy fire and consecrate this rite on our behalf."

A tumultuous swell of cheers from the crowd hailed Gwenhyfar as she rose from her seat and walked through the purple dusk to stand before the fire. The flames leapt high, casting golden light upon her face as she slowly began the ancient ritual of the queen's revolutions around the fire. All eyes were locked upon the slender form of the queen, their embodiment of the Goddess, as she circumambulated the now roaring blaze. When the last round was complete she raised her hands, and a reverent hush muted the expectant throng.

"My people," she called in a resounding, steady voice, "a new year begins. The sun will journey through the houses of heaven once again, bestowing life and light upon our people, upon the trees and beasts and fields. Let us celebrate with joy and gladness the ever-renewing spiral of life, the great cosmic order ruled by the three forces from which all things are born, grow, and die to be reborn again. Let us give thanks for the cycles and seasons, for the abundance of gifts we receive each day from the generous hands of our goddess! Let our seeds be made fecund for the year ahead!"

A deafening roar of approval swept through the crowd as Gwenhyfar bid the druid and priestess to continue the rite. Resuming her seat upon the dais, she sat at the king's right side with her ladies Carys, Ghleanna, and Bloedwyn beside her. At the king's left side stood his first knight, Lancelot. The other knights were gathered around, making a royal tableau that included Bedevere, Peredur and a brooding Mordred, who hovered about trying unsuccessfully to get close to the king. Much to the his chagrin, Arthur's seneschal and foster brother Cai stood behind the king awaiting any request he might have during the ceremony.

A host of knights and ladies of the court stood or sat nearby. Excited maidens and lads of the king's castle, the people of Caerleon, and a growing crowd of pilgrims from the surrounding farms and villages watched as seeds and acorns were offered by Ariana, then oils and essences that blazed in the fire, causing flames to lick and leap high. A reverent hush fell upon the expectant thousand or more gathered for the rites of the coming spring as Hadyn walked forward to pour the offerings of ewe's milk and then blood.

When the last drops of dark viscous liquid had spilled out upon the fire and Hadyn raised his arms in a shout of victory, the people broke into a wild cacophony. Satisfied that they had fulfilled the hungers of the goddess, some faces were enraptured or smiling broadly while others were streaked with tears of lamentation as they called out Brighid's name, evoked Her blessings with prayers of supplication, or shouted Her praise.

When the goddess had been well sung and all offerings were made, the shadows of twilight had long faded into the indigo of a clear, starry night—a rare sign of Brighid's pleasure. The beeves and lambs were put on to roast over smaller fires nearby, while the driving rhythms of drums mingled well with the felicitous sounds of pipes, lutes and bells to take over the night. Mead and ale began to flow and cups were filled then refilled. Joyous noise, revelry and dancing around the Imbolc fire would grow, becoming wild and frenzied throughout the night.

Just before dawn, the roasted meats would be served to all, along with salted flatbreads, flecked green with early spring herbs that were kneaded into huge mounds of wheat and barley dough prepared by thirteen women. These women had white or gray-streaked hair, which earned them the honor of sitting at small fires that burned in a circle around the Imbolc fire, where they deftly patted and shaped each flat round that was then baked on hot stones. Their job was not finished until they had amassed a mountain of breads, enough to feed everyone at the predawn feast.

The night deepened to black, revealing fiery stars that gleamed in familiar constellations scattered across the velvet sky; their dim radiance softly illumined the swelling crowd. Smoke drifted on the breeze and added to the mystery of the night as couples ran between the thirteen bread fires, the six roasting fires, and the immense sacred fire at the center of all. Music permeated the air, and there were many circles of dancers who plied their joy with shining eyes and ruddy cheeks.

Arthur and Gwenhyfar watched, presiding over all with cups of spiced wine in their hands. At one point Arthur leaned in to Gwenhyfar and whispered, "Do you remember, my queen, when we were much younger, and we danced wildly around the fire ourselves?" With a glance and a smile, she squeezed his hand lightly.

Arthur's charisma waxed brightly as he relaxed in camaraderie with Cai, Lancelot, and Bedevere. On the other hand, Gwenhyfar was extraordinarily somber, and yet she exuded a quiet radiance and poise. Bloedwyn noticed that the queen seemed happier than she had been in many moons. As a sliver of moon rose higher in the sky and the drunken ecstasies of the dance and amorous advances among couples grew more raucous, a smoldering glance lingered between the queen and Lancelot and was not missed by knowing eyes. Even the ever-loyal Cai and Bedevere noticed and shared a penetrating look between themselves. Mordred rustled impatiently beside Bedevere, thrusting his elbow into the knight's side.

The moment spurred Cai to stir and cough lightly then bend down to whisper in the king's ear, "Sire, the hour grows late. May I assist you in some way...?"

With a smile Arthur turned toward the queen, taking her hand in his.

"My queen," he invited, "it is time for us to retire."

Before she could respond, Mordred stepped forward.

"Father, allow me to see the queen to her chamber."

Arthur looked in stern surprise at the young man before him. Sixteen years of age, his shoulders were broad and his waist thin. His dark hair and eyes belied the Pendragon blood that ran in his veins—he did not favor his father at all, but was wiry with a perpetual scowl, pale skin and dark hair that he wore pulled back in a leather queue. The king's chagrin was visible. Lancelot said nothing but exchanged a quick glance with Gwenhyfar, who had remained still in her seat at the interruption. With a sharp flick of his finger, Arthur dismissed Mordred.

"I will accompany the queen myself. It is no business of yours, Mordred." Then, more kindly, he urged, "Now go and celebrate with the other boys your age."

They watched as Mordred reluctantly turned away into the darkness, heading toward the stables. Arthur shrugged and laughed but the sound was uneasy. He turned to his seneschal.

"Cai, have you made everything ready in our chambers? The queen and I will celebrate a renewal of our marriage vows on this Imbolc eve."

"Yes, Arthur," Cai bowed his head, "all is made ready, exactly as you asked. Roasted meat from the fires will be brought to your quarters with hot bread and mulled wine just before dawn for you and the queen to enjoy."

The Pendragon nodded in approval, then, with a word to Bedevere and Peredur, the knights dispersed among the crowd to join with their ladyloves or a damsel, to drink, sing, dance and eventually tryst amidst the groves and thickets or in a hayloft, or, if they were lucky, in the warmth and comfort of their chambers within the castle.

Satisfied that all were now engaged in Imbolc festivities, Arthur extended his hand to Gwenhyfar, who dismissed her ladies with an encouraging word to Ghleanna and the ever-solicitous Bloedwyn to enjoy the night and dance around the fire. The two younger women vanished within seconds, leaving the king's first knight and his seneschal with Lady Carys to watch as the king and queen departed through a crowd that cheered and called out blessings to the royal couple, making way for them to progress through a throng of revelers. Even as they moved through the burgeoning crowd, they were pelted with early spring flowers, gingerly touched by rough but gentle hands, and besieged with a hundred murmured or shouted blessings.

"Well, Sir Lancelot, what is your plan on this Imbolc evening?" Cai turned to Lancelot with a smile playing about his lips, pulling Lady Carys close to his side.

"Me?" Lancelot returned lightly. "I am as I always am. Alone, by choice."

"I would have thought the Lady Elaine of Astolat would be here to pursue you, as she has so often over the years!" Carys teased, but her brown eyes were soft and friendly. The shadows of the flames flickered upon Lancelot's face as he replied.

"In truth, the Lady Elaine and I have not shared a bed for several years. She wanted a commitment that I could not give to her. My life is given in service to the king and his queen, my lady."

"Hmm. Yes, it has always been so, hasn't it? Though at least you do have a son. Galahad must be well over ten years now." Lady Carys smiled.

"Yes, he thrives, living in Listinoise with his mother, Elaine of Pelles." Lancelot's answer was cool but amiable. "And what of your Imbolc celebration, Sir Cai?"

"I will retire with the Lady Carys," Cai replied. His twinkling eyes sought those of Carys as his arm tightened around her waist. "We will have a late supper and drink a toast to our union. Then...who knows?" Carys laughed sweetly and hugged Cai, who planted a sound kiss upon her cheek.

"Well, Sir Cai, Lady Carys, I bid you both goodnight and a joyous Imbolc." Lancelot bowed and disappeared into the darkness that surrounded the bright and wilding scene of the sacred fire.

The Rending of Veils

Entering Arthur's quarters, Gwenhyfar was impressed with the preparations arranged by Cai, who had sent the serving maids earlier to light countless beeswax candles and stoke the fireplaces with huge logs against the growing chill of the night. Bidding their king and queen a happy and fruitful Imbolc, the maids withdrew quietly.

Gwenhyfar walked to the inner chamber, where another fire blazed on the hearth and sconces and candles burned bright around Arthur's bed that was hung with sheer silken curtains of a saffron hue. The stone floor was strewn with sweet herbs of early spring, scattered atop the new rushes, and the bed covers were turned back and the pillows plumped and lush. A flagon of golden wine with two rare glass goblets sat upon the table near the fire.

"It's good, is it not?" Arthur stood at her elbow. "This is for you, my queen, the place where you and Lancelot will join. A fitting arbor for the conception of a new Pendragon, is it not?"

Gwenhyfar said nothing, but turned to face him.

"And you, Arthur? Where will you be?"

"I will remain in the outer chamber," Arthur informed her with a curl of a smile, his attempt at levity, "where I will enjoy this fine wine brought from the south of Gaul while I study the new maps of Alba. Then, perhaps I will sleep awhile upon the couch there."

She gave an irritated soft snort at this news. A thread of fear shot like lightning through her belly, causing her breath to quicken. Calming herself, she gazed steadily at the king.

"Sleep? With Lancelot and I in yonder room?"

As he opened his mouth to respond, the soft sound of three taps came from the outer door, drawing them back into the sitting room of the king's inner chamber. Arthur called out, "Come in," and Lancelot walked in, closing the door behind him with a firm hand.

"Were you seen by anyone?" Arthur asked.

"I am certain I was not seen coming here, but suspicion floats on the air like the smoke from yon fires," Lancelot replied. "Certainly Bedevere and Peredur suspect something, and Mordred is more troublesome than usual. Cai is no fool, and has the eyes to see, but as you well know he and Bedevere are loyal to you. Of all the knights, they are friends to me as well."

Arthur chewed his bottom lip thoughtfully between his teeth as he walked to the fire. "Come, let us warm ourselves and share a cup of this fine wine."

When they were settled as Arthur arranged, with Gwenhyfar and Lancelot together on a low couch, he sat opposite them to pour three cups.

"To love, life, and progeny," he offered, holding his aloft. When Gwenhyfar and Lancelot stared at him in dismay, he laughed.

"Drink! Drink up. It is far too late for misgivings, my dear ones. Faith is the magic that dissolves the obstacles the gods place before us." Quaffing his own cup, he wiped a sleeve across his mouth and smacked his lips, watching as they drank, satisfied that they had sipped the wine.

"There is another offering to be made tonight."

In his hand appeared a small carved wooden ball in which three strands flowed together in an intricate design that interwove as one. Holding it in his palm and turning it carefully, he continued.

"This is one of three talismans given to me by Nimuë years ago. She told me to use these only when I need the assistance of the Old Ones. We have already beseeched Brighid's blessing. Now I will offer this into the fire, with a prayer to Ceridwen, your own favored deity, Gwenhyfar, to ask for Her blessings for the three of us..."

Before either could move or speak, Arthur had tossed the talisman into the fire, where it was quickly consumed in flames. As it burned a sweet fragrance filled the air and a golden glow suffused the room, enveloping the three who watched in amazement as the power of the talisman was unlocked and released in the moment of its destruction. A faint otherworldly melody chimed, a carillon born in the unseen world, and Gwenhyfar shifted in her seat. As she looked around in wonder at the transformation in the atmosphere, her champion was quiet, absorbed in his own thoughts.

Arthur raked a hand through thick, gleaming hair as he watched the ball incinerate. When the remaining white ashes fell onto the pile of burning logs, his eyes fell in speculation upon the couple at his side. His fair face was framed by an unspoken question, and after some moments of silence, the king stood, taking Gwenhyfar by the hand.

"Come, my love, to the bed of your champion, my best knight, where you will conceive a child, a son who will continue our work to unify this great isle, Briton."

At the king's gesture, Lancelot rose as well and received the hand of the queen in his own as Arthur delivered her unto him.

"Now go, and rejoin me for the feast, just before dawn."

Walking to the fireside table strewn with maps, the king picked up a finely wrought vellum, unrolled and stretched it out. He watched as the two walked through the heavy wooden door to his bedchamber. Lancelot turned, looked into the king's eyes and bowed his head, then disappeared behind the closed door.

Dropping the vellum, Arthur sank to the bench, picked up the cup of wine, and sat as still as the sacred wells of Annwyn, his eyes narrowed and his lips pursed. His body slackened in a pose of deep reflection, as if he waited for some inner sign. After some moments, he took a deep breath, rose up, and walked into the chamber adjacent to the one now inhabited by Gwenhyfar and Lancelot. Entering a small closet, he pulled back a wall hanging to reveal an ornate iron grill of clever design, through which he could see into the bedchamber. He had gone to great lengths to have his stonemason prepare this secret view, and now he was satisfied to find that it worked quite well.

Gwenhyfar's fair skin glimmered in the half-light of candles and fireplace as she slipped the blue velvet gown from her shoulders and stood waiting. Lancelot's eyes were luminous dark pools as he watched every nuance of her moves. Pulling his shirt over his head, he approached bare-chested to place his hands on her shoulders in a caress that brushed away the silk of her undergarments that slid down over full breasts as he folded her body into his arms.

Moving his hands over her curves and hollows, he then took her face between his palms to kiss her deeply again and again. Leaning back to look into her eyes, she saw tears glimmering there.

"The hours of the day have never been so long from yesterday till today, cariad," he breathed, his hands roving back to her breasts to fondle lightly the roseate nipples.

Arthur gave a silent gasp. He could hear their breath coming faster and their sibilant whispers or the sharp sounds of their pleasure cries. He could see the queen's breasts rising and falling with her breath, the way she drew him forcefully against her, the silken brush of warm flesh against flesh, eager mouths and the spilled nectar of their kiss.

Pressing his face hard against the grill, Arthur watched in agony as Gwenhyfar pulled urgently at the laces of Lancelot's britches. Desire suited her well, bringing out the goddess who lived within. Gazing intently at Lancelot, her face was framed by dark waves of hair that swung below her waist, her cheeks were flaming roses set in pale cream. Her wide set twilight eyes were twin stars of compelling luminosity that matched in force the fervid intensity of her hands as she worked to set him free.

As Lancelot's head fell back in ecstasy and his breath came in gasps at the pleasure of her kisses, Arthur's pulse raced. His breath came hard and fast as he watched the knight seize her arms and pull Gwenhyfar to his chest with a low moan of desire as they half stumbled to the bed to fall pell-mell into its soft pillows and quilted recesses.

Slowly, Lancelot kissed the length of her until he arrived at the dark mystery between her thighs. With a bright cry of abandon, Gwenhyfar arched her neck, her head deep in the pillows as she twined her fingers in Lancelot's hair. Within moments—or was it years?—they had changed places, and Gwenhyfar sat astride her knight, eyes glowing and chest heaving with gleaming tumid breasts and ruby nipples, a sheen of sweat upon her brow and unrestrained joy written across her face.

Swallowing hard the stone of envy that lodged in his throat, Arthur watched their inevitable surrender to ride the cresting waves of pleasure and sweet pain that had no beginning and no end. These were not new lovers. Indeed, it appeared to him that they had only opened the floodgates to a river of ecstasy that flowed eternal between them.

The lines around his mouth deepened in a grimace of agony, mirroring the inner battle he waged. He was pierced within by a stab of jealousy. It surged within him, a strange new feeling, one he had never known. A mood, as strange and heavy as a chartreuse sky before a storm, afflicted his mind. With one hand he gripped the golden dragon that hung on a thick chain at his chest, grasping with the other the iron frame of the casing through which he saw, with an aching gasp, the folly of his design.

The lovers lay upon the soft silk of the pillows with hands touching lightly. They had passed the night in ardent embrace, as one wave of desire led to another and then another, urging them on to fulfill the commands of their bodies, ruled by the heart. In this way they drank deeply of each other, discovering an unquenchable thirst, an inborn need to know and rejoice in one another. Finally they slept entwined for a while, dreading the hour when they would have to part.

"The feasting bell will soon toll, my love," Gwenhyfar whispered, moving closer to his warmth. "Listen! Do you hear the owls calling outside?" She smiled, then sighed with pleasure and pain mixed.

"I am soaked in your seed, and gladly my darling," she whispered, "not for the tanaiste the king would have me bear, but only for the love of you and everything that you are. I want to be immersed in you, to drown in you, my Laëllon."

The corners of his eyes crinkled in happiness as he turned on his side to envelop her in the circle of his arms. Squeezing her gently, he whispered in return, "By all the gods and goddesses, Gwenhyfar, you are mine and I am yours. Nothing can tear asunder this love, for it is a gift, born from the depths of our souls, where we are not two but one."

She nestled against his chest, her hands taking pleasure with fingers tangled in the soft dark hairs that curled there.

"We have loved before this life," she replied softly, "and we will love again." Her voice became wistful as she reflected. "In the days and weeks ahead, it is uncertain when we can be together again...but I will call for you when I can."

As the interlude of their loving waned, the burden of their obligations came to sit upon them like buzzards landing on a tree, but nonetheless they rested in quietude, absorbed in one another, until they heard the distant repetitive gong of a large bell announcing the beginning of the Imbolc feast. It was still dark outside, and they knew that before the masses gathered to partake of the blessed food, the first portion would be delivered to the king's quarters. It was time to rise and join Arthur for the meal.

"Gwenhyfar, my love," Lancelot whispered, leaning in to meet her lips with his own. Pressing their cheeks against one another, hands smoothing back disheveled hair, both black and brown, they clasped each other in an aching embrace. As desire surged between them once again, Lancelot extricated himself slowly, taking her in with his gaze. He held her face in trembling hands for a brief moment, breathed deep to secure his resolve, and then pulled away to rise from the bed.

Within minutes they were dressed. They splashed water on their faces from the large clay bowl near the bed and arranged themselves well for presentation to the king. Gwenhyfar twined the tangled length of her hair in a chignon and fastened it with a carved wooden stick from her pocket, then combed Lancelot's hair with her fingers, tying it back in a queue with a scrap of soft leather. Smiling into his eyes, she whispered.

"My champion, you have touched me at the deepest core of myself, and I will never be the same. My heart beats with yours, Laëllon, now and always."

He bowed, a chivalrous hand upon his heart. "My queen." Then, looking up with tender regard in his eyes, he smiled. "I am yours, cariad, now and forever."

Visitation

The outer chamber blazed with light. Servants had already come and gone, and the feast was arranged upon the long table where Arthur sat. His face was haggard, and his bruised eyes fastened on the queen as they emerged from the bedchamber. Gwenhyfar walked swiftly to the king's side and leaned up to kiss his cheek. He did not pull away, but flinched and then gestured to the food.

"Come, let us share the Imbolc feast." His voice was oddly sharp and commanding. Not knowing what to say, they obeyed wordlessly, taking seats that he offered as he picked up a silver fork. "Allow me to serve you."

Moving to the table, Arthur took up a beaten silver plate and piled it high with meat and bread, then sat on a stool near Gwenhyfar and across from Lancelot.

"Let us share this plate," he invited. "Eat."

With an inquisitive glance at her husband, Gwenhyfar took a half round of bread and a small piece of lamb.

"Well, I hope you have accomplished our aim!" Holding the platter of food out to Lancelot, Arthur snapped awkwardly, as if issuing battle instructions to one of his soldiers. The stab found its mark, and Lancelot looked long at the king as he took bread and meat from the proffered platter. Looking away, unable to meet the eyes of his closest friend, Arthur served his own plate then dropped it on the table to move beside the fire, where he looked them over warily. It seemed to Gwenhyfar that there was a chasm, a great unknowable distance, between the king and herself that had never existed before.

"You think I don't know how it is for you, but I do," he stated flatly.

Gwenhyfar recoiled in shock at the bitterness in his voice as he continued in a half-snarl.

"Love beats between you like ravens on the wing. I was a fool to believe that you did not conjoin," he shot an accusing glance at Lancelot, who sat still and pale as starfire, "when you brought her back from Meleagant."

He straightened his shoulders and stared at Gwenhyfar. "Well, my queen, you warned me, didn't you? Now it is done."

Putting down the plate, Gwenhyfar stood and moved to his side. Placing her hand upon his chest, she looked up, her face beseeching.

"Arthur, please, don't do this. I have always loved you and I love you still. You have asked me to love Lancelot as well, and I have done so in obedience to your command. We were not together when Meleagant abducted me. It is the truth that we have stayed apart all these years!"

Reaching a hand to his face, her whisper was urgent. "Arthur, this is not easy for any of us. It is dark outside still, but when the sun rises, things will look differently to you."

Her face was wreathed in sorrow. Lancelot said nothing but watched the king with dark, unreadable eyes. Arthur turned to Lancelot, but his next words were waylaid as the same chiming sound resounded, just as it had when the talisman burned and the atmosphere in the chamber had turned suddenly lambent.

The air stirred and thickened, and Lancelot stood up, pulling the knife he wore sheathed at his thigh and hefting it in his hands. All three were frozen, captured by the suffusion of bright power that coalesced as a pale form took shape, withering then growing until it appeared almost human, becoming recognizable as a woman with wild red-gold hair and enormous eyes the color of the pools of Avalon, so blue they were almost black.

"Morgan!" Arthur gasped. Shock rebounded among them at the visitation, which had now taken on a flesh and blood aspect and breathed the same air as they did. The woman was dressed in a gown the color of forest berries. She carried a carved rowan staff in one hand and scrutinized them evenly, her calm gaze falling not unkindly upon them. Over one shoulder lay a thick woven shawl fringed with the tails of silver foxes.

"I will hear no more of this, Arthur," she ordered mildly. "You, my brother, have opened this door. Do you remember the old Roman tale of Pandora's box? Our mother, Ygraine, once told me that story, many years ago. So, the box is open and now we must live with what comes out of it. You three are joined together by destiny and now further by the power of Nimuë's talisman, which you burned only hours ago, thus summoning me here to intervene in this madness."

Arthur's face had gone ashen and his mouth opened in surprise, but he quickly regained his usual aplomb, responding courteously with a bow. Lancelot had gone down on one knee in a salutation of reverence, sheathing the knife and bowing his head. Gwenhyfar smiled and inclined her head in grateful acknowledgement of Morgan's timely appearance.

"Sister," the king began, "I will not ask what brings you here since you have already told us, at least in part, I suspect. But now that you are here, what can I do for you, or for Avalon? Will you partake of the Imbolc feast with us?" He gestured to the meat and bread that had grown cold. "Or have a glass of wine before further discussion of your unannounced arrival?"

Raising one eyebrow, Morgan smiled. "Diplomacy, is it? I heard what you said to your queen and your first knight. All of it. You are wrong and should ask their forgiveness."

She stared at him, locked in a brief battle of wills, until Arthur relented. "You are correct," he stated simply, and turning to Gwenhyfar then Lancelot, he bowed graciously, but his voice was low and strained as he intoned, "Forgive me."

With a solemn face and open heart Gwenhyfar accepted the apology, and Lancelot nodded once in acknowledgement. Morgan laughed, then sweeping past the three to the couch, she sat down.

"I warned you, brother, but you chose to misunderstand me. You led Gwenhyfar to believe that I was in favor of this idea!" She snorted with frustration then paused.

"Now things will unfold as fate will have them. Do you really think you are in charge, Arthur? The three forces—creation, preservation, and destruction—are ruled by a great Intelligence that orders the Cosmos, whose arms and legs are the very gods and goddesses we honored on this night past. We are all ruled by inexorable laws, including that of causes and effects." The power of her gaze raked over them, and Arthur wiped a hand across his brow, discomfited.

"Well, at any rate, I have some news that I must share with you. Please sit." She gestured to Gwenhyfar, indicating she should take the seat beside her. The two men pulled up hassocks and sat nearby.

"As we know," Morgan began, "the invasion of Roman values and beliefs in our world has changed Briton—a land of magic so ancient that even the priestesses of Avalon do not remember or understand it. The influence of Saxon invaders plays a role in these changes as well, but it is the peculiar sophistication of the Romans, with their Christian religion, that erodes the ancient ground of Briton, going back to the lost land of Atlantis, which long ago disappeared beneath the sea. Myrrdin and Nimuë carry in their blood the last remnants of the Old Ones who once guided the light of Avalon and carried the wisdom of this island. Arthur, you and Laëllon and I are their protégés, the last of our kind, with Taliesin."

She paused, whether for effect or to gauge their minds remained unclear, even as she looked slowly from one to the other as the three sat still, rapt and captured by her words. Seconds ticked by before she began again.

"The Romans are capricious, aggressive, and carelessly cruel. They care nothing for the true life of the soul. They allow their minds to rule, not the heart. Sadly, they have knowledge that is beyond the bounds of their wisdom. Though they have brought about their own downfall, their influence in the world not only remains but spreads, an avaricious growth; it has caused much disturbance in the subtle field of Avalon and all that Avalon stands for."

She rested a hand upon Gwenhyfar's, then lifted her staff, which leaned upon the edge of the couch, to hold it upright in her hand. "Myrrdin and Nimuë are gone. They have left Avalon, leaving a new Lady to preside there...none other than myself. Yes, I am the Lady of the Lake. While my beloved mentors and guides have left me with their burden, they have taken refuge from this world, with all its strife and difficulties, to live in solitude and meditation."

Lancelot stirred. "You know where Nimuë is?"

"She is with Myrrdin. He has found the cave of crystal that he has long sought, and they are dwelling there, somewhere in the lost forest of Broceliande, across the water in Bretonnia."

Arthur rubbed his chin with one hand. "Then we are lost," he lamented. "Without Myrrdin's help and advice, and with Nimuë gone..."

Morgan's smile was filled with irony as she interrupted. "Yes and no. We are lost, and we are not lost. Do not forget what Myrrdin has taught us. He has imparted wisdom to each one of us. He has guided our lives for twenty, thirty years or more—as in your case, Arthur, for whom he manipulated reality that you might be born in this time and place! And we have all paid a price for that, have we not?

"But, the true moment of reckoning is yet to come. The cost of this current venture is high." She stared intently at

Arthur. "The cosmic order will exact its coin."

Gwenhyfar interjected, "What price do you speak of?"

"I cannot say exactly how we will pay, only that we will." She faced Lancelot. "You will play a part in this, Laëllon, as will Arthur and Gwenhyfar, such is the way your fates are interwoven. But all three of you will suffer. And if that is not enough, you should know that Avalon is receding further into the mists that surround it.

"The time is coming when the tidal sea will be tamed, the waters will recede from the marshes leaving a fertile plain, and the lake will be no more. Avalon will still exist upon the Tor as a gateway to the Otherworld, but only in another dimension. It will become harder to reach as its vibration changes and Avalon resides beyond the earth.

"Avalon cannot and will not match pace with the progress of the world but undergoes a transformation of its own that will change everything—our lives, history, the consciousness of human beings and even the planetary body on which we live."

Morgan stood, and they saw that her form was becoming transparent. Picking up the staff and holding it aloft, she summoned her will to stay. "Listen! I have very little time before I am pulled back to Avalon, where my body of flesh and blood lies protected by Iona, my apprentice.

"In the times to come I will advise you as I am able, and I tell you now, Arthur, there will be no tanaiste for you! You are rash and foolhardy at best. As Gwenhyfar warned you, she cannot bear another child. And if by some miracle she did, you would do better to hope for a girl, who can carry on as sovereign queen of this land. Do you realize the geasa of Gwenhyfar's line, going back for generations? Her spiritual obligation is as great as yours, but you are blind, arrogant, and ambitious, seeing only your own glory."

Morgan's voice had become serious and edged with a tone that only remorse could embrace. "Now Arthur, you must stand behind your decision to bring these two together in love, for in love they are. Be the king you were born to be. Let them go."

Arthur's mouth was drawn in deep lines as he listened and registered the impact of Morgan's hard truth. Gwenhyfar leaned forward urgently.

"Go? I cannot leave my people, my land!"

Morgan glanced at her with dispassion.

"And where would we go?" Lancelot pressed.

"To Alba," Morgan answered without hesitation.

"The land of the Picts? They are our enemies," Gwenhyfar gasped, "and known to be brutal in defense of their land."

The Lady of the Lake raised one hand, and her form flickered in and out of their vision. "There are places in Alba that are not controlled by the Picts, but we will speak of this at another time."

Focusing on Arthur, she counseled. "Do not despair. Someone else will come to you, Arthur. You will not spend your days in solitude. Be valiant, let chivalry, noblesse, and justice be your guides. Let them go...and the sooner the better."

Then she was gone. The silence she left in her wake reverberated like a clap of thunder, pulsating within the chamber. Gwenhyfar was the first to move. She looked at

Arthur, whose face appeared as a sculpture in stone, then at Lancelot, who was remote and taciturn, and yet his face was illumined as he met her eyes.

She could hear the birds singing and knew that the rays of the dawning Imbolc sun glistened translucent upon bare treetops, but the new day did not touch them. Their world was shattered, their hearts stunned into a quandary so deep that none could put it into words. Finally Gwenhyfar uttered a small cry, as if she awoke from a dream. Then she spoke with the authority of a queen.

"I will retire to my rooms. I pray we will each contemplate deeply what the Lady of the Lake has said."

Betrayal
529 C.E.

Return to Camelot

Cai wiped beads of sweat from his brow and pulled in the reins to slow his horse, lathered and blowing from the hard ride, to halt beside the king, whose mount was already drinking at the stream. They sat astride their steeds in a companionable silence for some moments, the spring day filling their senses with soft light, the green of tender leaves that danced lightly on the wind, and the drift of feathery seeds on the mild air.

With a sign from Arthur they dismounted and lounged together, at ease on the grass while their horses grazed in the verge at the river's edge. Even in relaxation, Arthur's tall form was imposing. His exceptional height was well formed in body, with long bones and powerful, pliant muscles. Thick hair hung about his shoulders and glinted golden in the sunlight that shone on his tanned and glistening face. Although countless scars gave testimony on the flesh of his body, his beauty and strength appeared unscathed by years of war. Even so, his seneschal could not fail to see that the king's blue eyes were troubled.

"Tomorrow we set out for Camelot," Cai ventured. "May I speak with you about a pressing matter, before we return from hunting this day?"

Arthur glanced sharply at his foster brother, then nodded once. Cai took a deep breath and plunged in, knowing full well that the king was not going to like it, since he had skillfully avoided this conversation with his seneschal for two weeks or more.

"Thanks to the gods, Gawain and the knights have been victorious in Ynis Witrin," he began cautiously, "driving away the rebel Cornovii. Their leader, Gorlon, is dead, his band of warriors are routed, Father Donnan and the monks have survived and are safely reinstated in their church. Our men who died, Gordon and Rory, did so with honor, though they are sorely missed and grieved."

Cai swallowed hard. " I understand why you made the decision to move court back to Camelot—it is wise to return and assert your rule after such a rebellion. You will arrive in Camelot with Gwenhyfar, Lancelot, and the rest of the company in three days' time, and I pray to the gods that preserve us, the reunion will go well."

Arthur listened, watching his horse with narrowed eyes. "Exactly what are you saying?" He faced Cai and eyed him steadily.

"It troubles me that Gawain and the knights lingered in Ynis Witrin, unwilling to return when you ordered them back to Caerleon four weeks ago. I am grieved by the atmosphere of suspicion and rebellion that grows among them. I sense that the relationship between the queen and Lancelot has caused a permanent rift between the knights of the Round Table, and that you will not be able to repair the damage this time. I am afraid that the hard-won unity of your kingdom is threatened."

Seeing the king grow tense, Cai sighed. "Arthur, I must have your permission to speak candidly, as your brother and friend."

"Proceed," Arthur snapped.

"Gawain, Agravaine, Gaheris and the others—they are not going to turn their heads the other way when you arrive with Gwenhyfar and Lancelot. I would wager gold that Mordred has somehow sent a message to them, and they already know..."

Arthur looked sharply at Cai, but the seneschal plowed ahead. "Gawain's temper is legendary, and he has no discipline over the passions that rule him. You must know that he has coveted the queen and sought favors from her for years. He lusted for her at the Beltane fires and at Imbolc. It infuriated him when she turned him away.

"And now it appears you condone a love affair between Gwenhyfar and Lancelot. Why are you allowing such blatant behavior? What has happened to you? To them? It's true I could see that it was coming, but it would be prudent to be discreet, or even better, to keep their affair secret."

"Enough!" The king spoke softly, though the word was forced out between clenched teeth. "I will not explain myself. I appreciate your brotherly concern for me, but I have my reasons for what I allow and what I don't allow. I will handle Gawain and his brothers. And we will speak no more of this."

Standing, he offered a hand to pull Cai to his feet. "Let's ride on. I will be glad to be reunited with all of my knights again."

Within seconds they were galloping down the trail, with Arthur in the lead and Cai following, his face creased with worry.

Three days later the king, his noble company, and his court arrived at the hill fort of Camelot at midday—a long train of horses, manes braided and decorated with flowers, their flanks covered with bright embroidered tapestries dyed in the king's colors of purple and gold, interspersed with painted war chariots and wagons carrying furniture, musical instruments, weapons, food, and household goods.

Arthur rode proud astride his immense gelding, with Lancelot and Gwenhyfar on their steeds to his right and left. Cai, Peredur, and Bedevere rode close behind, then came Gwenhyfar's ladies, Carys, Gleanna, and Bloedwyn on their mares. The rest of the knights and ladies followed, with Mordred skulking at the rear beside Blane, Lancelot's squire, Farquar, and a passel of young men in training to be warriors. Behind all these rode or walked the court at large—the king's astrologers, bard-poets, jugglers, builders, and mathematicians; his musicians, cooks, bakers, tailors, courtiers, the pages of the knights, healers and herbalists, messengers, chamber maids, scullery maids, serving maids and lads, and assorted folk who traveled with the royal company.

"Look at yonder Tor. It has a mystic beauty, does it not?" Bloedwyn whispered to Ghleanna, who had never been to Camelot before. "It is the place of Avalon, where it is said the gods and goddesses dwell." Ghleanna arched her neck to look across meadow, woods and marsh to the green flanks of the high hill that dominated the surrounding countryside.

Gwenhyfar rode with confidence and ease among the company, smiling warmly at the girls and boys who ran up to press bouquets of wildflowers into her arms with grubby hands. She stopped the train several times to see the new babies, blessing them by taking them into her arms, showing them to Arthur, then gently handing them back to their mothers before signaling the train to continue on. As they made way through the streets many of the people cheered to see the king and queen again, and the crowd surged close to touch their horses or feet as the royal couple passed by.

But Lancelot was uneasy to see that Gawain, Agravain, Gaheris, and Gareth were nowhere to be seen. He noticed that some of the local men stared and grumbled, whispering to each other under their breath, while others turned away casually as soon as the king had passed, going back to their work or the taverns where they played at chess and gambled with cards. Cai also watched the crowd, and it seemed to him that his fears had been well-founded, and that intrigue and gossip flew between the lanes and houses like wraiths that chilled the air. Arthur smiled and waved to his people. As far as Cai could tell, he was oblivious to all.

The Knights of Lothian

Arriving at the fort, most of the knights were still conspicuously missing. Only Lady Garwen, Sir Bors, and Sir Accolon had come forward to greet the king and queen as they dismounted. After the customary salutations, Bedevere and Lancelot accompanied the royal couple to their quarters while the court was unpacked and arranged so that business as usual could continue. Cai was already conferring with Sir Bors, who informed him of a growing list of local people who begged for an audience with their king. Disputes to settle, land to divide, debts to be paid, and arguments resolved would come before the Pendragon in the days ahead. In the meantime, Arthur sent Peredur to search out Gawain and request his presence before the king.

An hour later, the hulking red-haired Lothian knight of renown sat before the king in his privy chamber and listened as Arthur requested his nephew to accompany him during the royal audience in the afternoon. Gawain's demeanor was cold and remote as an ice-bound highland lake.

"Nay. I cannot do your bidding today, tomorrow, or during the next days, Arthur." His face was surly as he surveyed the king with eyes hard and implacable as black amber. "Tomorrow before dawn I leave on a hunt with my brothers."

The king did not flinch but parried. "Change your plans, Gawain. I have just arrived, and I want you at my side to attend to my needs. Though I have heard from others, I have not yet received your report on the battle with Gorlon and his ruffians. You can go to hunt at any time."

Arthur pulled his sword from its scabbard. "Caliburn needs a good sharpening. You have always seen to this sword for me, nephew." His command was soft, and he looked up at Gawain from beneath his brows.

Tension hummed between them and the moments beat by like a hawk on the wing. Finally Gawain leaned forward and spoke between clenched teeth.

"I know what is going on between your queen and Lancelot. We all know. The news reached us here and spread like a pox among beggars. Deal with the traitors, Arthur."

The Pendragon shoved the sword back into its scabbard. Visibly agitated, he charged ahead to wrest control of the situation.

"I cannot believe that you, of all people, son of King Lot of Orkney, born and bred in the highlands among the Picts, with Ygraine's blood running in your veins, now pay homage to Christian ideas of infidelity and sin. By all the gods, Gwenhyfar is sovereign queen of Cymru! The power of the Goddess runs in her veins. Lancelot is the queen's champion; it is a relationship of honor that goes back centuries, rooted in the sacred customs of our ancestors."

Gawain snorted. "Times have changed, Arthur, and continue to change. The ways of Rome have infected us all, including you. You and I both carry Roman blood in our veins—no one knows the real truth of Ygraine's ancestors. The sentiment in Camelot, where the church of Ynis Witrin influences the daily lives of the people, is different than Caerleon, where you rule the queen's lands and people with a soft hand while she takes the lead." His eyes lingered on the sword Caliburn for a moment.

"Do not invoke the power of the Goddess in your attempt to rule me. The old gods and goddesses are dying. Avalon is on the wane. Its time is past. Rumor has it that Myrddin and Nimuë are gone. Now my mother's sister, Morgan, is the Lady there."

Gawain barked out a harsh laugh. "I am no more fond of her than I am of Gwenhyfar!" He paused then snarled out, "You are right, uncle. The teachings of that Christian zealot, the monk they call Padrig, has brought about many changes here, none of which I care a whit for. I do not believe in sin, but I do believe in power and the right to rule. I am not going to stand aside for Lancelot. Or a Cymry queen.

"The forces of Myrrdin, Nimuë, and Avalon, which have guided your reign as the Pendragon, are old and decrepit. There is a new power surging here, and I am its vanguard, the herald of its coming." He bared his lips and hissed, "I am its champion."

Without another word, Gawain stood and walked briskly to the door, and then he was gone. Stunned, Arthur sat unmoving, his eyes upon the sword that lay cold in his hands. It seemed to him that Morrigan gave a laugh, somewhere between bitter and taunting—as if the goddess of war and fate danced, an unseen demon, a shapeshifting imp that tittered wickedly in the shadows of the room.

For a moment madness gripped him, and he muttered to himself. "Get hold of yourself, man. You are the Pendragon." Then his thoughts turned to Morgan's words. "Let them go. And the sooner the better," she had said. He passed a shaking hand over his forehead, rubbed his face. The weight of ten millstones dragged upon his chest. His breath was labored, encumbered by regret and fear as cold as a ball of ice in the pit of his stomach, as he stood up and walked out toward the audience chamber, where Cai and Bedevere awaited him.

Arthur moved through the afternoon and evening like a man who had been routed at battle. He avoided his queen and first knight and would hardly meet their eyes, leaving the table abruptly at the evening repast with the excuse that something he had eaten gave him a bad stomach. But most telltale of all was the fact that the knights, Gawain, Agravaine and the others, who had been sent to Camelot two months before to free Father Donnan and his monks from Gorlon, were absent. Everyone with eyes to see knew full well that there was a schism brewing among Arthur's companions.

Gwenhyfar watched the king leave with a growing sense of dread. She spoke quietly to Lancelot, who was seated on the other side of the king.

"This does not bode well. Something has happened."

Lancelot's keen eyes swept around the room as he answered with a feigned casual air, "Aye, he is sorely troubled. I will talk with him later. For now, we should both go, separately, you to your quarters, take Bloedwyn with you...and I, to the stables to find Blane. I am training the young paladins early tomorrow morning and will make preparations." They rose and parted ways without a backward glance to one another.

Intrigue and Infamy

The next night the entire court was invited to a celebration organized by Lady Garwen in the great hall to welcome home the king and his court. The musicians were in fine form, and wine flowed easily, with mead and ale, to cheer the company as they feasted. The long wooden table was adorned with platters of roasted wild pig, partridge, duck, and trout dressed in lemon. Fresh flatbreads of wheat and barley dripped with butter compounded with crushed herbs fresh from garden and woodland. Mounds of wild greens—dock, sorrel, cress, dandelion—cooked with woodland mushrooms swam in a golden broth of duck fat in the crockery bowls.

Before long the dancing began as the bards sang one song after another, accompanied by the musicians on flutes, harps, drums, and pipes. The merriment continued as the moon rose in a dusky sky, even as Arthur, who had been quiet and brooding as they dined, rose early to say goodnight. He had peremptorily refused Lancelot's request to meet, but they did not need to be told that something had happened at the Pendragon's meeting with his nephew.

As Gwenhyfar watched the king's broad shoulders disappear into the hallway that lead to the stair of his private quarters, Cai saw the queen turn to her champion and lean her head in toward him to whisper with apparent urgency. The seneschal sighed and looked away, consternation lining his face. Carys whispered, "What worries you, love?"

"Yonder lovers worry me, my darling. Everyone can see that they are besmirched with one another. Already the king has quarreled with Gawain, who has left with his brothers to go on a very untimely hunt when the knights should be gathering around Arthur, as always. Such an insult to the king, who has only just now arrived back in Camelot, cannot be misread by anyone!"

Carys watched the queen and her champion from beneath long blonde lashes. "Though it may well be true what you say, don't be so hard on them. We do not know the truth of the matter. The king looked miserable throughout dinner and did not talk with our Lady Queen once. Most unusual. People are going to notice and they will gossip and talk viciously. I am sorry for them all. I do not know what has happened, or what changed things for the three of them."

Cai's frown deepened as he growled. "It does not presage well for the future of the Round Table or of Arthur's court."

Just then Cai's attention was taken by Lady Garwen, who approached seeking advice about arrangements for the king's supper the next day, while across the hall Mordred pulled Blane into a dark corner after Arthur had disappeared down the corridor. He laid a casual, clammy hand upon the young knight's shoulder.

"Gawain and his brothers, as well as Bors and the others, are nowhere to be seen," Mordred whispered furiously. "You are Lancelot's squire. How can you bear this? Does it not sicken you to serve him when he cuckolds the king?"

Blane shrugged Mordred's hand away from his shoulder. Taking a step away from the thin, wiry youth, he realized he had been caught off guard. Resolving inwardly that he would not allow that to happen again, Blane responded tersely, "Do not belittle the queen in such a way! You and I have trained for years under Lancelot's instruction. Verily, he has been my teacher since we were ten years of age. Show some respect! It is not your place, or mine, to say such things, and especially when we do not know the truth of the matter."

"Bah," Mordred asserted, leaning his hand against the wall behind Blane, "you are a fool for Lancelot, blind to his charms. He has enjoyed power for too long. His time is up, and he will soon be brought low. As soon as my uncle, Gawain, returns from the hunt. You will see, my friend. Things are changing … to my mind, for the better. Gwenhyfar has gone too far, and this is not Caerleon. Her warriors of Dyfed and Morganwwg and Gwent cannot help her here."

Mordred shoved off from the wall and sauntered away toward a group of giggling maidens who hovered in another corner of the great hall, where wine and ale were served. Blane watched as he disappeared into the crowd.

"A puffed up bastard cock with no real power," he muttered aloud.

Blane drew himself up and looked to the king's table, now absent of the Pendragon, where Gwenhyfar and

Lancelot sat together. He walked across the great hall toward them, and with a bow of deep courtesy to the queen, he then inquired of Lancelot.

"Is there any way I might serve you tonight, Sir Lancelot? I would be honored to attend to any necessity you or my Lady might have."

Blane had come to Lancelot through Gwenhyfar, as he was the son of Sir Caradoc, king of Gwent, whose lands and people were far away in Cymru, north of Caerleon. Sir Caradoc was loyal to the Pendragon in battle, but his first allegiance was to the queen and the Cymry royal line. With the blessings of Gwenhyfar and Arthur, Lancelot had chosen Blane as his squire two years before, after years of training. At sixteen years of age, Blane was turning into a fine young knight. Now, as he spoke to the queen's champion, his face beamed with the appreciation of many years with his mentor. Lancelot looked at his protégé with a smile of pride.

"Thank you, Blane, for your noble service. It would be most helpful if you would escort the queen and Lady Bloedwyn to her quarters. I will go for a ride to enjoy the full moon tonight. I do not require anything—I will stable my horse when I return. Please attend to me in the morning at first light, in my rooms. Until then, I bid you a good evening."

Lancelot and Gwenhyfar rose from the table. With a bow from her champion, she made her way—with Blane as escort and Lady Bloedwyn following behind—through the crowd that parted to let her pass. The gathering grew quiet as all eyes followed the queen, who walked gracefully from the great hall, the black waves of her hair cascading down her back. Lancelot stood at attention until Gwenhyfar was gone, then joined Sir Cai and Lady Carys for a glass of wine at their table, making sure he was visible to all. After a genial toast, Lady Carys turned away to talk with Lady Garwen and Lady Dindrane, who had arrived that day to rejoin the king's court.

"There is danger on the air," Sir Cai muttered under his breath, leaning in to Lancelot to guard his words. "Everyone is watching you and Gwenhyfar. I've warned the king and now I'm warning you. Stay away from her, Lancelot. It's not going to go well here in Camelot for either of you. Even with the influence of Avalon, which wanes daily as the Christians take over, the sentiment here is different than in Caerleon, where Gwenhyfar is the queen of her people."

Lancelot gazed at Cai for a moment, then tossed back the wine in his goblet. "Surely Arthur has told you the truth of how we came together at Imbolc past. You cannot be so ignorant, Cai, of what is really going on."

Cai shook his head. "Arthur has told me nothing! He himself is blind to the fact that he stands on quicksand. We are all going to pay a big price for this affair."

Lancelot frowned. "It is not an affair, Cai. Arthur has bound me to Gwenhyfar and himself in a formal rite blessed by the powers of the Old Ones. I will not say more, as it the Pendragon's place to tell you himself. Things are not what they appear to be, and I suggest you talk with the king. I bid you a good night."

Cai's mouth hung open in surprise. Unfolding his full height as he rose from the table to take his leave, Lancelot made a courteous bow from the waist to the three women who looked in his direction. "Good night, my Lady Carys, Lady Garwen, Lady Dindrane. May you be blessed with a peaceful sleep and sweet dreams." Then, with a nod to Sir Cai on his way out of the hall, he was gone.

Disappearing into the labyrinth of corridors within the fort, he came out under the night sky near the stables and stood, his heart sunk low from the disturbing conversation with Cai. Gazing up at the stars and then out over the shimmering vast honeycomb of lake around the Tor, he knew he should not go to Gwenhyfar. He saddled his horse and galloped away down the road to the south through the forest, but after midnight he came trotting into the tilting yard and took his horse into the stables for bedding down with oats and water.

Minutes later Gwenhyfar heard a sound and knew that Lancelot had entered through the door that led to her antechamber, now shrouded in shadow on the far side of the room. Moonlight streamed through the sheer muslin hangings of the open window and lit the bedclothes in bright shafts of silver light. Lying quietly, she watched as her champion shed jerkin and peeled off leather pants, then his tunic of spun flax. She held her arms out to him and welcomed his warmth as he slipped under the quilts and pressed his body against hers with a groan when he discovered her naked.

"Laëllon, I yearn for the moments when we can join," she whispered, pulling him tight against her body.

"By the Goddess, cariad, I tried to stay away from you this night, and I cannot. My blood sings for you,

Gwenhyfar! I am on fire, my body aches as if it will die in separation from you…"

Lost in a storm of kisses and the sweet fire of commingling flesh, their loving was desperate, deep, and fast as they came together like a tempest over the Severn Sea. They tried to smother the cries and moans that came from their lips unbidden, lest someone should hear, but they could not still the paroxysm of love that gripped them.

Afterward they slept in each others' arms, until, a full hour before dawn, he pulled himself away in an agony of parting. Quietly, cautiously, Lancelot made his way down the hallways to his own quarters, where Blane would shortly arrive with food, hot water, and ale.

In the following days the court was settled in the stronghold of Camelot and running smoothly, with Lancelot and Cai in command, since Arthur was oddly absent in more ways than one. At times no one knew his whereabouts; at other times, he was in his rooms or seen galloping away on his horse, usually with Bedevere, Bors, or Peredur at his side.

The denizens of the court and Camelot village noticed that their king did not spar with the knights in the tilting yard or exchange humorous repartee and pleasantries, or visit them at their work during the day, as he was known to express his affection for his loyal subjects in such ways. Nor did they enjoy the glow of noble friendship that had always shone between the king and his first knight. Instead, each went his own way during the day. Lancelot was pre-occupied and distant, even with Blane and the other young knights-in-training, while the king appeared glum and distracted. At eventide, when the rest of the court gathered for supper in the great hall, Arthur often took the meal in his own quarters, and Gwenhyfar did the same.

Very few in Camelot were happy to be rejoined with the bastard son of the Pendragon, who even at his young age had a reputation as the harbinger of bad news. Mordred was seen skulking or striding from one place to another around the fort or in the village, whispering or talking surreptitiously at meals with the younger knights who spent time with Gawain. Mordred often disappeared for a whole day at a time, while Lancelot watched him from afar with growing trepidation, his instincts piqued and tingling with a sense of foreboding.

Despite deep-rooted tensions and brooding factions among the knights and courtiers, many people remained unaware of any problem among the royals. Springtime was upon them, with a harmonious interplay of sun and rain that coaxed the orchards and forests to bloom in a luxurious display of colors and scents. Already the gardens were providing early spring onions, greens, and cultivated peas, as well as tender young parsnips and carrots as the beds were thinned to make room for summer's growth. They anticipated an abundant harvest of blackberries and apples, raspberries, gooseberries, and bilberries, and the woods were filled with wild strawberries that ripened with each passing day.

The king's gardeners were adept at cultivating many of the trees and vegetables that had been introduced from faraway lands by the Romans, and a small cherry orchard within the fortress walls just outside the great hall was the gardeners' pride and joy, as its flowers and fruit gave the king great pleasure. The cherry blossoms were a beauty to behold, and their petals drifted on the air in the soft wind of spring days.

Arthur's chief cook, Cynan, managed the king's kitchen with a firm hand, under the wise administration of Lady Garwen. The generous harvests of past years had been well-stored, and he was satisfied to have a good stock of barley, oats, dried legumes, and wheat that would easily carry through until the next summer's harvest. Cynan was savvy at bargaining, and he procured exotic ingredients from the merchant ships that sailed north from the Mediterranean Sea loaded with goods to trade or sell—saffron, cinnamon, and many other spices that were both delicious and healing, almonds, dried figs, apricots, and dates, and on occasion lemons and oranges.

On this day Cynan received a message from the king that set the kitchens into a flurry of activity. Gawain and his brothers were returning to Camelot! News of their arrival spread through the lanes and back paths of the town, and soon everyone was buzzing with excitement that the king had ordered a special return feast, in which all the knights of the Round Table would come together with their Pendragon for the first time in months. Everyone would partake, even the peasants and workers who would eat in the orchard outside the great hall.

Cynan planned to make one of the king's favorite dishes, stewed lamb with apricots, onions and carrots, thick with spices and tangy salt from the sea. Servants hurried about insuring that the great hall was well swept, scoured, and new rushes—mats woven from river reeds—were laid across the floors and strewn with sweet-smelling herbs. Fresh tapers and sconces were in place and ready for the onset of twilight, the tables were oiled and soon to be laden with food. A high table for the king and queen was set upon a slightly raised platform, so that everyone in the vast hall could see the Pendragon and his Lady throughout the evening's revelries.

At the appointed hour, the sun was low in the sky and the air was cooling when the Pendragon's court and local inhabitants of Camelot began to gather for the feast. As evening shadows hovered under trees along the forest edge and bonfires burned among the wattle and daub huts of the lake village, the vast hearths of the great hall were heaped with wood that blazed with merry abandon.

Soon Arthur arrived with his queen and her champion. Even with his strange moodiness, the king was golden as the sun, tall and elegant in his long woolen cloak of purple embroidered with gold. His first knight, on the other hand, shimmered with the mystery of distant stars; he wore the colors of Avalon, of the forest and the sea on a full moon night.

Gwenhyfar was dressed in the full regalia of her royal line—she had donned a heavy silk gown in the sea green and rose red of Cymru, artfully accented with bright Pendragon colors of purple and gold. Her thick hair hung in a long, complex braid laced with seed pearls suspended on silver threads, and from her neck hung three strands of large sea pearls that gleamed softly against her breast. A slender golden crown set with moonstones encircled her smooth forehead. Around her hips she had strapped a finely worked leather belt and scabbard that cradled her graceful shape; in it was sheathed a short but well-honed dagger. On both wrists she wore wide bands of copper, gold, and silver crafted in strands of three interlacing currents symbolizing the three forces that rule life, each one inset with snow quartz, sea pearls, and the rare blue crystal called sgòthan na mara—the light of the sea—by her people.

Taking her seat beside Arthur at the royal table on the raised dais, she was pale but radiant as she looked out upon the gathering of knights, ladies, courtiers, merchants, and artisans. With a nod from the king, the musicians began to play and Sir Cai stepped forward to serve wine to the king and queen with his own hands. Lady Garwen and Lady Carys were seated beside Gwenhyfar, and further down the table the queen's young kinswomen, Gleanna and Bloedwyn.

Lady Garwen leaned near with a warm smile, her hand upon Gwenhyfar's arm. "My queen, you are shining tonight. Please let me know if there is anything you might require."

Gwenhyfar squeezed the woman's hand, but her eyes did not leave Lancelot as he approached, bowed to the royal couple, then took his seat beside Arthur. For the first time in weeks Arthur turned to his first knight and placed his hand upon Lancelot's shoulder. Joy and surprise flickered across the champion's face as he turned toward Arthur, who leaned in close to speak in a low, firm tone.

"Lancelot, I want you to go to Avalon tomorrow. Speak with Morgan. Ask her to meet me in Camelot three days' hence. You are the only one I can send on this mission.

The others are no longer able to find their way through the labyrinths of lake and mists around the Tor, or locate the entrance to that realm. Nor can they be trusted. Depart before the sunrise in secret."

Lancelot responded with a quick nod. "As you wish, my Lord."

"Alone and in secret," Arthur restated with a meaningful gleam in his eyes. "Say that I need her help. She will understand."

"It will be as you say, Arthur." Lancelot bowed his head.

Just then a fracas erupted at the entry of the hall and within seconds Gawain came striding in with Agravaine, followed by Gaheris and then young Gareth behind him. Bors entered behind them. Serving maids carrying dishes of food scurried to get out of their way as the towering men, swords clanging at their sides, stalked across the hall to their usual table below the king's dais.

"Hail to the Pendragon," Gawain called in a loud voice. "King of all Briton! And, of course, to his lady consort, Gwenhyfar."

The great hall fell silent at the troubling tone behind Gawain's words of greeting that left out any of Gwenhyfar's traditional titles—Queen of Briton, Queen of Cymru and Dumnonia, Queen of the Summer Country, Sacred and Blessed Cauldron of Inspiration, Ceridwen's Daughter, and so forth. Attempting to ameliorate the situation, Gareth stepped forward with a bow.

"We greet you, Arthur, and welcome you and your queen back to Camelot, where we have re-established peace in these past months."

His attempt at chivalry was a scant help, but it was usurped by the fact that Gaheris looked down at the paving stones of the floor, his face unreadable, while Agravaine's stare was bold and unsmiling. Lancelot sat with his hand on his sword hilt, but Arthur smiled and inclined his head.

"It is good to be here, indeed," he responded. All eyes were on the king as he blatantly ignored the insult and the tense faces of Gawain and the others as well as their impudent manner.

"Sit and relax," Arthur gestured magnanimously. "The wine from Bretonnia is very fine tonight, and there is ale aplenty to celebrate. A fine feast of the hunt, prepared by Cynan himself for your return, will soon be served."

Before Arthur had finished his welcome or Farquar could come forward to assist them, the four knights made a ruckus as they settled at the table where Gawain poured generous libations of wine with rowdy glee. Their flagrant dismissal of court etiquette was appalling, and while the stench of it lingered at the king's table, the smell was quickly washed away on the tide of revelry that surged in the great hall.   The Orkney brothers were soon greeted by Lady Dindrane, Lady Gloriane, and Lady Amrys, with a flutter of admiration from a bevy of young ladies of the court, who sat at nearby tables. The ladies smiled with allure at the knights or whispered among themselves as they looked at the men appraisingly, if not with open desire.

Lancelot leaned toward the king and spoke in a low voice, "Arthur, this is unacceptable. I should call them to dual for such an offense to your honor and the honor of the queen. Let me do so, now!"

Putting one large hand on Lancelot's arm, Arthur demurred with down-turned lips. "No, Lancelot. I will not endanger you in that way. It is not only Gawain but his brothers Agravaine, Gaheris, and young Gareth, as well as the score of young knights who follow their lead. And I do not yet know where Bors stands in all this. You cannot take them all, and Gawain would gladly see you dead.

"This has to be handled with politesse. Morgan will be here soon, and we will take her counsel. You should retire early and sleep, so you can leave well before dawn, in the secrecy of night. Or even better, leave now—as soon as you have taken food. You know the way like you know your own heartbeat—travel through the night to Avalon. I will anxiously await word from you."

Gwenhyfar glanced in growing frustration at the two men who sat beside her in terse conversation, wondering what Arthur was doing now, but the lads arrived with the feast and Farquar began to serve their plates and bowls. The king turned his attention to his plate, and Gwenhyfar dared not lean around him to engage Lancelot or catch his eye lest the crowd take note of them. With a strong look at Arthur, she picked up the wooden spoon and lifted it to her lips, but her roiling stomach rebelled at the thought of food, however delicious.

Within minutes Lancelot had bolted down a bowl of lamb stew and rose to step down from the Pendragon's dais. With a bow to the king and a burning quick glance at Gwenhyfar, his fist pressed against his heart, he turned to leave the great hall. His sword swung at his side as he strode purposefully through the crowd of people still feasting at their tables, not stopping to speak to anyone.

Gawain watched him go, then looked at Gwenhyfar with narrowed eyes and a subtle leer that curled upon his upper lip. The glint of satisfaction in his eyes as he stared at the queen curdled her blood, leaving her cold and shaking inside. With the skill gained in long years of training at her mother's knee, Gwenhyfar calmed her rapidly beating heart with deep, slow breaths. Lifting her head proudly, she looked out over the revelry in full play throughout the great hall, picked up her wine goblet and sipped.

After a few moments, Gawain and his cohorts guffawed and joked loudly among themselves again, then rose to dance with Lady Dindrane and some younger damsels of the court. With one eye on the dancers, Gwenhyfar leaned in toward Arthur and spoke loud enough for his ear alone.

"We must talk, Arthur. Where have you sent Lancelot? What is going on?"

His face was limned with consternation as he glanced at her and sighed. Following her lead, he feigned—what appeared to all others—a pleasant conversation between the king and his queen. From the corner of his eye, Arthur saw that Cai openly watched all that transpired, nor did he try to conceal the anxiety engraved upon his face.

"Gawain and his faction are plotting sedition," Arthur admitted in a rush of words. "I have sent Lancelot to Avalon with a message to Morgan that I—nay, we—need her counsel. I have asked her to come, and she will. Of this I am sure." His reluctance to speak of the situation at all was not missed by Gwenhyfar, who watched warily as he smiled and nodded to a courtier who came near the king's table for the Pendragon's blessing. Having received it, the man maneuvered back into the flow of the dancers, his lady in hand.

Gwenhyfar sat back in her chair and took another deep breath. To her eyes, everything seemed fraught with danger. A murky pall was cast upon dancers, musicians, and all the happy people who drank and chatted gaily in their finest clothes, celebrating unaware of the dark storm that brewed beneath the surface. For some moments she watched and waited, as Cai approached to whisper in the king's ear. Arthur listened then turned to Gwenhyfar.

"It is best that I retire for the night now, so let us leave together," he suggested, "to make a show for everyone. No need to heap dry tender on Gawain's fire." He rose and took her hand, and they swept out of the hall. At a gesture from Gwenhyfar, Bloedwyn followed cautiously, with Cai following to see the lord and lady to their separate quarters.

The Chains that Bind

"My Lady! What has happened? Sir Lancelot left so abruptly, the other knights, the friends and brothers of Gawain, are behaving so badly. Dread thoughts are creeping into my mind, and I have the sense that we have lost our way somehow." Bloedwyn's words spilled out as she combed the queen's hair. Gwenhyfar put down the heavy strands of pearls she held in her hand.

"Bloedwyn, you must calm yourself. We must prepare, for there will be difficult times ahead. I want you to pack a bag of necessities, one for you and one for me, in case we have an urgent need to leave Camelot. Clothes, travel food for three or four people. Do you understand?"

Tears formed in Bloedwyn's eyes, trembled and shone in the lamp light, then rolled down her smooth cheeks as her brow creased in sorrow.

"My Lady, our lives have been so blessed, so wonderful…my heart breaks with sorrow that this has happened, and I don't even know what it is, exactly, except that it centers around you and Sir Lancelot. I fear what tomorrow will bring. I have a deep foreboding that haunts my mind and weighs like a stone on my heart."

Gwenhyfar pulled the frightened girl to her breast and smoothed her hair. "Shush, shush my darling, my little flower."

With her arms around the queen's waist and her cheek pressed to her breast, Bloedwyn wept. When the tears had stopped, Gwenhyfar sat back and released the young woman. With an affectionate caress to her cheek, Gwenhyfar lifted Bloedwyn's chin and smiled into her eyes, wet-lashed and red.

"Do not fear, Bloedwyn. The Goddess sees us through all the comings and goings of this life and the afterlife to come. This earthly realm is where we are born to learn over many births and deaths, where our souls are forged from iron into pure gold. Even the Christians understand something of this. They say that Jesus said, 'Do not put your treasures on earth but in heaven, where moth and dust do not corrupt.'"

Taking the comb from Bloedwyn's hand, Gwenhyfar pulled it through her own long tresses. "That is good advice, isn't it? Except, of course," she gave a light laugh, "we do not despise this earthly existence, as the Christians do. We enjoy it fully, with the blessings of our benevolent Goddess. And while it may be true that Morrigan laughs now at our folly, beloved Ceridwen will not forsake us."

Bloedwyn gave a tremulous smile as she moved away to pull back the covers on the queen's bed. Taking a silken nightgown from its hook, she laid it out upon the coverlet and smoothed it gently. She then tended to the fireplace, adding logs to the low fire that burned, which had been started earlier by the chambermaid during the feast, when the weather turned brisk after dark.

"Mostly likely a storm is brewing at sea," Bloedwyn chatted, recovering well as she checked to see that the queen's water flagon was full for the night, and that she had fresh water with which to wash in the morning. She then helped Gwenhyfar remove her heavy gown and held up the silken nightdress. Its weight fell easily over the queen's head and slithered down her shapely body.

"Perhaps we will have rain tomorrow," Gwenyfar replied evenly. Bloedwyn stared at the queen, whose pale face was framed by tendrils of black hair.

"You were especially noble and beautiful this evening, my queen," Bloedwyn sighed with a smile, her dimples showing sweetly in her round face. "I was proud to be your lady-in-waiting. No matter what tomorrow may bring, I am happy to serve you, as always."

Gwenhyfar returned the kindness with a warm smile. "Bloedwyn, I thank you with all my heart for your love and care. Now, I want you to sleep well, for we will need our energy for whatever the future holds for us. I bid you goodnight, cousin."

She watched as the young woman took up her cloak and departed, closing the heavy door behind her. Finally alone, the queen shoved the heavy iron bolt across the door, then blew out the candles one at a time and crawled between the sheets. Despite the fire, there was a sea-chill in the room, and she longed for Lancelot's arms to comfort and warm her on this night.

Though covered with a heavy silk screen and thick muslin curtains, the moonlight came through the window to suffuse the bed with a bright glow. Gwenhyfar's thoughts wandered over memories of their lovemaking, only three nights before. It had been warmer that night, and the moonlight coming through the open window had melted over their bodies in a silver sheen.

"Laëllon, my champion." Her whisper was sibilant as she wrapped her arms around her body as if to hold him tight. "May Ceridwen see you safely to Avalon and return you to my side as soon as possible."

She lay for a long while, staring into the moonlight, until finally she turned on her side with a sigh and closed her eyes. The relief of sleep came finally, some hours before dawn.

A gray pall, strange for a late spring sky, reflected Gwenhyfar's dread as she dressed for the day in a simple dark blue woolen gown that turned her eyes the color of forest shadows. She sat patiently while Bloedwyn plaited her long hair in three braids and then wove them together, knotted and fastened them with a long silver pin at the nape of the queen's slender neck. When the young woman offered a small glass vial of delicate, sweet-smelling oil, Gwenhyfar declined.

"That is not necessary, Bloedwyn. I must face this day as I am. But I will wear my silver stag brooch and the moonstone circlet to hold my hair back from falling into my eyes, as it escapes even your careful braiding!" She laughed sweetly, then grew solemn. "Have you done what I asked of you last night? The preparation for travel?"

Bloedwyn's gaze revealed the forlorn cast of her features as she answered. "Yes, my Lady, I have prepared several bags early this morning. And I will speak with the stable boy about the horses. May I attend you somewhere first?"

Gwenhyfar lifted her chin to glance at Bloedwyn. "I am going to sit with the king in his audience chamber this morning. Yes, you may accompany me. We will go there straightaway, then you must go to your tasks."

When Gwenhyfar entered the audience chamber of the great hall, Arthur sat alone, slumped upon his formal throne—a heavy oaken chair, carved with a bold dragon in flight across the back, and the sword, Caliburn, in relief from the handrests down the length of the chair's thick legs. He appeared to be brooding, hunched over, his chin on his fist with his elbow resting on his thigh. Beside him was a smaller chair, also carved but in the symbols of the Cymru—winged dragons, tiny wrens, owls, and clusters of cenhinen pedr, the golden bell-like flowers that bloomed in the woodlands and vales of her native land. The Romans called this flower "narcissus," because its scent was so sweet, its beauty so alluring. It had great meaning for Gwenhyfar—the distilled fragrance of its essence had been cherished by the queens of her line for countless generations—but even so she had declined it when offered by Bloedwyn on this onerous day.

"Gwenhyfar," he called out, looking up as she approached. He unfolded his length to greet her with a kiss to her cheek, offering a courteous hand to her elbow as she lowered herself into the queen's chair.

"Have you slept well this night?" he inquired.

"As well as can be expected, I suppose," she answered.

He could see the shadows beneath her eyes and the fine lines drawn around her mouth, and his heart clenched. His thoughts were darting and cloudy, he lacked his usual crisp clarity. Was he responsible for all this? Or did the queen and her champion spur this on, catalyze the events that had gained momentum like an avalanche that begins with one small rock. It had all seemed so clear before, and now nothing was clear to him. He rubbed his jaw in reflection as she spoke.

"I will not be relieved until Lancelot returns from Avalon with news from Morgan. Surely you must feel the same? Arthur, I fear we are hanging by a slender thread that could be cut by Gawain at any time."

Even as Arthur inclined his head to signify his understanding, the double doors to the great hall were flung open with such force that they crashed into the stone walls before the sentinels could catch them. Gawain and his brothers, Mordred, and a score of lesser knights swaggered in, their hands on the hilts of their swords.

"We have come for the queen! She is accused of treason against you, Arthur, as she is known to be plotting with Lancelot to take over your throne," Gawain shouted, his voice ricocheting around the hall. "Relinquish her to us now."

Arthur recoiled, his face the color of cold ashes. His lips were pressed together in a straight line across his face and his brow knit. When he did not move but stayed frozen as a highland hemlock after a winter storm, she looked at him in alarm.

"Arthur! Rouse yourself, man!" Gwenhyfar grabbed his arm.

The king opened his mouth to speak then gaped blankly at his nephew, as if in shock from a mortal blow. The nightshade of memory, Gwenhyfar's gleaming flesh in Lancelot's arms, crowded the mists of his mind. Finally he shook himself, like a man coming out of a dream, and began to speak, but his voice bore only a faint shade of the command she knew him to wield over the years.

"She has done nothing wrong," he stated in response, but his tone rang flat, as if he sought to convince himself.

Gawain snorted with contempt. "You are under her power, Arthur. Look at you—a king who speaks when his queen tells him to! Hand her over, for the sake of Briton, for your own good."

Arthur's blue eyes flashed at the insult. As if shaking off an unwanted cloak, the king raised himself from the royal chair to his full height, gaining force as he did so. Gwenhyfar watched in wonder and dread as fragments of the man she had known all these years flickered ephemeral then coalesced before her eyes.

"My personal affairs are not your business, Gawain. Cease this insanity now! Return to your quarters, all of you. We will meet later, when Lancelot has returned, to talk this out."

Cai and Bedevere ran through the doors with Blane and Farquar; Bloedwyn, Carys, and Garwen came close behind. They rushed toward the knot of men that stood on the paving stones below the platform that served as a royal dais for the chairs of the king and queen. Pushing through,

Cai attempted to get between Gawain and Gwenhyfar, but his heroic move was to no avail. Gawain plowed toward the queen, shoving Cai back into the crowd as easily as he would a child.

"No! You are wrong, Gawain," Arthur shouted, his eyes drawn toward Gareth, who stood rooted to the stones beneath his feet. "Gareth, don't listen to your brother," he charged. "Stop this! He has gone mad."

Gawain snarled, "You are the one who has gone mad, Arthur. Mad and soft, letting this seòrsa siùrsach have power over good men. You, Lancelot, Cai...and others. She even tempted me once, but I was strong enough to say no."

Gwenhyfar's voice rang out across the mayhem. "You are a liar, Gawain! You are the one who is committing treason, not me. You want the throne for yourself. This is nothing more than a ploy..." She stood tall, hands clenched at her side, fury raging across her features.

With a crazed leap toward the dais, Gawain grabbed her by the arms and pulled her down. As she fell toward his chest, his arms clamped around her like iron bars. Arthur came to life with a shout to Cai and Bedevere—"Help her!"—but along with Farquar and Blane they were held at spear and knife point by the bloodthirsty knights who clustered around Gawain.

Gwenhyfar cried out, struggling to free herself of his grip. The man was huge, taller than Arthur, and broader of shoulder. His black eyes glittered and spittle gathered in the corners of his mouth, downturned and bitter as gall. As strong and able as Gwenhyfar was, she was no match for Gawain, nor was any man in the room except for the king, who in his younger days could best any man. But now, Gawain held her as easily as she might hold a struggling babe in arms.

Bloedwyn had forced her way through the surrounding clot of courtiers, who were reluctant to manhandle a lady of the court. She slipped unseen past Gawain's men and beat her fists upon his back, tears streaming down her face. He turned with a snarl, then snapped at his brother Gaheris, "Get this wench away from me. Take her outside."

It was then that Arthur jumped down from the dais and made to draw his sword, but Agravaine was standing with his own drawn, and his conscience did not stay his hand from stabbing the sharp tip into the king's heart. Arthur looked down in shock at the dot of blood that blossomed on his linen shirt.

Agravaine's deep voice was cruel as he growled, "You have lost yourself, uncle. This is for your own good. We are here to defend your throne."

Clinching Bloedwyn in a grip under one arm like a rag doll, Gaheris jeered, "Aye, t'was most helpful of you, Arthur, to send Lancelot away on another knight's errand. It was the signal we waited for, which showed the time to act. She will stay in the dungeon until we are ready to conduct her trial."

With a struggling Gwenhyfar pulled along easily behind, Gawain stalked toward the great doors, Gaheris ten paces behind with a terrified Bloedwyn in hand. Once outside, the knight shoved Bloedwyn into Lady Garwen's arms, snapping, "Keep her out of this!" He moved fast to keep stride with Gawain and the others as they hurried toward the dungeon, Garwen and Bloedwyn running behind them.

Arthur was still held at sword point by Agravaine and a host of men, while Gareth, who had stood staring at the king, turned and walked away.

The slamming of the iron door clanged painfully in Gwenhyfar's ears as she fell against the stone wall of the dungeon. The last thing she saw before her world was encased by iron and stone was Bloedwyn's tear-streaked face, next to the horror and shock on Lady Garwen's. It had all happened so fast. She had thought they had some days, maybe a week to plan, but Gawain had moved in a swift strike, a bird of prey.

There were no tears on her face as she gathered her strength to stagger further into the dungeon and drop to her knees on the hard stone floor. Kneeling there, bone against rock, her heart opened in the weak rays of sun that shone down through one high, barred window. As Gwenhyfar began to pray, her words took form and flight from the deepest recesses of her heart. One tear ran its course down the curve of her pale and dirt-smudged face.

"Ceridwen, Breo Saighead, Bright Arrow! Mother of All, be with me now. Fire of Inspiration, Poetess, Muse, Sun and Sunlight, Water, Rivers, Sea…" She shuddered, then breathed deeply of the air that smelled cleanly of rock, dirt, moss, and of something old and dark as well—bones, blood, must and mold. She raised her hands in supplication as the words spilled out unbidden, a liturgy of praise learned long ago at her grandmother's knee.

"My Mother, Prophetess, Mistress of all crafts, Great Healer, Bestower of hidden knowledge; Mother of metallurgy, She who smelts and sculpts the gold and silver, who pounds the herbs to make medicine, who courses within our blood as the Fire of Life itself!"

"She who is the Sun, the springs of water that gurgle forth to run free from oimbelc, the Womb of Creation. She who is both beautiful and ugly. She who transfigures Herself from the death of winter to the rebirth of spring. Mistress of the Mantle, Great Ceridwen who hangs Her cloak upon the Rays of the Sun, Keeper of the Cauldron, your daughter, Gwenhyfar of Dyfed and Cymru, invokes your protection!"

Gwenhyfar wiped the tears from her face, then lowered her head to rest her forehead on the cold stone floor with hands clasped, arms stretched above her head. Passion spent, she passed the next hours sitting quietly, leaning against the rock wall as she watched motes of dust float in a shaft of sun that moved across the dungeon floor from the high window. At first she planned every detail of her escape with Lancelot, then thoughts of Arthur took over. She was bewildered and then betrayed by his strange hesitation to defend her. Inwardly she ranged from anger and rage to sorrow and worry for his well-being until, finally, her mind and heart became curiously quiet.

Trials and Tribulations

It was just past midday when she was roused by the sound of men's voices shouting, the jingling of keys in a lock, the grating of iron against rock. Mordred and Agravaine stepped into the dungeon cell.

"Get up!" Agravaine ordered, bending down to grab Gwenhyfar's arm with his hand. Shrugging away his touch, she stood up and smoothed the hair back from her face, looking him in the eye.

"There is no need to put your hands upon me. I will come of my own free will."

He curled his lip with contempt, then pushed her from behind as she walked past him toward the door. Blinking into the sunlight as she emerged from the dungeon, she saw Gawain and several of the younger knights standing beside a large oak tree.

"Well, Lady Gwenhyfar," he laughed, "you are not so sure of yourself now, are you?"

She gave him no answer, but lifted her head and straightened her back as she walked surrounded by Gawain and his knights, Mordred at her heels. Drawing near the great hall, she saw many people gathered outside in the cherry orchard. Arthur was there, and she was shocked to see that he stood in bitter silence with a cluster of his closest knights, watching her walk toward him until Mordred grabbed her arm, forcing her to halt a few feet away. Her eye caught the bloodstain on Arthur's shirt near his heart and she wondered how he had acquired it. Nearby were Blane and Farquar, who strained to reach her, but they were held back by the swords of Gaheris and three others. Beside them stood Lady Garwen, Bloedwyn, and Ghleanna. Ghleanna wept, while Bloedwyn's rage was foremost.

Love and sadness seeped into Gwenhyfar's heart at the sight of so many familiar faces that looked out at her, most of them stricken with grief at her plight. The court astrologers and herbalists, the healers, cooks and bakers, many of the courtiers stood with looks of horror or tears streaking their faces. She saw Dafydd, the stable boy who cared for her horse, the washerwomen, serving maids and lads, children of all ages whose faces, usually bright and happy, were now fallen low, perplexed and downcast with sorrow. Standing with Gawain and his fellows were Lady Dindrane and Lady Amarillys, their faces haughty and cold, and a score of knights under Gawain's command.

"People of Camelot!" Arthur called out in a loud voice. "My nephew, Gawain, accuses the queen of treason. Sir Gawain and Sir Agravaine have called for a court hearing. Let us hear what the knights have to say, as it is our law."

Gawain shouted and gesticulated, his face a parody of righteous rage. "The law must be satisfied. I say what we all know—that the queen has taken Sir Lancelot as her lover and they are guilty of plotting treason against the king! Gwenhyfar seeks to depose the king and place Sir Lancelot upon the throne. The penality for treason is death, and I ask for it, demand it, to preserve the peace and the life of honor that we have won under the Pendragon's sigil. Look around you, there is no one here to speak for this woman. She is alone. Even her so-called champion has forsaken her!"

Just as Arthur opened his mouth to speak, an earth-shaking clap of thunder rent the air, then another, followed by a blinding flash of lightning and a booming crash that shattered their senses, the thunderous roar rumbling until it finally trailed away on its journey into the distance. A few of the villagers fell to the ground in panic, covering their heads from the fear of being struck, while others cried out in dismay as a thick mist appeared, moved by an unseen force that swirled the fog about them until they could not see.

Frightened mutters and alarmed shouts, the clang of weapons drawn to no avail filled the white void of mist that obscured their sight until, just as suddenly as it had come, the mist cleared, leaving only silver wisps that floated among the sunlit trees. Petals of cherry blossoms lilted on the air, and in their midst stood a small woman with wild and knotted red hair. Her eyes were as piercing and predatory as those of the little white owl that flew to her shoulder and perched there. In her hand she raised high a gnarled rowan staff. Her robes were pale, the color of the sky at dawn, and about her shoulders was draped a woolen mantle fringed with silver foxtails.

Gawain took a step forward, his sword raised and an angry scowl upon his face. Morgan gazed at him solemnly. Thunder growled in the distance, an angry giant hard to hold at bay, but the sorceress raised her staff and uttered, "Peace." Two fingers, curled around the staff, were lifted easily toward Gawain, who fell back, a tremor of alarm crossing his face as his sword clattered to the ground. He stared at his hand, incredulous.

"Gawain, nephew. Son of Lot and my sister, Morgause. You are quite adept at fomenting darkness, are you not? You have caused a great disharmony in the subtle web of life that binds us all. It is your deeds that have drawn me here."

Glaring, Gawain stared at Morgan, who shrugged, as if she played with a very small creature. "The king and his queen," she began, "and their first knight are under the protection of Avalon. Make no mistake about this. I will not tolerate your behavior, nephew. You should satisfy your ambitions with becoming king in Lothian. Surely my sister Morgause will welcome you in Orkney at any time. I suggest you go there, away from Camelot and Caerleon. Take Mordred," she cast a withering eye toward the glowering youth, "with you."

She turned and held a hand out to Gwenhyfar, speaking to the crowd. "The charge against your queen is ridiculous." The people listened, shuffled and whispered among themselves as confusion gave away to dawning relief.

"This is nothing more than a family squabble. Everyone disperse, go back to your work and forget about this mishap of understanding."

Gathering Gwenhyfar to her, Morgan walked away with the queen at her side, the white owl flying to the treetops and disappearing in the forest. As they moved toward the king's keep, Gwenhyfar whispered, "Where is Laëllon?"

"He is riding hard to arrive as soon as possible. I do not think that Gawain will desist. It is only a matter of time. Let us go, straight away, to your quarters."

Arthur arrived shortly, an anxious Farquar at his heels, after the women were settled beside a small fire set by Blane, who had withdrawn with a solicitous and tearful Bloedwyn to stand guard outside the door to the queen's chamber.

"What is wrong with you Arthur, that you cannot rally yourself to properly defend your queen?" Morgan snapped, whipping around to confront her brother as he entered the room. Gwenhyfar sat upon a low couch, her face drawn and livid, eyes brimming with sorrow and anger.

"What do you know of how a king works?" Arthur's shoulders were tense as he defended himself, rebutting her accusation. "I handle my knights as I deem best. Gawain is dangerous, to be sure—he ordered Agravaine to hold me at sword point!" He plucked at his shirt where the bloodstain showed rusty brown. "But now I have it under my control. Perhaps you don't understand the maxim, keep your friends close, but keep your enemies closer."

"Hah! You do not have it under control, Arthur," Morgan hissed. "Gwenhyfar spent this day in Camelot's dungeon. In fact, you have lost control of your own destiny. This will come to no good in the end."

He barked in defense, "Your prophecies of doom are not helping, Morgan. If I did not know better, I would think you want this to go badly. What exactly is your interest in it all, sister? Is this your revenge, finally come down to it?"

"You are a fool, Arthur. I stand before you as Avalon, and Avalon has no interest in petty illusions of revenge. Avalon is eternally committed to the good in us all and to good for all. You dare to accuse me? You should attend instead to your own jealous pride. What has happened to you, brother? There was a time when you had nobility, wisdom—when Myrrdin saw the Great King in you."

He stood immobile, eyes upon Morgan, his breath coming in tortured gasps, emotion like a small feral beast clawing within his belly as he clenched and unclenched his fists. Seeing him so, Gwenhyfar's heart quailed with pity, and she moved to his side, taking one hand into her own.

"Arthur, my love, my king. We can mend this somehow. But we must stay united. You and me and Lancelot. It is the only way forward."

Shifting his eyes from Morgan to the queen, for a moment something flickered in his face, a softening of the line of his brow, a small relaxation of the muscles that spasmed in his cheek. His mouth crumpled, his lips turned down in bitter sorrow, and his eyes shone with the water of unshed tears. A knock on the door dispelled the moment, and Sir Lancelot entered, taking in the scene with one penetrating look. He closed the door on the anxious faces of Blane and Farquar that peered in behind him, then turned to regard the king.

Lancelot's face was dreadful, fervid and bright as he fell upon Arthur with a glancing blow. They struggled, clenched in strong arms as each wrestled with the one they loved best above all others—except the queen who now forced herself between them at the risk of taking their blows to her own body.

With Morgan's help, they were pulled apart, and they stood, two warriors poised for death, facing one another with heaving chests and reddened eyes, cheeks flushed from the power that pounded through limb and muscle and heart. Moments ticked by in a vacuum punctuated only with the sound of their breathing, and as they faced one another, they were suddenly unable to move, flummoxed by the burning distillation of their passion, suspended in time and steeped in the raw truth of all they had wrought between them—past and present, with an agony of prescience toward the future, the chimera of what would surely come. It was as if they could hear, somewhere in the Otherworld, the resounding crash of their golden life as it shattered into the ruin of their folly. In that moment, they knew that Camelot, and all that Camelot stood for in this world—and all that Camelot could yet be—was lost.

Avalon
529 C.E.

Refuge

There was no time for regret, and remorse would dawn later. Only the urgency of the moment pulled them back into action. Morgan looked from one man to the other, then to Gwenhyfar. Then the Lady of the Lake spoke with sober deliberation.

"I deem we are no more than four players," she sighed heavily, "caught on stage in a great theatre. We are at the crossroads, at the in-between point, when it becomes known that the inevitable extremes of fate are upon us."

She gestured toward the door. "Is it not so?"

Morgan opened the door to find Lady Garwen standing with Blane and Farquar, hands poised to knock. Asking them to send for wine and food, she closed the door and turned back to the threesome that stood immobile and mute.

"We live within the burning friction of the conflict. So, Arthur. What will you do now?" He said nothing but stared at her, a man in shock, caught in the trap of his own device.

When Lady Garwen and Bloedwyn had come and gone with comestibles, the atmosphere congealed into a dismal quiet. They partook of the food in scant measures, too desolate to eat, until Arthur rustled in his chair. As he opened his mouth to speak, all eyes turned to him.

"Tis not safe for you, Gwenhyfar, to remain in Camelot right now. This much is clear to us all, but—by the gods that breath my life!—I will not give you leave to depart in exile. This madness will pass. But tis true that even your ancestral stronghold of Caerleon is not safe. Gawain and his brothers will surely search for you there." He glanced at his half-sister, who sat impassively listening, eyebrows arched.

"Morgan, I ask you to take Gwenhyfar and Lancelot into your protection. Let them stay in Avalon until I can resolve this problem with Gawain. I still believe it can be done. At least give me the chance to work with my knights. I will send them on a merry chase to Bretonnia across the channel. They will easily believe that Lancelot has taken you to his lands there. It will give me time to work with them, to set things right."

With a penetrating look at Arthur, the sorceress sat unmoving. Lancelot's face betrayed sheer disbelief as he watched the king, while Gwenhyfar walked to the window and stood looking out, pulling a woolen shawl tight around her body. Outside the twilight wreathed the trees in shadows, swallows swooped and dove to feed on insects that hovered in the courtyard air below the windows of Gwenhyfar's apartment. A distant bell rang out, carried over distance through the gathering mists, and she cocked her head to listen.

"Father Donnan is calling the monks to their evening prayers," Gwenhyfar reflected. "What do the Christian monks know, I wonder, about the dire problems of the royals? Does gossip and intrigue reach their ears? I think it does."

Morgan walked to the window. "You are wondering, do they support the queen, or would they lend themselves to her downfall and death? I think not."

Gwenhyfar shifted uneasily. "I remember the Christian zealot who came from Erin, called Padrig. He died before Arthur went to war with the Saxons. His teachings have caused divisions between Britons who worship the goddess and the gods of old and the Christians, whose numbers proliferate more and more each year. They are so sure that there way is the only way. No, I do not think they will help me."

Morgan listened, watching the queen's face with a solemn gaze. "There are factions among the Christians. Some despise the goddess and fear Avalon, others have a broader view. I know Father Donnan very well. Father Donnan is a wise man, and his monks are fair and good men. Some of them are holy men. They do not follow the ways of the wandering monk, whom they called Patrick, for I knew him much better than I wanted to."

Gwenhyfar said nothing more, but sat down, lowering her head to hide her tears. The minutes dragged through a brooding silence, until Morgan picked up her staff.

"Hmph," she huffed. "A fine mess, indeed. Well then, there is nothing to do but carry on. No need to spend more precious magic on a swift return, the way I came here. I will stay here tonight with Gwenhyfar. Ask Bloedwyn to prepare, and she will come with us to attend to the queen's needs. Lancelot, you and Blane have five ponies ready, and when the Great Bear turns toward morning, we will meet you at the stables, hopefully when most are deep at their slumbers. We will make our way to Avalon then, while the mists of night give cover."

Arthur leaned forward. "Sister..." he began. Morgan interrupted him.

"I give you the summer to resolve this, Arthur, because you are the Pendragon, foretold by Myrrdin Emrys, who is wise beyond us all, and who set you on course to be King of Briton. When Myrrdin returns, and I pray that he does, I can assure him that I have given you a chance to reconcile your wrongs."

Gwenhyfar and Bloedwyn crept to the kitchen through the inky dark, where Lady Garwen awaited them holding a candle and a cloth bag of food.

"This should see you through the day, until you get to Avalon," she whispered, handing the bag to Bloedwyn. "My Lady, what happened yesterday is like a worm that eats at my heart. If there is anything at all I can do for you in these weeks ahead, send a message with Blane, and I will do whatever you bid..." Her kind brown eyes welled with tears, and Gwenhyfar reached a hand to her shoulder, then drew the older woman to her breast for a quick embrace.

"Now, we must make haste!" Gwenhyfar hurried out the kitchen door, Bloedwyn close behind. Stars twinkled overhead as they scurried over mud-packed ground to meet Lancelot and Blane, who held their horses, leather reins in firm hands, as they waited at their agreed upon meeting place behind the stables. Passing the palisades of the fort and slipping out the back gates, they followed Lancelot into a thick fog as they descended into the boggy meadows, where they carefully picked their way on sure-footed ponies through misty predawn shadows and across water logged moss and peat.

After a time, the first light of dawn shone pale on the eastern horizon just as Lancelot located a labyrinthine path laid out with thick timbers that led through the marshes surrounding the lake. As they skirted the waters and kept to solid land as much as possible, they moved through thick swaths of white mist, now and then catching glimpses of treetops washed in the sun's early gold. The Tor glinted in the distance, a bright beacon that reared above rosy pools of mist floating upon its flanks.

By midday the mists had receded as they reached the wattle church, surrounded by small huts laid out in a circle upon a dome of land that stood above water. The monks were busy going about their work in the vegetable garden, tending animals, or spreading handfuls of thick mud to reinforce the wattled exterior of the church. Two of the monks cast curious glances or looked askance at Gwenhyfar and Lancelot, guessing their identities, while another came forward to welcome the Lady of the Lake and beg her to stay to break the night's fast with them.

She declined, saying that she was urgently needed in Avalon, but would most certainly come another time. However, they could keep care of their horses for them, as they would soon need to cross a stretch of water by corricle to Avalon. Leaving their horses at the stables with one of the brothers, they were turning to leave when Father Donnan came bristling out of the forest, a basketful of mushrooms and wild edibles in hand. Seeing them, he hurried forward to greet the visitors.

"My Lady of the Lake! It is with pleasure that my eyes fall upon you once again." He smiled broadly, setting down the basket and taking her hands in his own. "What luck! I returned from the white spring just in time to see you. Morgan, you all must stay and take food with us," he insisted, looking around at the others, taking them in with a glance.

"I have already declined the gracious offers of the brothers, Father Donnan. We are on an urgent mission and cannot stop to visit, but I hope to see you tomorrow night, in Avalon."

Father Donnan's canny eyes lingered on Gwenhyfar, and she knew without doubt that he had recognized her, even with the hood of her mantle pulled low over her face, for indeed the monks had met Arthur and his queen on many occasions over the years. He smiled hesitantly and bowed, saying, "My lady... And is that Sir Lancelot? All praise to Blessed Mary! I am honored to see you again."

Lancelot moved forward and grasped the priest by an arm, a warm greeting in his eyes. He spoke quietly, leaning in close to the priest's ear.

"Father Donnan, I am honored as well to see you again, indeed. But in truth we must go, for it is the Lady's life that hangs in the balance," Father Donnan looked in concern at the queen, who stood with quiet dignity, hands at her side.

"We will speak more of this tomorrow, when you

come for the full moon rites," Morgan countered with some urgency. "Now, Father Donnan, allow us to depart, for we must reach the safety of Avalon as soon as possible."

Father Donnan gave a sage nod of his head, then added, "Yes, we will speak tomorrow, and until then, my friend...you were never here." He met Lancelot's eyes and then Morgan's, and turned away toward the monastery with a jocular wave of his hand and a casual, "Fare thee well, then, friends."

Avalon

They trudged through a beech forest, making their way among trees and brambles along what seemed to be an indiscernable path. Morgan led this way and that until finally they came upon a timbered walkway that led across a boggy stretch of marsh and wet meadow to the shallow lake. At high tide, the walkway would be covered with salty water that now lapped gently at the shore where two corricles were pulled aground and tied with ropes to nearby trees. Loading their bags, they climbed in and paddled across the glassy stretch of lake that reflected the sky in shades of blue and silver. They were damp and tired as they came ashore, hefting their bags and clambering up a path through dense forest that grew uphill. The path continued steadily upward a thick tangle of thorn hedges that surrounded Avalon in a high, impenetrable wall.

Cut deep into the hedge was a heavy wooden gate. It was impressive, carved with an intricate design of interwoven knots. Gwenhyfar gasped with pleasure as she saw the outline of a symbol carved into the center of the seasoned oak. It was almost obscured by a layer of fine green moss, but she made out the two interlocking circles with ease and exclaimed, "I know this. It is a sigil of the goddess!"

Lancelot explained, "Tis an ancient symbol of deep meaning to both Avalon and the Roman Christians, who call it vesica pisces."

Morgan nodded absently, distracted for the moment by the need to attend to their entrance into the guarded sanctum of Avalon. She knocked with her staff in a pattern of three swift rapts followed by three more, then repeated the series again twice, each strike against the solid wood emphasized in a peculiar rhythm that gave away to a dance of beats, until she stopped and called out.

"Saorsa chun dul isteach ar an Oileán Úlla!"

"Freedom to enter the Isle of Apples," Laëllon whispered, answering to the curiosity and awe that moved across Blane's face. The door swung open with ease, held secure in the hands of two male guards dressed in dark woolen tunics.

"An Lady an Loch thíos anseo!" They could hear the resounding joy in the voices of many who crowded around and others who came running, eager to greet or touch Morgan's feet, hair, or the hem of her robe.

"How did they know she was coming?" Blane whispered to Bloedwyn, who shrugged in wonder as they watched the convergence of no more than twenty people, some of whom were small and slight, with hair the color of night, the bark of trees, or white as snow. Others had red or gold hair; they were tall and moved like swans.

"Come now!" Morgan scolded. "I have only been away overnight!" She stood out as different among them all, her small frame moved fast as a dragonfly in flight, and her ruddy hair shone in the sun. She was older than most who swarmed about her, and her dark eyes glittered with unearthly power. As she affectionately greeted and then pushed away the eager denizens of Avalon, the white owl sailed down to land on Morgan's shoulder.

In the wake of Morgan, Lady of the Lake, they were permitted to enter, and, as she strode up the path at a fast walk, they followed her eagerly into the sacred land of the goddess. Gwenhyfar and Lancelot kept up with ease, while Blane and Bloedwyn spurred themselves to catch up, as they had slowed down to gawk in wonder at the sights around them. They made their way up a well-worn, wide stone path through an apple orchard in full bloom, which sprawled across the wide green hillside. Far above them, it seemed, the Tor rose, mysterious yet solid.

Everywhere the opulence of spring cast its soft glamour upon the land. Birds swooped and called or thrilled from the limbs of trees. All things green burst forth and flowers sprang in profusions of blossom—thick clumps of white daisies and a maze of golden buttercups, nodding in the gentle breeze, intermingled artfully with the violet-blue of tiny waxen bells. Beyond the apple trees they caught glimpses of bracken and banks of heather blooming in purple splendor on the rising flanks of the Tor.

Ahead Gwenhyfar saw a rambling collection of mud and stone houses, more like a honeycomb than a fort or dùn, with several larger stone and wattle huts nearby, some of them shaped like beehives. Some had thatched roofs of thick straw with timbered walls and doors of wood.

Everywhere were pathways of stone or timber, making for an ease and joy of walking. Gwenhyfar imagined that during storms and rains, when the lake rose, the maze of pathways made it easier to traverse from one part of Avalon to another.

Beyond the dwellings, a paved stone pathway widened as it led up the spacious green expanse of the Tor. With great curiosity, Gwenhyfar saw that the path curved gracefully around the hill in a sculpted spiral that led to the summit. At the top of the hill was a tall, stone tower-like structure of unusual workmanship; it reminded her of the brochs that Laëllon had described, which he had seen in Caledonia when traveling there so many years ago. And yet it had the influence of Roman artisans in it. She looked at it with interest, making a mental note to ask Morgan about it later.

Moving toward a maze of stone buildings, Morgan called out in a trilling ululation. Almost simultaneously, three young women emerged from different buildings, each one lifting the heavy woolen tapestries that covered the doors to keep out the cold and frequent mists. The tallest of the three came running down the hill, long amber hair flying in waves behind her lovely, coltish form.

"Beannachtaí, Bean draíochta... Morgana!" She grabbed the diminutive priestess around the waist and whirled her around. The formidable Morgan fussed, with a sharp tsk of her tongue against her teeth, but then relented, relaxing into the embrace and returning the girl's hug with warmth.

With shining forest-brown eyes and skin the color of spring honey, exquisite features, fine arched brows and full lips, the spontaneous joy that spilled from the young woman, hardly more than a girl, made her beauty and charisma almost overwhelming. And yet she seemed utterly unaware of the effect she had on others as she turned toward Lancelot and the strangers with a pure and innocent smile of welcome.

"This is Iona," Morgan introduced, holding the girl's hand with affection and smiling at her with pride. "She is my apprentice. Iona will be Lady of the Lake when I am dead and gone. But that will not be any time soon," she added hastily, with a wry smile and humorous wink for Bloedwyn.

Iona smoothed her dress—a long voluminous robe of plain soft wool dyed pale green, gathered at the waist with a belt of braided leather, fringed and spangled with silver beads. She pulled back loose strands of thick wavy hair as she looked at each one in turn and said, "Welcome to Ynis yr Afalon," she said with a small bow, glancing at the tall knight who stood, relaxed and smiling, pleased to be home.

"Sir Laëllon du Lac I know, but I have not met his beautiful Lady, Queen of the Cymru, of Dumnonia, and all Briton...though I have heard much!" She bowed to Gwenhyfar, whose heart was touched in a deep and satisfying place by this new acquaintance, who seemed familiar, as if she had known the girl forever.

Two other young women walked up, their faces lit with smiles for Morgan and her companions. Introduced as Tressa and Cara, they were apprentices in training who cared for the shrines and altars of Avalon and studied in specific areas of the priestesscraft. Herbalist, keeper of plants and caretaker of nourishment, ample Cara informed them that supper would be served at dusk, then took her leave to attend to the kitchen and the cooks while Tressa remained, beaming at them, impish and small as a wren.

"Tressa plays harp very beautifully," Morgan smiled kindly at the dark-haired youngster who was only a few inches taller than the Lady of the Lake. "You will hear her play when Iona sings while you are here. The full moon comes tomorrow, and we will perform our usual rites, to which you are most welcome. Now, Tressa, back to your harp. Taliesin will be looking for you. Iona, and the rest of you, please come with me."

As Tressa walked away, Morgan took Gwenhyfar's arm in her own and walked in companionable conversation with her while the others went ahead with Laëllon. "Tomorrow we worship the goddess as she manifests in the golden orb of the full moon," she commented with a broad sweep of one small hand.

"We will be honored and pleased to attend," Gwenhyfar responded with a faint smile. She stopped and turned toward Morgan. "Lady Morgan, I have not properly expressed my gratitude for the sanctuary and protection you have offered to me." Morgan shrugged and pursed her lips, her eyes seeking a distant horizon beyond the Tor.

"You and I serve the same one—and that is why you are under my protection, Gwenhyfar, child of Ceridwen. All the ancient deities take shelter here in Avalon. Of course, there is also Laëllon's love for you—he is a son of Avalon, and we take care of our own. Beyond these good reasons, by the goddess, our destinies are entwined in myriad ways,

Gwenhyfar. But there will be time to speak more of this later." She took the younger woman's hand in her own and turned back to the path to catch up with the others.

Arriving at the largest of the round houses, Laëllon held back the heavy linen drape that covered the doorway to allow the women to enter, then stooped to walk through the portal himself. Inside it was dark, and Iona moved quickly to open windows covered with woolen tapestries. Light poured into the room, and Gwenhyfar noticed that the level earthen floor was hard and well polished beneath her feet. There were carved wood chairs, a low divan, a long wooden table with benches, a fine loom with a half-finished weaving in blue and red wool, two spacious fireplaces with stone mantles.

Lutes and lyres of varying sizes hung upon the walls along with round hand drums. A crock of wildflowers adorned the table, and bundles of drying herbs and hanks of spring onions hung near the scullery and kitchen fireplace, where a bucket of fresh water sat upon a wooden counter. Green mounds of fresh herbs grew in crocks beside the window—mint, the balm known as sweet melissa, and thyme. On one end of the room was a doorway leading to another room. Gwenhyfar could see that the place was well lived-in, and for the first time in days, she began to relax.

"Sit, and be comfortable in my home," Morgan commanded, not unkindly. "Now we must consider your safety for the next four months, as Arthur has until autumn to settle accounts with Gawain and his faction."

After Iona had served hot tea and sweet oat cakes, they spent the rest of the afternoon making a plan: In seven days, Blane would make his way back to the hill fort of Camelot, where he would talk with Lady Garwen and the young ones, Ghleanna and Farquar, to get the news without revealing the queen's exact whereabouts. In fact, he would aid in the king's plan, spread the gossip that Lancelot had taken the queen to his castle in Bretonnia, Joyeuse Garde, across the narrow sea. Blane would remain in Camelot until he received word from Lancelot to return to Avalon, and while there, he would find out what the Pendragon was up to while Laëllon and Gwenhyfar were sequestered within the sanctuary on the Tor. Morgan assured them that, despite factions among the Christians, Father Donnan was trustworthy. She would personally arrange for him to receive news from Blane, if needed, which Father Donnan would find a way to pass on to Morgan.

When the sun hovered on the western horizon, soon to sink into the sea, Cara and Tressa arrived with food. They were joined by Iona and a young man called Andras to partake in a supper of partridge cooked with mushrooms, served with flatbread. They ate together, the young women of Avalon answering question plied by Bloedwyn and Blane, while Morgan, the queen, and her champion listened. Occasionally Morgan interjected something, but it was the young ones who carried the conversation, for the day had been long and hard. Noticing that Gwenhyfar's face was drawn and pale, Laëllon intervened.

"Lady, it is time for you to rest. You have not slept for days. Allow me to escort you to your quarters." He stood and held a hand out to the queen, who had been uncommonly quiet throughout the day. She took it without complaint.

"Iona and Andras," Morgan instructed, "take Laëllon and the queen to her lodge. Provide whatever she needs. I bid you rest well, Gwenhyfar. We will meet again on the morrow."

Summer Idyll

The full moon had come and gone, and then another month passed in which Gwenhyfar and Laëllon flowed easily through daily life on the Isle of Apples. Indeed, the orchard fruits were growing round and blushed rosy from the sun that shone more often than usual during the days of the summer. Mornings on the Tor were often overshadowed by mists, but by late afternoon the sun shone bright through fast-moving fluffy white clouds that scudded across the sky, sped along by a breeze that brought with it the salt of the sea, and the Tor was unveiled and majestic for some hours of idyll.

During the days they came to know Taliesin, the druid bard, astrologer, and star master who taught the children who came from the Summer Country and beyond—as far away as Alba and Irlandis—to learn from him. Revered scholar, musician, mathematician, and master of lore, Taliesin had been the disciple of Myrrdin, like his ally, Morgan. He had long ago mastered the arts of astronomy, star lore and cosmic cycles, as well as the crafts of music and song. Taliesin lived in the stone structure on the crest of the Tor, which was, as Gwenhyfar learned, a temple of ancient star knowledge. The druid was also a fine bard whose voice was renowned for its ability to touch the heart as he played lute and lyre and drum with accomplished skill. It was Taliesin who taught Iona and Tressa the fine points of music even as he sometimes helped with the instruction of the smaller children of Avalon, who were eager to play their harps and drums and flutes.

With meeting Taliesin, Gwenhyfar came to know more of the renowned schola of Avalon. Laëllon had been educated there as a boy, and gifted children from old Celtic families—some strong with the ancient blood—were sent to learn the arcane arts in hopes the knowledge of the Old Ones could be preserved, even as their world changed with every wave of invasion, and now Roman and Anglo-Saxon influence was pervasive. Gwenhyfar was touched by the sight of children of all ages, who could be seen throughout the day scampering about on errands, busy with tasks of learning, laughing gaily at play, or with heads bent over their instruments.

Over the weeks Gwenhyfar and Laëllon had grown close to Morgan's three apprentices and Andras, and with the gardener of Avalon—Tammas, who worked magic amongst the vegetables and herbs and passed on his knowledge of wild edibles and mushrooms of field and forest to generations of young ones. They met a woman with hair and eyes the color of storm clouds, whose name was Corey, who was Morgan's right hand and facilitator of all matters of daily business. It was Corey who kept the essential wheels of life turning on Avalon, linking the various tasks and elements together to make a working whole.

Each day as the summer sun sank toward the west and the tides rushed inland to flood waterways, marshes and estuaries, the mists began to rise again and the levels of the lake changed with the cycles of the sea. In the evenings the inhabitants of Avalon often gathered in the great hall of the sanctuary with lutes, pipes, harps, and drums. Window hangings were thrown open and the sound of music flooded the Tor. Their revelry was infectious, and even the tight knot in Gwenhyfar's belly relaxed as she danced with Laëllon on many nights of music and song, their bodies unrestrained, their faces flushed with unfettered happiness.

Oftentimes Tressa played harp and Andras the drum, and Iona's voice sailed out, sublime and sure, bringing heaven down to earth, as it seemed to Gwenhyfar. The three young apprentices were the delight of their people, the joy of their hearts in the evenings of sweet ecstasy, when the queen was held safe in the refuge of the Lady of the Lake, who ruled supreme on the Apple Isle.

During the long summer nights of endless twilights, it seemed to Gwenhyfar that she could feel the heartbeat of the Old Ones—an atmosphere of mystery blended with a palpable presence that permeated feast, song, drumbeat and salty air with an invisible sheen, a hidden wash of gold, a subtle burning fire that appeared in light forms of moving circles and complex whorls of entwined flow, perceptible only to the vision of her inner eye.

The inner sight was most strong when Taliesin played harp or drum and sang, and his voice, refined and subtle yet bold, unfolded great epic poems, the deeds of heros and heroines, of gods and goddesses and the Tuatha Dé Danaan of Erin, who worshipped the goddess Danu. In Taliesin's songs, she learned more of the daoine sìth, the people of the mounds, who were known in Avalon as the Old Ones.

The druid's stories in song were accompanied by strange and marvelous music that carried their hearts away on a river of sound and feeling until their joys and sorrows erupted in wild dance and rhythmic romps or liquid mystic flights to haunting melodies. Many voices joined to resound through walls and thatched roof until, long past midnight, they poured out into the thick night air seeking their beds, surprised to see how far the stars had wheeled across the sky, or that a summer storm flashed its lights in cloud castles that hung low over the Tor. Then, returning to their small house, Laëllon and Gwenhyfar came together with fervent passion, free to explore and discover the endless landscape, the valleys and peaks of their love, melting together afterward in a lull of peace and rest they had never before known.

One evening past midsummer's eve, not long after the solstice had been celebrated on one particularly marvelous night, instead of a summons to the great hall, they received word from Iona to come to Morgan's house to sup with Father Donnan, who had arrived with one of the monks from the monastery, Brother Paulinus, pulling behind them a lamb with long soft fur as black as peat.

"For you, Morgan," Father Donnan smiled as he greeted the priestess. "I know how you enjoy the black wool for your loom."

"Tis true," Morgan chuckled, "the black sheep have lovely wool for spinning and weaving. I thank you, Father Donnan."

Morgan bent down to stroke the lamb's long ears, then called for Cara to take the animal away. "Put her in the southern pasture with the other sheep," she instructed as she turned toward the door to greet Laëllon and Gwenhyfar.

"Ah, here is the queen and her champion," Father Donnan smiled. He bowed from the waist as Gwenhyfar approached, Laëllon just behind her, tall and protective, brown eyes alert and gleaming.

"Queen Gwenhyfar, Sir Lancelot, I am honored to greet you both once again, and under more favorable circumstances than when we last met!" Father Donnan smiled, holding out a hand to the monk who stood beside him.

"And this is Brother Paulinus, a Roman by birth, but with the soul of a Celt."

Gwenhyfar smiled, acknowledging the young monk with a nod of her head as Paulinus laid a hand flat against his breast and bowed. Laëllon said nothing but stared for a moment at the visitors, then assisted the queen as she settled upon the long bench across the table from the monastery guests. Morgan took a seat at the head of the table in a chair. Iona sat on the bench at her right hand and Laëllon at her left beside the queen, who waited with quiet dignity for the discussion to begin while Cara served cider, a bowl of hazelnuts, and honeyed barley cakes. Andras lit several candles on the table, then sat beside Iona with a sidelong glance and a tender smile. They had handfasted at the recent solstice rites, and everyone in Avalon basked in the springtime of their love.

Outside a gust of wind rose, blowing in through the open window, strong enough to stir the ashes in the fireplace, now cold. A simple knock came at the door, and Andras rose to answer. A soft murmur announced the arrival of Taliesin, who glided through the door to the table, where he stood beside Morgan to take them in with eyes the color of an ice bound sea. His hair was long and brown as bark except for white swaths that flared at his temples. Despite the white hair, his face appeared young with smooth brown skin, except for the fine lines that embellished the outer corners of his eyes. These crinkled easily with a smile that lit his mobile features.

"Taliesin," Morgan greeted him without rising. She gestured to the seat at the other end of the long table. "Welcome, and please take a seat. I am glad you are here."

He chuckled. "How could I not hear the call you sent? It was quite loud, sister. I was in the temple, contemplating a star chart for Avalon in the year head. I hope I am in time to hear the news," he drawled softly as he bowed to the queen. "My Lady Queen," he intoned, "and Sir Laëllon. I am always pleased to see you. And Father Donnan knows well the pleasure I take in his company."

Father Donnan bowed his head, hiding the humorous curve of his lips that quivered beneath his beard as he remembered many a night over countless cups of mead or wine. Both priests, Christian and pagan, were known to love their cups. Moving efficiently, Taliesin took a seat and sat patiently waiting, his eyes on the Lady of the Lake.

Morgan's eyes lingered on Taliesin then roved over the circle of guests toward Father Donnan.

"Please," she insisted, "enjoy the cider. We have been blessed by the Goddess with an excellent apple harvest for some years, and our cider is both plentiful and strong this summer. As you know, Cara and Tammas are skilled at brewing and fermenting spirits. Even you, Father Donnan, may be surprised at its potency," she glanced around the table, "so drink carefully if you go too easily into your cups."

Father Donnan chucked amiably. "I believe you know very well that the monks of Ynis Witrin are known for our capacity to enjoy spirits of all kinds! We thank you for your kind invitation and your hospitality, which is abundantly fine as always." He lifted his cup to Gwenhyfar and Sir Lancelot, then Morgan, Taliesin and the others at the table.

"Sláinte mhaith," he toasted them in the style of Irlandis, his homeland, and crossed himself. With a wink, he cajoled, "It is always best to ward away evil spirits at the beginning of anything." Taking a draught, he put his cup down on the worn wooden surface of the table and smacked his lips in satisfaction.

"Excellent, indeed. But we have not only come for the pleasure of your good company, Morgan." He glanced toward Laëllon. "Blessed Mary brings us here with news from your page, Blane, which you will want to hear. In fact he has told us that Arthur has sailed with Bors the Younger and Sir Peredur to Bretonnia to join with Gawain and a host of knights—who left a week after you took flight from Camelot, almost two months ago. Gawain was in a fury to look for you." He looked steadily at Gwenhyfar.

"It seems that the king convinced him that you, Sir Lancelot, had taken the queen to Joyeuse Garde after

Morgan intervened on that rueful day in Camelot. To make matters more interesting, we also heard that the Arthur told Farquar, who told the Lady Garwen, that the king intends to keep Gawain and the knights there as long as he can, sending them on a political mission to the castle of King Bors the Elder, and giving them heroic tasks to fulfill. The Pendragon plans to return in two weeks' time with Gawain and the rest of the party. Though unsuccessful so far, the king still has hope to reconcile the conflicts that have caused grief to our queen." He bowed his head to Gwenhyfar.

"I tell you now, Sir Lancelot," Father Donnan continued, "no one wants harm to come to our queen. The villagers of Ynis Witrin and people of Camelot are deeply disturbed by Gawain's actions against you. We have come to give you this news and to ask, will you receive our help?"

All eyes turned to Sir Lancelot as an expectant hush fell upon the gathering. Lancelot's eyes shifted from Father Donnan to Gwenhyfar, who gently covered the knight's sun-browned hand, which rested upon the table, with her own. Their eyes locked together, solemn and intimate with the knowledge of one another. Finally Lancelot stirred and Gwenhyfar took her hand back into her lap.

"I have pondered the words, Morgan," Lancelot began, "which you spoke to we three—Arthur, Gwenhyfar, and myself—night after night, seeking the starry heavens for an answer to my questions. My heart tells me there is no way out except by the course of action you have offered to us. Gwenhyfar and I must leave. Yes, go into exile. Leave Camelot, leave Caerleon, leave Briton. We cannot go to Joyeuse Garde, for Gawain will find us there easily. Even the vast northern regions of Cymru, Powys and Gwynedd, are not safe from Gawain's reach. No, we must go further, travel north to seek a haven, somewhere in the secret places of Alba." Lancelot put an arm around Gwenhyfar, though his eyes were steady on Morgan.

"Gwenhyfar and I have pondered about this on many nights, awake until dawn. We have wondered, planned, sought solutions. The rupture it will cause to leave without the king's blessing is a wound from which I will never heal. I am vowed to serve as Arthur's first knight, and I will remain so for the duration of this life." Laëllon's speech was soft but firm and bold, and the timbre of his voice grew fierce with passion. "But as I live and breathe, as blood moves through my veins, I will not risk my queen's life! I will die fighting to protect Gwenhyfar from Gawain, Agravaine, Gaheris, and any other knight who follows their course."

All around the table heads nodded slowly in somber agreement. Morgan had listened carefully, one hand resting flat with fingers spread upon her heart. She nodded once to Laëllon to acknowledge his words, then gestured to Iona, who stood and disappeared into the room in the back of the house. Moments passed and they sat mute, waiting, with only the sound of their breathing to stir the silence where Laëllon's words vibrated still, until Iona returned with Morgan's staff. She placed it in the hands of her mentor, who took the hard length of wood and stroked lovingly its polished whorls and carved gnarls.

"I tell you now, Laëllon and Gwenhyfar—Taliesin and I can help you escape, but if there is a blood battle, we cannot harm or kill. The Old Ones can only intervene in these events with great delicacy. Beyond a certain line they will not venture, for it goes against the cosmic order.

"For some reason, I have not been able to penetrate the veils to see the outcome of our fate. I have peered into the mirror of my chalice time and again and asked, but the goddess does not speak, and yet she is relentless and demands our obedience to the heart of the matter. It is at great times such as these, when so much hangs in the balance, that the forces of light ask us to choose our path with care, for we are responsible.

"And so, from the silence of the goddess, I surmise that we must decide for ourselves. We must act according to the pulsations of our own hearts. We must find our own way to be true to ourselves. The obligation and the consequences belong to us—and most of all to you, Laëllon, Sir Lancelot du Lac, and to you, Gwenhyfar of Cymru.

"You will not be remembered kindly by history, my friends. But then, neither will I. Even so, you have many allies who are willing to help you carry this burden. Now, Father Donnan has offered his help. Will you accept it?"

Gwenhyfar stirred. Her simple linen robe, woven in Avalon, slid across her thighs as she moved. She raised dusky blue eyes to the Christian priest.

"Laëllon and I must go into exile before Arthur and the knights return from Bretonnia." She paused, then stated, "It is with gratitude that I accept your kind offer."

The decision was made, and it was shattering. The occupants seated around the table heaved a soft breath that swooshed around them, and the intimate shared wind of their travail was felt throughout Avalon and across the Tor and beyond to the meare pools and estuaries and the briny marshes. For those who had the ears to hear, the sound of their suspiration crossed the river Brue and spread, on to the restless sea in the west, and then to the north as well, where the Elders—the sarcen stones of Sorviodunum—dwelt in silence, and east to the Great Horse of the chalk hills. All the hidden powers of the land sighed in a shared knowing, interconnected and luminous as the sun and moon, now soft with sorrow in mute recognition, a reverberation of awareness resounding with the certain end of a holy world that had for eons been.

Father Donnan sighed loudly, an echo of the deeper breath they shared. "Brother Paulinus comes from a Roman father and a Celtic mother. He was born near the river Exe south of here. He spent his first ten years there, in Dumnonia, and the next ten on the islands of the northwest coast of Alba. He knows these lands as intimately as he knows his own skin. He can help you find the way north into Alba. With him will be Brother Caedmon. He is a true man of God, despite his name," he chuckled.

Gwenhyfar smiled. "We could use a 'wise warrior,' at any rate, to keep Laëllon company."

A grin stole across Brother Paulinus' face. "If the truth be known," he offered shyly, "Brother Caedmon is well accomplished with the dagger he keeps beneath his robe. Of course he does not use it unless it is necessary to save a life. He would be here today with us, but he travels back from Aquae Sulis, where some of our brothers live. He will arrive within a few days, if not on the morrow."

Morgan interjected, "Another wise warrior soon arrives to succor our cause. I have seen in the mirror pool that Sir Accolon returns within three days." Her eyes fell upon Lancelot. "He will help us."

"A more worthy knight I do not know, my Lady of the Lake, nor one more loyal to you," Lancelot ventured. "I have always enjoyed a friendship with Sir Accolon, and I will rejoice to see him again—and to fight back to back with him, if it is necessary."

"There are dangers," Morgan cautioned, "because we do not know exactly when Gawain and his warriors will appear, or when they will realize that you were in Avalon all along. When the truth dawns upon Gawain, he will be enraged. We will see a greater fury in him than we have ever known. We cannot trust that you will remain hidden from their eyes. There are powerful sorceresses in Bretonnia who can see us, despite the veils and cloaks and subtle mists which we," she glanced at Iona and Tressa, "with Taliesin, have cast about the Tor and maintain with every breath we take. Not every seer is a friend of Avalon. Many will scry for gold and silver…or merely to siphon off force from this place of ancient power."

Lancelot shifted his weight upon the bench, rising to stand and pace to the open window. Deep twilight cast purple shadows upon the Tor, causing its mystic heights to brood with the coming night. A light breeze wafted through, and just outside they could see the bright glow of lanterns and the smaller fires of cooking pits strung across the meadow toward the rambling honeycomb of the Avalon sanctuary. Children ran back and forth, chasing fireflies and each other with easy laughter in the last play of the evening before they were called to supper and bed.

"It would be different if Myrrdin were still here with Nimuë," Morgan mused, sighing in a rare moment of such candor. "Their combined powers could ward off any seer's prying eyes, but they are not here—or anywhere, for that matter. They have gone beyond my capacity to see them."

She took a drink from the cup in her hands and they waited, knowing she had more to say. "I take their disappearance as a sign of more changes to come. Now, Taliesin and I do as we are able, with the help of our apprentices." Taliesin listened silently, his face unreadable.

Father Donnan coughed. "A prayer then. May your Gods and our God, your Goddess and our Blessed Mary, be with us in this travail. Beloved Mary, as you love the Lord Jesus, keep Queen Gwenhyfar safe from harm and strengthen her champion, Lancelot du Lac, in all their vicissitudes and efforts to preserve our queen. We ask in the name of Blessed Mary, may Thy Will be done. Mar sin, go mbeadh sé."

With a signal from Morgan, Cara and Tressa brought food to the table and Andras served their cups with more of the effervescent cider. After a simple supper of oat bread, cherries, and sheep cheese served by Cara, the company soon dispersed to retire for the evening. The next day the preparations for travel would begin.

The Seneschal's Advice

Cai stretched his back and yawned, luxuriating in a rare moment to enjoy his own bed in Camelot with Carys, after weeks on the road to Bretonnia and back with Arthur. He ran his hand down the length of the soft flesh on her naked back. What a relief it was to be home. It had been a harsh, hard-driven journey, by horse and then by boat across the narrow channel and back again, with a long, stress-filled interlude in between, in which the king struggled to manage Gawain and his faction. Worst of all was the task that fell to Cai of attempting to support and uphold his king.

After the interlude of their loving, Cai and his lady had talked for a while as the dawn slowly melted the shadows of the room into early day. Carys moved to get up, knowing Cai would soon leave to break his fast with Arthur and attend to business that had accumulated in Camelot with the Pendragon away in Bretonnia—and plan the banquet in honor of the return of the king and his knights, which would be held that night. Indeed, there was much to be done. Her thoughts fled toward Gwenhyfar.

"Cai, we must do something to help Gwenhyfar. It is her very life that is in danger! Now that Gawain and his errant knights have returned from Gaul sooner than Arthur thought they would," she warned, "surely the news that the queen and Lancelot have been given sanctuary in Avalon has reached Gawain's ears." She slipped on a robe and poured water into a bowl for her morning ablutions.

"Dindrane, who sleeps with Gawain, confided to me last night that he will confront Arthur today. Gawain will not take it lightly when he realizes that Arthur sent him and his warriors on wild goose chases and continues his attempts to ameliorate Gawain's charges toward the queen. Arthur has never told Gawain the truth, and now his warriors are back in Camelot itching for action."

Cai stretched his arms out, rubbing them with some languor. "Arthur has urged them to make peace and forget about the past, to move forward as knights bound in brotherhood. Today he will attempt to buy more time; he plans to divert them by saying that Gwenhyfar had disappeared with Lancelot and were seen going northeast, toward Cynnit."

Carys shook her head in disbelief and reached for her linen undershift. Her face flushed as a wave of anger shook her inwardly.

"How can you be so casual? Are you the man of chivalry, whom I have know for so long?"

"Do not fret about it, my lovely lady. It will be over soon enough, one way or another," Cai replied firmly, rising from the bed to pull on leather britches.

"How can I not worry, Cai? It may be that you are too cavalier, darling. Gwenhyfar is innocent. You and I know this to be true, as she finally admitted to me that her joining with Lancelot was Arthur's command, to conceive a tanaiste. We both knew her words rang with the truth, knowing Arthur the way you do, and hearing the things he has said to you these past two years, since the time of his wound."

"Carys," Cai lowered his voice to a forced whisper, "please do not speak of that. We have all labored to keep the Pendragon's secret. And Gawain already suspects—if he knew the full truth, this insurrection would turn into a full scale war."

Carys shrugged. "At this point, I do not care if the Pendragon is found out. He deserves what he gets."

Cai stared at her. "That is treason, Carys," he muttered thickly.

"My darling, the king has allowed Gawain, Agravain, Gaheris and the rest to believe that he has been cuckolded by Lancelot." Cai squirmed inwardly at her ruthless honesty. "He has put Gwenhyfar's life in danger. I have known the queen and her champion for many years, stood beside them in war and in peace. I know who they are, Cai, and I will stand beside them now. Please understand that I will not abandon them, even if it means you and I are on different sides—if you must stand beside Arthur, and he is not able, or willing, to do the right thing."

Walking to her side, Cai took her hand in his and kissed her firmly. "My lady, you must do as your heart commands, but I would be sorely grieved for this to come between us. I beg you, do not misinterpret my words, for my heart is torn with grief. I am only trying to find my way, hoping that I will be able to do as my own heart bids if the moment comes when I must make difficult choices."

Raising her hand again to his lips, he then moved away to don his leather jerkin and buckle his sword about his waist. Walking to the door, he turned for one last glance at her, and Carys returned his bittersweet smile with one of her own.

Striding down the hall, his heart ached for them all. It was a tangled, sorrowful web they were caught within. Each one of them had played a part in the destruction of all they held dear and sacred—the chivalry and honor of their knighthood, the integrity of the Round Table, the reign of Arthur Pendragon, their glorious pagan queen, Gwenhyfar, and her champion, Lancelot—best of knights, whom none could defeat in combat.

He thought of these past golden years of Camelot and Caerleon, and of his wife and their sons, and of their little daughter Kelemon, living safe and unharmed by court intrigues at his castle in southern Dumnonia. It had been over a year since he had seen them, but then his place was at the king's side. And, truth be told, he had always preferred the company of the Lady Carys. Now, even their love was affected by the poison that had taken over the court, beginning with the wound inflicted upon the golden king who ruled at the center of their lives.

Cai had known and loved Arthur from his earliest childhood memories. They were brothers, if not by blood, then at heart. He could not take sides against Arthur, regardless of the cost. And yet, he could not foresee what course Arthur would take—would he tell the truth about the affair of the queen and her champion, and take the violence of Gawain and the Orkney brothers upon himself? And when the time came, would Cai, the king's seneschal, be forced to betray Gwenhyfar and his friend, Lancelot, if Arthur took Gawain's part? Taking a deep breath, he steeled his resolve and strode forward to meet the Pendragon.

Gawain listened with Agravaine and Gaheris while Mordred delivered his news with dark glee. The king's bastard had waylaid the knights on their way to the stables, risking the wrath of Gawain's renowned impatience and insisting with bold confidence they had to speak in Gawain's private quarters. Now he sat at the table, drumming his fingers upon the hard oak of its surface. He glanced at Agravain, who watched him steadily as he sharpened the blade of his dirk.

"So, they were in Avalon all along. My kinswoman took them in," Gawain growled with smothered fury, his eyes narrowed. He slapped his leather riding gloves against one hand, and the sharp noise resounded as if he had struck a face. "I should have known. This whole thing stinks with Morgan's interference. Damn Lancelot and both of those women!"

Mordred shifted his weight from one foot to the other. "We should have known that Arthur was lying for them. He came all the way to Bretonnia, he led us on with his incessant talk of peace and politics. My father deceives us because he has been deceived. He has either gone mad or he is bewitched by the queen. What can be said of such treachery?"

Unable to contain his nervous excitement, words frothed from his mouth like water over a broken dam. "It confirms the fact of the queen's treason against him, does it not? And Morgan is in league with them as well. Avalon should be put to the torch. Yes, the king has gone mad. He does not know what is good for his own self."

Gawain stared at Mordred, his face distorted by a grimace of wrath. Agravaine watched his older brother with studied dispassion, testing the edge of his blade with one finger.

"What will you do now, Gawain? Go east to Cynnit as Arthur suggested?" His words dripped with sarcasm. "Or go hunting for a few days, blow off some steam?" Agravaine paused. "Or ride straightaway to Avalon?"

"We will go to Avalon!" Gawain replied, rubbing his chin. "But not until night. Tonight we go to the feast and act as if nothing has happened. We will make Arthur believe that we have fallen for his ruse, that we are leaving for Cynnit in the early morning. He will relax his vigilance, and we will take them all by surprise. We will leave the feast early, pretending that we go to our beds after the long journey." He snorted in disgust.

"Let Arthur believe he has bested us. Then, under the cover of midnight, we will make our way across the marshes and the waters of the lake. My page, Gliglois, knows the lake like his own mother's face—he grew up among the lake villagers of Ynis Witrin. He can guide us. Then, we will take them by surprise in the early hours of the morning."

Mordred jumped up with enthusiasm from his seat near Gawain. "I will be ready to leave with you!"

Gawain turned a steady slit of an eye upon his half-brother. "No Mordred, you will stay here, where you can be useful to me. When I return, you will know exactly what has transpired in Camelot." When the young man protested, Gawain's voice became harsh. "Enough, Mordred! You will do as you are told."

Early evening arrived with a pearly sunset to the west and the smell of the sea on the air. The preparations for Arthur's return feast were well underway when Cai arrived at the king's quarters, his face creased with worry. Arthur was dressed for the banquet, wearing a long purple tunic edged in gold, gathered at the waist with a finely-tooled leather belt with a round bronze buckle—a dragon swallowing its tail in intricate detail with interlocking knots, held in place by a central pin. His hair hung long and golden about his shoulders, and around his forehead was the king's golden circlet inset with amethyst stones. He was amiable, shining with confidence as he offered a chair, but his seneschal refused, saying that there was little time before the banquet would begin.

"We must talk, Arthur. The court is brewing with intrigue. Insurrection among your knights, the queen disappeared with Lancelot, Gawain on a rampage..."

"Gawain has calmed his bowels," Arthur interrupted briskly. "He and I spoke on the voyage back from Bretonnia to Camelot and again this morning. The situation has been ameliorated."

"No, Arthur! It is not 'ameliorated.' Just now I heard that in fact Gawain was told this morning—by Mordred!

How does he know such things?—that Gwenhyfar and Lancelot are hiding in Avalon, under the wing of Morgan. Gawain plans to leave in the middle of the night to ride for Ynis Witrin and on to the Apple Ise for a surprise attack."

This news seemed to hang suspended in the air while Arthur stood mute and tall as the oak trees outside his window. Seeing his king, who always knew exactly the right action to take in the heat of danger, appearing dismayed, even shocked, Cai's heart contracted. Even so, he was obliged to tell him the truth.

"Tonight at the banquet you will see Gawain and his gang of knights leave early, begging to rest. Hah! We know that is an unlikely situation. Gawain does not leave a banquet to 'rest.' When that happens, you will know that a tragedy will soon occur. He will steal away to Avalon and take the queen. I tell you, Arthur, as brave and skilled as Lancelot is, he cannot stand against the brothers of Orkney and the following of knights they have gathered to them."

Arthur stared at Cai, breathing through parted lips with a slackened jaw. He sat heavily in his chair and stared into space. Cai watched with growing alarm as moments passed and beads of sweat broke out on the king's brow. Arthur raised one hand to wipe away the droplets that gathered at his forehead.

"What will you do, Arthur?"

"There is little I can do beyond what I have done. We will have to see this through, see how it goes." His voice was low and thick as he spoke.

"What is it, Arthur? What holds you back, brother? Surely you do not believe that Gwenhyfar has betrayed you, that she and Lancelot are committing treason, as Gawain charges?" Cai gaped at Arthur. Where was the decisive battle leader, the fierce warrior he had known all these years? He could see that Arthur was trenchant and closed, the muscle in his jaw working hard, his fists clenched.

Finally the king spoke, his voice soft and grave. "I am eaten from inside by the worms of doubt and grief. Cai, I saw them together that night. I watched from yon peak hole that looks into my bedchamber. I saw the truth of those two, Gwenhyfar and Lancelot," he spat out their names, "and I cannot shake it from my mind. I think they lied to me. What I witnessed told me that they have been together all along." He breathed out, his words coming in a rush of air.

"Ridiculous, Arthur!" Cai hissed, his voice hushed and strained. "It has been common knowledge among your closest knights that they stayed apart these years since Lancelot rescued Gwenhyfar from capture in Meleagant's castle. Lady Carys also knows the truth of this. No, Arthur, this conjoining between them...it was your design. She did what you asked her to do. Did you expect her to hate every minute of it? Come on, man," Cai pleaded.

A trenchant silence ensued, then the king whipped around. "How do you expect me to handle sedition? I am bound by my kingly oaths! Perhaps it is as you say, that I am caught in my own design." His fierce rebuttal ebbed, his words stumbled and he choked on unshed tears. "By the gods, Cai!"

Cai thrummed with anger and outrage as he waited, his eyes boring into the king's in raw confrontation. They sat immobile until, finally, Arthur relented with a groan that conveyed the anguish that churned within him.

"How could I have been so blind? You are telling me the truth, brother. It is all my responsibility." He bent over, covered his face with his hands and wept.

"My queen!" The bitter wrenching sound of his sobs finally abated. Arthur looked up in appeal, eyes bright with hot tears, comely face contorted in pain. Cai's roiling passions were supplanted by sorrow and then pity as he watched and listened to the confession that came pouring out.

"I live in agony that she loves him and not me! I have lost her, Cai, and I am devastated by the ruin I have brought upon us. How will I live without her? What I have wrought? And now, even her life hangs in the balance because of me. Brother, what will I do?"

Cai steadied himself and responded gingerly, aware that the king's state of mind was unstable and could turn again at any moment.

"You are tortured by jealousy and pride, Arthur. The rules of chivalry—the unwritten code of this court, of Camelot itself—demand that you clear your conscience and do the right thing. Stand beside her ancestral right as queen to bed her champion, as you have bed so many yourself, and as you commanded her to do. Appeal to the old way and stand against the nonsense of the Christian ethic that takes over our people, which Gawain uses to his own purposes.

"You must rally support for Gwenhyfar. Send word to Caradoc, Dinadan, Galeron, many of the other knights—Bors, Bedevere, Peredur, and Escanor support you..." Cai continued with calm persuasion.

"No!" Arthur snapped. "They are all away, many of them on quests of their own, and I will not call them back to me to battle their own brothers-in-arms. A fight to the death among the knights of the Round Table is not the answer—and that is what it would be. I will defend Gwenhyfar myself, when Gawain brings her to court with his accusation, seeking a judgment. That is my plan."

Cai shook his head, his face lined with sorrow. "Arthur, you must face the fact that you are no longer a match for Gawain. You deny the truth of what is happening, Arthur, and it will come to no good."

"I will handle this, as I must," Arthur whispered in response. Seeing Arthur's face closed in a tortured mask, Cai knew he could push no further. After a long moment, the king's seneschal and foster brother bowed. Turning on his heel to walk out, he whispered, "So be it. It is on your head, Arthur."

Into the Mists

The festive atmosphere of the banquet was augmented by the merry sounds of harps and lutes and the beat of drums that swelled the air as a steady stream of food and drink were served. Cynan and his cooks had prepared a score of dishes to please the king and his court, but no one missed the aching fact that the queen and her champion did not sit on the dais with the king. Instead, he sat with Cai and Lady Carys on one side and Bedevere on the other. At his customary table, just below the dais, sat Gawain with his brothers and their contingent of rebels.

After steaming roast legs of beef and lamb were served with hot bread, wine and ale, with a gesture from Arthur, the musicians started a lively tune and many of the courtiers rose to dance with their ladies. Honeyed cakes piled in layers dripping with thick cream and decorated with eatable flowers from garden and field arrived on laden platters; now the merriment would begin in earnest and go on well past midnight, but, instead of choosing a maiden from the ladies waiting to dance, Gawain and Gaheris stood up with Agravaine and Gareth and turned toward the king.

"Arthur, we will leave now," Gaheris drawled, his voice rife with irony. "After our long journeys, we will rest for the hunt tomorrow."

Arthur felt Cai's muscles tense, but the king responded with calm reserve. "Very well. I will see you after you return, tomorrow night."

Some of the courtiers stopped and stared at the rude knights, while others watched from the sidelines as their hasty departure made its mark upon the evening. As they shoved their way through the crowd of dancers toward the huge double doors of the king's hall, even Gawain's full beard could not hide the way his lips turned down, a grimace hidden within his full beard.

Two hours before daybreak, the moon shone bright behind low-hanging clouds as warning horns jarred the peace of Avalon and ricocheted up the Tor. A stab of fear shot through Gwenhyfar's belly, jolting her awake.

"Tis Gawain, I know it," she whispered urgently, reaching for Lancelot. His arms tightened briefly around her then he whispered, "Dress quickly, Gwenhyfar, we will leave by the back paths."

Tossing back the blankets, Lancelot moved fast to put on britches, shirt, jerkin and jacket. He strapped on his sword, pulled on his boots and sheathed his knives, one on each ankle and one on his thigh, while Gwenhyfar struggled into a dress, pulled soft leather boots on her feet and grabbed the bags she had packed for travel, which she kept at her side every night. She strapped her own leather girdle and knife about her hips, pulling it snug. Slipping a woolen mantle from the peg by the door, she was ready. Her hair swung in a long braid, and as she smoothed the loosened strands that fell across her face, Lancelot could see that her eyes were wide, the pupils dilated.

Holding a finger to his lips for silence, he stood at the door and listened, opened it to look outside. Seeing the way clear, he grabbed her hand as they ran from the house toward the back gates of Avalon that led upward toward the Tor. Within minutes they passed Morgan's house, where they almost collided with Morgan and Accolon, alert and moving in haste. Accolon had arrived the evening before, and they had supped together and talked late into the night. Now his sword was drawn and his face was grim. Morgan carried her rowan staff in hand.

"By the Goddess, Gawain and his knights breached the gate," she muttered.

"We will take the secret paths around the north side of the Tor." Pointing uphill, Lancelot's whisper was hoarse and urgent.

The other knight nodded tersely. "I will go to defend Avalon—take Morgan with you."

"No!" Morgan objected. "I will go with you, Accolon. Lancelot, you and Gwenhyfar make your way to Father Donnan. He will help you escape. I will deal with Gawain myself, with Accolon's help."

Andras and Iona emerged out of the swirling mists of the predawn dark, eyes huge and gleaming. "How can we help?" Andras asked.

"Go to the house where the queen has been staying, make it look like you sleep there," Accolon responded. "They may search Avalon, and we don't want to draw any attention to an empty hut with a still-warm bed. If Gawain or his men come, divert their attention as best you can."

With a brisk nod, Lancelot grasped the queen's arm and moved quickly. They were swallowed by darkness even as Iona and Andras hurried toward the cottage where the queen and her champion had lived for the past two months.

Morgan and Accolon arrived at the gate of Avalon to see the bard Taliesin, his face tight and strained in the flickering light of the torches. He stood before Gawain, who appeared like a spectre of death in the swirling mists with Agravain and Gaheris on either side. A host of ten knights crowded behind them with swords drawn and crossbows nocked and aimed, arrows pointing toward the druid. Around Taliesin were the men of Avalon, holding nothing but flaming brands.

"Again, I tell you, we will not harm Avalon or any of its inhabitants," Gawain shouted, "if you turn over the king's whore. Defend her and you will suffer. Give her to us, and we will leave you in peace."

Pushing past the protective circle around Taliesin, Morgan's eyes flashed with fury as she stood face to face with her nephew. She raised her staff, and the cry that came from her throat rent the night and chilled their bones. A sudden wind rose and lashed at their cloaks and hair. Their horses neighed uneasily and stamped, pulling at their reins.

"Those who you seek are not here." Morgan's voice was bold and steady. Accolon stood at her side, sword glinting in the light of the firebrands. "Go ahead, you can look all you want. See to it that you behave honorably—as knights of the Round Table—in our sacred spaces."

No one spoke a word. Gawain stared at Morgan, his face a mask of ice.

"Come," Taliesin echoed. "See for yourself," he invited, picking up on Morgan's cue. "The sun will soon arrive to chase away the shadows in our dwellings, our great hall and kitchens and music rooms, making all visible to you."

"Do you think me a fool, to wait until the sun rises while they get away? Agravaine, Gaheris—take the bard," Gawain ordered, "and go through all the buildings now. We will wait here for you. My kinswoman and her knight will stay here to keep us company."

Minutes passed, fifteen then thirty, while the knights made their search and a tense silence thickened, broken only by the neighing and stamping of nervous horses amidst the group that clotted uneasily about the gate. Morgan took a seat in the gatehouse with Accolon standing nearby. Gawain grew agitated and impatient, pacing and glaring about. The still shadowy shapes of trees, buildings and gardens emerged from the dark swirl of fog that dwindled in wisps. Finally, Agravaine and the others returned with Iona and Andras, who walked with uneasy faces toward the clinch of knights and people who hovered anxiously around the Lady of the Lake.

"There is no sign of them, Gawain. It seems they were not here after all," Agravaine shrugged. "All we found were these acolytes, still sleeping up in one of yonder huts. They say they are Morgan's apprentices, and newly handfasted."

The men laughed raucously. "That is why they were still abed—even with the sound of warning horns!"

Gawain eyed the young couple with suspicion, then turned black eyes upon Morgan. "I do not believe it. These two were covering for them while they got away." He hefted his sword into its scabbard with a violent thrust. "You will not save them with your magic this time, Morgan," Gawain growled. "Sooner or later, I will track them down, and I will see to it that Gwenhyfar and Lancelot suffer. And when I find out that you have lied to me, you will suffer too, kinswoman and priestess or no."

He stalked through the gate toward his horse, held steady in the hands of his squire. Jumping upon the back of the stallion, Gringalet reared and stamped the ground as the other knights mounted their steeds. Without a backward glance, they disappeared into the rising mists of morning, moving toward the lake and Camelot.

As soon as he was gone a cacophony broke out in the release of held tension. Morgan called for quiet and order. "People of Avalon, take heart! Return to your homes and your morning tasks. Carry on as usual." As people dispersed, she turned to Taliesin, her face filled with worry.

"Taliesin, I must leave. I ask you to stay here while I am away, hopefully for not more than a day or so. Iona, Andras, you will come with Accolon and me to Father Donnan's monastery. Ask Cara and Tressa to have travel food ready quickly. We leave straightaway, after we have broken our fast."

Drops of sweat ran down Gwenhyfar's temple as she hustled to keep up with Lancelot, who glanced over his shoulder at her or reached out a hand to help her catch up, as he charged up the Tor through a dew-drenched darkness that soon faded to morning's twilight. Once they had ascended, she managed to keep pace with him as he fled across the northern flank of the hill.

As they began their descent, the mists were softly gold from the sun that had just broken free of the horizon to illuminate, from behind rose-tinged clouds, the mist-encumbered world that opened before their eyes. While Lancelot stopped to deliberate on which path to take down the Tor, Gwenhyfar glimpsed Ynis Witrin and beyond through shifting fog—the low hill "islands" that rose out of the lake, the timber and wattle church and clusters of hermit's huts, and beyond that, Wirral Hill to the west. Looking behind them to the southwest they could make out the distant dim shapes of Camelot.

The beauty of the scenery did not calm the anxious thudding of her heart. She wiped her forehead with the hem of her gown and nodded briskly to Lancelot, who whispered, "Beloved Lady, there is no time for words. We go there." He pointed in a westerly direction toward a faint path that disappeared into thick fog. Trudging along behind him, she surrendered her own senses, now compromised by the shroud of mist, to the certainty of his sure steps. As they descended, the fog grew thicker as they approached the lake, and she soon saw that Lancelot had chosen a path that led directly to the point where the inhabitants of Avalon kept corricles tied to nearby willows. He deftly untied the ropes that tethered the smaller of three oiled-hide boats and turned to reach a hand to help her in. He shoved off and jumped into the corricle, groping for the paddle that was lashed to one side of the boat.

    The corricle emerged from the lake at the other shore where they disembarked. The secret trails of Ynis Witrin opened to Lancelot's keen memory, and when memory failed, his native instincts took over in movements that were agile and silent as a stag. She marveled at his skill and poise in the wildwoods, realizing that this was the blood of the Old Ones that ran in his veins. Morning had arrived in its full glory, making it easier for her to imitate his footfall as closely as she could, although she could not walk as Laëllon did—inevitably a twig snapped or leaves crunched lightly underneath her careful steps.

    They made their way along a narrow path that led through oak, birch and alder thickets, over narrow stretches of spongy moss banks between pools of water that reflected a changing sky in shades of gray-blue intermingled with the brown of earth and fallen leaves. The marshy waters, still or flowing, were flanked with stands of water reeds and occasional green mounds of watercress where a sweet water streamlet ran swift and clear. Blackbirds sang their sweet songs, and at one point they startled a covey of ducks that flapped away in alarm, sensing a hunter in their midst.

    As they drew closer to the wattle church, the sun that had shone brilliantly at daybreak and for two hours after had now disappeared behind billowing dark clouds that would spill rain before midday. Distant thunder rumbled as they broke free of the forest and walked toward the church.

"Queen Gwenhyfar, Sir Lancelot!" Father Donnan hurried toward them from the church door, concern creasing his face. "I saw you approaching...something must have happened to bring you here like this." He eyed their disheveled, leaf-flecked hair and rumpled clothes, the flush of exhaustion on Gwenhyfar's face and the determination on Lancelot's.

"There is little time for explanation, Father," Lancelot responded. "Suffice it to say that before dawn the warning horns were blown in Avalon. The queen and I left by the back trails of the Tor. Morgan and Accolon stayed to deal with the intruders, without doubt Gawain and his followers. No one else would dare to breach the gates of Avalon in such a way."

Father Donnan led them toward the kitchen, calling out to Brother Tellemond, who waited nearby to assist. "Go to the stables and ready their horses as well as two more mounts, for Paulinus and Caedmon. On your way, tell the other monks to attend to their duties and leave us be." Turning to Lancelot, he said, "We have kept your horses well-fed and ready for travel since I saw you last. Paulinus, there you are..."

He turned to the young monk who arrived out of breath. "Find Brother Caedmon, prepare yourselves to leave immediately."

Paulinus took one look at the tall knight's face, then hurried out the kitchen door. Turning to Lancelot, Father Donnan inquired, "Will you at least take a bite of food before you leave?"

"We can ill afford the time, but we must eat to keep up strength—and we are both ravenous." Lancelot escorted

Gwenhyfar to a seat at the refectory table. A round of cheese, a platter of cold venison, and a loaf of barley bread appeared. They ate in haste while the cook, Brother Justinian, packed a cloth sack with food. Tucking an unfinished half loaf of bread and a hunk of cheese inside his jerkin, Lancelot stood, ready to leave.

"Father Donnan, I am grateful for your help," Gwenhyfar spoke, rising at Lancelot's urgent glance, "but I am concerned for the welfare of your monks and your church. Be warned that if Gawain finds out you have helped us, he will burn you out. He has as little love for the Christians as he does for his own people's religious beliefs. His god is power."

"Of that I have no doubt," Father Donnan agreed, following Lancelot who had hustled the queen toward the door and out into the yard. Paulinus and Caedmon waited with the horses.

"Pay close attention," Lancelot barked tersely at the young monks, lifting Gwenhyfar up on her mount and then jumping nimbly upon his own. "When I need your help, I will ask. Until then, do everything I tell you to do, without question. If we encounter Gawain, you must be prepared to flee without being seen. The welfare of this church depends upon your swift action."

Brother Paulinus opened his mouth to respond, but it was Father Donnan who answered for them. "Have no fear, Sir Lancelot. They are trained and trustworthy." He raised a hand in blessing. "Until next we meet...God be with you."

By midday Morgan and Accolon arrived at the church to discover that Gwenhyfar and Lancelot were well on their way, going westward with the monks. Father Donnan offered food, but Morgan declined. She left unceremoniously, Accolon at her side, and Iona and Andras at her heels.

Now she sat beside a hidden meare pool wherein she gazed, but nothing had appeared to her inner eye. She frowned and snorted in sheer frustration, glancing at Iona. "Nothing. I see nothing."

Accolon counseled, "Perhaps you are too disturbed to scry, and the sight will not come to you. Still yourself, Morgan, as you do, then try again." Clutching her staff, Morgan stood and paced, muttering, "Yes, you are right, as you often are."

He glanced at Andras. "It is very likely we will run into Gawain and his party of knights hell bent on a fight. We must be vigilant."

"What Accolon says is wise," Andras agreed. "Trying to catch them is suicide for us. Perhaps we'd best return to Avalon and guard our own flanks."

"And you, Iona? What do you say?" Morgan asked.

"I say return to Avalon and wait for a sign. If there is a part we have yet to play in this, we will know. A sign will be given." The young woman held one hand out to Morgan. "I know it is hard to let them go," she soothed, "but our first obligation is to Avalon—not to the queen of the Summer Country, as much as we love her."

Morgan listened, then leaned back on her haunches beside the pool. "There is much in what you say that is true," she began, "but we are not as separate as it may seem. What befalls Camelot, Gwenhyfar, Arthur, and Lancelot also befalls Avalon and all of us. We are bound together by the strands of fate. What do you say, Accolon?"

The knight shrugged. "As you say, we are all in this together. You, Lady of the Lake, must decide. As a Knight of the Round Table, for me, death for a just cause is honorable."

Taking this in with wide eyes, Andras slipped an arm around Iona; the two young lovers settled against a beech tree and watched as the priestess worked her magic. Breathing in a deep and even pattern, Morgan swirled the water of the meare pool with one hand and watched as the ripples spread then ebbed until the water became smooth and serene.

"We are like this pool," she mused. "Easily stirred, agitated by emotion, but then, if we let go and open to the moment, the serenity of stillness comes again." She bent over the water and peered into its blue-green depths.

After some moments, she spoke. "Ah, they are close to Wirral Hill, soon to cross the River Brue and the old bridge. I believe they are headed toward Beckery. Lancelot must plan to stay with the sister hermits there—I know them to be holy women. Come, Iona. What do you see?"

Iona leaned over the pool, catching her long braids in her hands as they fell toward the water. She looked for some moments, then sat up.

"I see Gwenhyfar, captured by Gawain. I fear she will die. But that has already occurred, has it not?"

"Hmm. The last time Gawain accosted Gwenhyfar, I was able to intervene. This vision belongs to a different time—one that has not yet occurred. Gawain will intercept them, and soon. If we do not move on, toward Camelot, she will die there. We must intercept the queen and Laëllon."

She paused. "Iona and Andras, this is where you shall go back to Avalon."

The young couple looked at each other, but it was Andras who spoke.

"Lady, please allow us to go with you. We wish to help. As you say, we are all connected in the web of life. Gwenhyfar's fate is our fate." Iona nodded solemnly, her eyes searching Morgan's face.

"Very well." Her keen gaze moved to Accolon. "And you?"

"At your command, my Lady."

Beckery

Late afternoon sun glinted upon stands of tall birch trees where they stopped not far from an old Roman bridge across the sluggish River Brue. Just ahead was Wirral Hill, and Lancelot jumped down from his horse to look closely for a pathway across the marshy river bottom. The knight listened, one ear to the ground. Looking up at the monks, his face was tense.

"Someone is coming. It sounds like a party of knights by the pounding of the hooves. Leave now. Take all of our horses, meet us at the monastery at Beckery, beyond Wirral Hill. We will seek sanctuary with the sisters there tonight. Pray the Lady Mary to help us. Now hurry!" The monks obeyed, turning their horses away, into the forest, as the knight helped Gwenhyar down from her mount.

"Quickly, beyond the bridge, to the glade," he urged. "We will take shelter there in the trees at the foot of the hill. Pray that they do not come that way." He watched as the monks retreated with the horses, melting into a copse of trees and thick brush, then he turned and plunged ahead in the other direction holding Gwenhyfar's hand and pulling her close behind.

Picking their way through a thick growth of river willow, the marsh ground was wet and soggy. It was slow going, but despite the sense of impending danger, Gwenhyfar could not but notice the beauty of the hill just ahead. She had heard the legend many times from Arthur, how the saint, Joseph of Arimathea, had first sailed up the Severn Sea to land near Ynis Witrin, and coming inland, had planted on this very hill a holy thorn tree, symbol of his master, Jesus, who once wore a crown of thorns at the time of his crucifixion. Now it seemed a fitting place for her plight to unfold.

They hid in a shady grove behind clumps of wild willow, birch and hawthorne, hardly daring to breathe. With one arm wrapped around her, Lancelot met Gwenhyfar's eyes and held them. At a clatter of hooves upon the stone bridge and a harsh shout, her eyes flashed with fear and then resolve.

Gaheris, renowned for his ability to track animal and man alike, had spotted the place in the bushes where they had pushed through. Gawain's voice rang out, "Scatter and find them."

Agravaine was on them within minutes. With his long knife held firm in one hand, Lancelot had the advantage—surprise, accuracy and a deadly intent. He struck just as Agravaine lunged for Gwenhyfar, who bolted to the left when Lancelot's knife came down to strike a deadly blow to the other knight. His armour shielded him well—the wound that would have taken his life left only a thin rivulet of blood seeping down over Agravaine's chest and shoulder plates. The shock gave Lancelot time to draw his sword, and within seconds the two knights were in the throes of combat, the clash of metal on metal resounding through the air. Gwenhyfar pulled her own knife from its sheath and crouched, waiting for an opening to plunge it into Agravaine.

"I want them alive!" Gawain bellowed as he crashed through the willows with Gareth just behind. Swift as a lion, Gawain reached out to grasp and quickly disarm the queen, jerking her hard against his chest and holding her captive, knife at her throat. She stood silently, chest heaving as she looked down at her useless knife, afraid to call out lest she disturb Lancelot's concentration. The two knights traded blow after jarring blow until Agravaine stumbled on a root and Lancelot grasped his arm. Twisting him roughly, Lancelot held Agravaine, sword trembling at his neck, and stood, panting, staring into the eyes of Gawain, who held the queen in a tight grip, blade at her throat.

"Well, Lancelot. Now what? One move from you and she is dead. In fact, pray give me an excuse to kill her now. Otherwise, I am beholden to bring her to Arthur, who in his right mind wants her alive. Revenge is sweet, they say. She is to be tried for treason. And this time, we will not fail."

His lips curved in a sardonic smile, eyes flashing with cruel delight. "Now, queen's champion, put down your sword and surrender, or she never makes it to the trial she so richly deserves."

Unable to move, wrapped tight in the unflinching grip of Gawain's arms, Gwenhyfar gazed at Lancelot with eyes of sorrow and resignation. Behind Gawain stood Gaheris with Griflet and three of the younger knights. Lancelot considered, grinding his teeth and working to slow his breath that came in gasps. He knew that he could take any one of them in single combat, or even two at a time, but he could not take all four, much less the addition of four or five burly young knights who waited at the bridge. He also knew with certainty that Gawain was good for his word—he would slit Gwenhyfar's throat at one wrong move from her champion.

"Alright." Lancelot released his grip on Agravaine, letting his sword fall and holding his hands up in the air. The knights moved in to grab the champion's arms and tie them at the wrist behind his back, quickly divesting him of his knives, picking up his sword, then pushing him hard toward the river. Gwenhyfar was also bound, and the lovers stumbled, roughly pushed and shoved by ruthless hands, toward the bridge.

His pride wounded more than his shoulder, Agravaine hissed. "Next time, Lancelot du Lac, I will kill you."

The late summer rain promised earlier in the day streaked the air with the first drops of silver as the knights and their prisoners made their way through the dusk along the wagon trail to the nuns' house at Beckery. Distant thunder ricocheted as they arrived under a steady drizzle to be greeted at the monastery gate by two women who introduced themselves as Sister Fiona and Sister Branwen. Branwen took most of the knights, leading their bedraggled horses, to the stables, while Fiona brought the rest into their timber and mud wattle house that stood next door to a small chapel surrounded by several tiny huts. They were met by the kind blue-gray eyes of Mother Brigit, who stood waiting under the dripping thatch of the roof.

"How can we be of help to you weary travelers?" She looked questioningly at Gwenhyfar and Lancelot, who stood with their hands bound behind them, dripping hair hanging in their faces. "Please," she turned her straightforward gaze toward Gawain, quickly ascertaining him to be in charge. "We are not a prison or jail, we do not pass judgment—what can this good woman possibly have done to deserve this treatment?"

Ushering them inside, she clucked her tongue and grabbed a clean cloth to towel the streaming rain from Gwenhyfar's face, then recoiled with a gasp. "Merciful Mary! You are the queen." She peered at Lancelot, then reached out to wipe his face as well. "And the king's first knight, Sir Lancelot. I have seen you both many times during the harvest festival in Camelot."

"That's enough!" Gawain commanded, his voice betraying irritation and envy.

Ignoring the order, she turned sharp eyes on Gawain. "What have you done? Sir, this cannot be right," she scolded. "Surely you are not a knight of the king's Round Table! Who are you that you dare to treat the queen thus?"

"Shut up, woman," Agravaine snapped. "Do as my brother tells you."

Gawain laughed. "It's none of your business who I am. You will give us shelter tonight, as it is you duty to do so with the king's knights when they come in need. And what we need is hot food and a place to sleep. We'll be away before dawn. Now, instruct your women."

Turning to Agravaine, he ordered, "Take Lancelot to the stables. He can stay with the horses. Tell Griflet and the other knights to keep watch and we will send food out to them." His scowl deepened as he glared at Mother Brighid. "Stop staring. This is not your business. Do as I tell you and we will leave you and your women unharmed."

She turned and spoke to a younger women standing beside her. "Food for all the knights, Miriam, and quickly."

Addressing Gawain, she spoke with calm demeanor. "You will need to sleep here, on the floor. It is the only place we have other than the stable. Unless you want to sleep in our chapel, under the knowing eyes of Blessed Mary and our Lord Jesus."

Gawain snorted in disdain, but Brigit's eyes had focused on Gwenhyfar, who stood wet and shivering in misery, now separated from Lancelot, who had been roughly shoved toward the stables.

Brigit's voice was steady as she observed, "This time of year the nights grow chill. It is warmer in here, sir. We will find whatever blankets we can spare and give them to you. Supper will come within the hour. Now, allow me to care for the queen, I beg you. She will need to relieve herself and wash…please."

With reluctance, Gawain assented, charging young Gareth to accompany the nun and the queen as they went outside toward the privy. With her head close to Gwenhyfar's, Mother Brigit whispered, "My lady, what can we do to help?"

Pretending to stumble and fall into the nun's protective embrace, Gwenhyfar whispered urgently in her ear, "Help Lancelot escape. There may be two monks of Ynis Witrin nearby who will help."

"Tsk, tsk," Brigit muttered, helping Gwenhyfar to steady on her feet even as Gareth, walking six feet behind them, ordered, "Stop talking! Attend to your business!"

Surrounded by Gawain and his brothers, Gwenhyfar was allowed to feed herself and then rest without restraints upon her wrists. She worried for Lancelot—was he given food? He must be cold and wet, hungry, miserable with anxiety for her. Hopefully, she was right that Caedmon and Paulinus had followed close behind and knew they were here. Knowing Lancelot, he was plotting his escape and making plans to free her from her captors.

Gwenhyfar's thoughts spun around that slender thread of hope as their supper—a simple stew of barley and mutton—was served by Miriam and Clara, two young novices by their looks, who gently cared for the queen as best they could. Mother Brigit ate nothing but watched as they ate, her lips pressed tight, her face etched in stern lines of care and concern.

After they had eaten, Gareth went outside to check on the men in the stable. He came in stamping wet feet and carrying a load of firewood, which he piled near the hearth, placing three stout logs upon the flames.

"How is it with the men?" Gawain asked.

"The barn suffices. They welcomed the food. Lancelot appears to sleep in a corner. His wrists are firmly tied. I told them to sleep, because we would be up and away before dawn," Gareth replied.

"Gareth," Gawain groused, "go back out and give my command that one of them must be awake and on watch all night. I do not trust Lancelot. He has been known to escape even the direst of circumstances. When you come back in, we will all sleep."

Gwenhyfar watched and listened from her pallet near the wall beside the fire, provided by Miriam. The rain had dampened the air to an early autumn chill. Mother Brigit had brought blankets to cover her and lovingly patted her face. With a wink of her eye, she turned away and disappeared.

"Where has she gone?" Gawain snapped.

"To the chapel," answered Miriam. "It is time for our evening prayers."

Clara added, "You can find her there with the sisters, if you want. She asked us to stay with the queen, as it is not proper to leave her alone here with men."

"Hhmmph." Gawain snorted, then lay down to sleep, turning his back on the women. The fire crackled and blazed, and soon the men slept soundly except for Gawain, who often rolled over to look at his captive and glance around the room, and Gareth, who rose twice during the night to add logs to the coals as the fire burned down. The little house was dark and smoky, and Gwenhyfar lay with eyes closed, senses piqued to agony, pretending to sleep. Now and then she dared to open her eyes and look around.

She was soon drawn to gaze up at a statue on the mantle of the fireplace, the carved wooden form of the holy woman known among the Christians as Mary. As the light of the fire flickered and shone upon the statue, Gwenhyfar remembered that the worshippers of Jesus had more than one goddess—or were they saints?— named Mary. One was the mother of their god, Jesus. The other was his companion, or was she his lady wife?

In the fire's play of shadow and light, she saw that this Mary must be the wife, as she carried not the baby Jesus but a skull in one hand and an amphorae in the other. This one, so the tale was told, was the one who had had encountered the spirit of Jesus in the garden, after he had died. Gwenhyfar marveled at the sculptor's skill in creating the image. Her long hair, partially hidden by a veil, hung loose to her waist. Her feet and hands were finely wrought and delicate. Her eyes gazed out of a face of compassion, one who has suffered and understands.

The smell of fear and violence thickened the air in the hut, and as her anxiety grew unbearable, Gwenhyfar mentally bowed in reverence to the Lady. A prayer rose up in her heart like fresh, clear water in a woodland spring. Lady of Light, she begged, help Lancelot escape his bonds and ride free.

Moments dragged into hours in which Gwenhyfar did not sleep but kept her eyes locked upon the Lady Mary. The night seemed endless, until finally the darkness was relieved by the faint glow dawn. Agravaine got up to leave, but within moments he charged back in, slamming the door behind him.

"Get up, all of you. Gawain, the fiend has escaped!"

"What! How in the name of all the gods..." Gawain stood up, flummoxed and furious, reaching to buckle on his scabbard and sword.

Gwenhyfar smiled inwardly, not daring even a breath that might draw their attention toward her. She knew Lancelot would be on his way to Camelot, planning her rescue.

On Toward Camelot

Sporadic shafts of light shone down through leafy branches as Lancelot urged his horse onward through groves of ash and alder, Caedmon and Paulinus just behind on their mounts, with Gwenhyfar's steed following behind them on a tether. He meant to arrive at Camelot before Gawain brought Gwenhyfar to the king and his court to be tried.

Luck had been on their side—or perhaps the Lady Mary answered his prayers. With the help of the good sisters of Beckery, Caedmon had snuck into the stable at the moment when the knight on guard fell asleep. He quickly freed Lancelot, who then stealthily pulled his sword from the side of the snoring knight who lay with the sword at his side. They had slipped away on foot, quiet as foxes, to the place where Paulinus held the reins of their horses. They made away an hour before Agravaine came to discover Lancelot's absence with a roar of rage and a resounding slap to the face of Griflet, the young knight who had slept on guard. Now they plunged ahead, splashing across the River Brue heading south.

"'Tis three leagues to Camelot, southwest of where we are," Lancelot replied to Paulinus, who had asked how far they had to go. We can make it long before Gawain arrives, if we move fast."

Just then the sharp cry of a hawk rent the air. The monks looked around in surprise, but Lancelot stopped his horse and listened, cocking his head, eyes alert. From his own throat came a similar cry, and again he listened for a response, falling silent as he held out one hand to still the questions of the monks.

"Wait here," he commanded, when the hawk cried once again. Jumping down from his horse, he tossed the reins to Caedmon then pushed through a willow thicket and disappeared into the forest.

Moments later they heard the sound of horses moving through brush, then Lancelot appeared, holding the reins of a horse upon which sat Morgan, followed by her three companions of Avalon. The seven merged, their horses huddling together, as they looked one another over.

"Well, here we are," Morgan commented with irony. "Lancelot told us what happened." She turned to him and asked, "Now what?"

"We go to Camelot, and we do whatever is needed to free Gwenhyfar so we can escape to the north." Jumping on his horse, Lancelot tapped his heels upon her flank, urging the mare forward. The others followed, with Morgan and Accolon in the lead.

An hour behind them traveled Gawain and his party of knights, their prisoner now both bound and gagged in

Gawain's fury over Lancelot's escape. He had threatened the sisters, shouting in Mother Brigit's face, but her calm, detached manner finally cooled his wrath to the point that he believed her story—the nuns had nothing to do with Lancelot's escape. After all, the king's first knight was known for his uncanny skill in escaping dire situations, as he himself had said. As they mounted their horses with Gwenhyfar riding on the saddle in front of Gareth, the nuns gathered outside their enclave with somber faces. Mother Brigit's eyes did not leave Gwenhyfar's as the horses clomped through the muddy yard. She lifted a hand in benediction and whispered.

"God go with you, Queen of the Summer Country!"

The companions made their way quickly with the reprieve from the rain. As they drew near the hill by the river Cam, upon which Camelot was built, Lancelot and Accolon rode side by side. Bringing his horse to a halt, Lancelot gave the order to gather around him.

"Let us consider carefully our next move. They must be an hour behind us, which means we can enter Camelot now and go directly to the king. Or we can wait for the right time to strike, when we have the advantage to take Gwenhyfar." He looked at Morgan, whose horse was stamping nervously.

"What do you say, Morgan? What does your priestess gift tell you?"

Morgan remained silent for a moment, gazing off into the horizon where layers of clouds foretold more rain. She looked to Iona, then around at the other companions.

"As able as we are," she began, "we are not strong enough to overtake Gawain and ten or more knights, including his wily brothers. And as to Arthur, when I last saw my brother I was astounded at his lack of clarity. Nay, we should not go to the king, but act in secret."

Accolon interjected, "I agree. It is best to hide and wait for the moment to strike." He paused, then suggested, "There are ways to get into Camelot without being seen."

Picking up Accolon's train of thought, Lancelot extrapolated. "Yes, Caedmon and Paulinus could go into the village first, find Blane, determine the best way to smuggle us in." He glanced from Accolon to Morgan. "Morgan, you should wait with Iona and Andras in the forest. Guard our horses for a fast getaway. You know the place—the hidden copse where the sacred pool lies, north of Camelot."

They weighed his words in silence, then Lancelot added, "There are those who will help us. I believe Cai, Bedevere, and Peredur and their ladies will help, maybe Bors as well. And many of the younger knights—Blane, Tristan, Dafydd, Gweir, and others—will be on our side. If only Sir Caradoc was in Camelot, he would help as well. He has always been loyal to the queen."

Their plan took form, and within an hour the monks were walking through the gates of Camelot, nodding to the guards upon the palisade then making their way into the busy market at the center of the village that surrounded the castle. It was late summer, the time of harvest, which was abundant this year, making the market all the more festive and bright with high spirits. They strolled past vendors selling vegetables of all kinds—heaps of golden squash and orange pumpkins, purple-topped turnips and white parsnips, mounds of broad beans and burlap bags filled with barley, oats, and wheat.

Some sold spices—cinnamon, saffron, coriander, and cumin—traded with the ships from the south, and yet others displayed pottery and beeswax or tallow candles, bags of salt gleaned from the estuaries of the nearby sea. Another stall sold pots of honey, while another hawked baskets of eggs, round loaves of bread, fresh cheese wrapped in leaves, or an array of cut herbs and flowers kept fresh in buckets of water. The market was lively and distracting, with blacksmiths, carpenters, and weavers at work, horses, chickens, and an occasional tethered cow, sheep bleating from a pen and wooden crates of geese, awaiting their turn under the butcher's swift knife. People of all kinds and ages milled about, going from one stall to another with baskets in hand, walking the narrow streets, or sitting at the inn swilling beer and mead.

Around the edges of the market square were small shops, where shopkeepers sold their wares: precious oils of all kinds, herbal tinctures and ointments, leather goods, woolens and the tailor's shop, next door to the stone hut where the midwife lived. Despite the color, action, and noise, the monks kept their attention riveted to the activity around the king's castle, where knights and ladies came and went on various errands or activities or leisurely walks.

Before long they were rewarded when a group of young knights came striding through the castle's tall double doors, banded with iron, which opened out from the central courtyard of the fort. One of them, with sandy hair and green eyes, matched Sir Lancelot's description of Blane, down to the colors he wore: sea green and rose red, which signified his alliance with the Cymry, as these were the queen's colors. The monks moved through the crowd with casual ease to follow the knights, and before long, they bumped into Blane, taking the young knight by surprise and knocking him off balance. He caught himself and turned to see who had jarred his progress.

"I beg your pardon, kind sir," the young knight said politely, reaching out to the monk who stood only inches away from his face. Paulinus pressed a note into his hand, and with a quick glance at the scribbled words, Blane looked up, eyes on guard.

"Meet me in ten minutes, behind the church," he whispered, then, in a loud voice, he cajoled, "A thousand pardons, brother, for my clumsiness!" He bowed and then sauntered, half dancing, down the street to follow his compatriots.

Two hours later Lancelot and Accolon lay flat between the cold clay of butter crocks, hidden under a thick covering of blankets and straw inside a covered wagon that rolled through the back gates of Camelot under the watchful eyes of the king's guard. Recognizing the driver as the young knight, Blane, they ordered him to stop.

"What have you got here, young sir? And why aren't you in the tilting yard, practicing your sword play?" one of them asked.

"You won't believe this," Blane laughed, "but Cynan, the king's cook, you know, talked me into bringing these crocks of new-made butter from the spring on his farm. It's not my usual job, to be sure! But it's for the Pendragon—a fine cake that Cynan plans for the king's feast, tomorrow night, and the kitchen boy is sick with a fever. So I agreed," he shrugged amiably.

"Well, along with you, then," they chuckled.

Lancelot breathed a sigh of relief. Perhaps the worst was yet to come—they would have to wait another hour, remaining perfectly still and quiet until darkness fell, to get out and make their way into the castle. Blane had told him the scuttlebutt along the village lanes, about a party of knights led by Gawain that traveled toward Camelot and would soon arrive with the queen. News about an impending trial spread from mouth to mouth, and people from all over the village clamored to come and see the high drama unfold.

Just as Blane's wagon rolled to a stop near the stables, trumpets sounded at the front gate, announcing the arrival of the knights with their prisoner. Gawain and Agravaine appeared, followed by Gareth and Gaheris. On the back of Gareth's steed rode the queen, bound and gagged with a dirty rag. A shocked hush blanketed the busy noise of the market as people stopped and stared, recognizing their queen. Some cried out in fear, sickened at the sight of Gwenhyfar in such distress. Others whispered among themselves, remembering what had happened only three months before. Others smirked, incited by the idea of trouble among the royals.

The horses' hooves clomped noisily, sucking up the wet earth of the marketplace as they made their way through the village, banners and spears held high in victory. As Gawain's entourage disappeared around the bend moving toward Arthur's keep, the market that had been suspended in fear and dread came back to action as vendors hurriedly packed up their goods and wares. People scurried away, eyes downcast, their faces marked with worry. Even though it was still an hour or more before sunset, the market was over. The scoundrels had fled to the taverns to swill their ale, and no one else had the spirit to continue.

Camelot
529 C.E.

Desperate Hours

From inside the castle, Farquar came running as the gates opened and the party rode into the courtyard. His mouth agape, he looked up to see that Arthur watched from a window in his apartment, his face grim and unreadable. As they descended from their mounts, Gawain took Gwenhyfar by the arm and led her inside. Farquar approached her, breathing heavily through his mouth, his face a map of desperation.

"Lady, Queen Gwenhyfar," he began haltingly.

Gawain snapped, "Do not speak to her. She is a prisoner held on the charge of treason. I will insure that she does not escape this time—she will be under lock and key until the morrow, when the trial will occur two hours after sunrise. Deliver this message to the king—tell him to make ready."

With a sweep of his hand, he commanded Gareth and Gaheris to come with him. Agravaine would handle anything that came up from the outside. As they disappeared into the depths of the stone keep, the castle of Camelot fell into silence, grief-stricken and deep.

Reaching his apartment, Gawain shouted orders to his brothers. "Wait out here, and stand guard," he pushed Gwenhyfar inside, following close behind. She stumbled toward the center of the room and looked around, then with a shove at her back, fell onto a low divan as Gawain slammed the door. She heard a bolt slide into place on the other side and knew that she was trapped inside with him. Gawain removed her restraints, and she scrambled back against the couch, trying to distance herself from his overweening physicality. She rubbed her wrists, but he laughed and pulled her abruptly to his chest, pressing his lips against hers.

"You want to know what it is to bed a real man, don't you?" His breath was harsh and stale as he panted, passion rising. He groped for her breasts as he shoved a hand between her legs. Struggling to get free, she spat in his face. Snarling, he slapped her, once and then again much harder. Her head swam and bright lights blossomed before her eyes. She tasted the metallic salt of blood, and for a moment she was utterly helpless against his strength as he manhandled her body, pulling her gown up and exposing her bare thighs. He ripped the fine linen of her undergarment and pushed her down.

Weeping silently at the act of sheer violence, she turned her face away and squeezed her eyes shut. As her body went limp in his grasp, his rage was fueled. He wrenched her chin toward him, digging his fingers into her cheeks then pinning her by the throat with one hand. Choking, she gasped for breath and pulled desperately at the hand that bit like iron into her soft flesh as he fumbled with the lacings of his leather britches.

He threw her back against the couch and lunged upon the length of her body. Shoulders, belly, and legs were crushed beneath his weight, and she shuddered as he rammed into the secret well of her and pounded at her body. There was no passion in the assault; his actions were fueled by a hatred she could not understand, and she lay passive under the battering he inflicted. An impulse to survive, stronger than the sickening revulsion that raged within, took over, and her mind retreated to a place deep within.

Finally it was over. Shoving roughly off of her, he stood up and wiped his mouth with the back of one hand, chest heaving with labored breaths as he pulled up his britches and laced them.

"You are not worth the trouble, Cymry queen," he looked down at her with lips drawn in a sneer, his red hair dripping with sweat. "I leave with the smell of you on my cock. But don't despair; there will be more before you hang for treason. There is a long night ahead." He stalked to the door and wrenched it open. Before he slammed it, she heard him say to a page, "Bring ale and food. And Gareth, do not allow that brat, Bloedwyn, to come anywhere near the queen."

Struggling to breath, numb and in shock, Gwenhyfar slowly wiped away the stain of him, straightened her gown and braided her hair, combing it first with trembling fingers. Grateful to be left alone, she whispered, her voice catching in a sob, "Laëllon." Misery overcame her and, as she worked, hot tears coursed down her cheeks. Immersed in dread, she sat in the growing dark until Gawain returned reeking of ale. She was relieved to see that Gareth, who had always been kind to her, was with him. They entered the room with a maid who came to cover the window, light a few tallow candles and a fire in the hearth. She carried with her a flagon of wine, some cups, and a plate of food. As the maid hurried away, Agravaine knocked at the door. He conferred with Gawain in whispers, then they abruptly left, locking the door behind them. She breathed a sigh of relief.

"Eat, lady," Gareth urged.

"Why would you care if I eat, since if you and your brothers have their way, I will die tomorrow?"

Gareth hung his head. She saw that he was little more than a boy, the youngest of the sons of Morgause and King Lot. He was as afraid as she was. Knowing that she had to keep up her strength, clinging to the faith that Lancelot had a plan and would rescue her, somehow, she ate a bit of the bread and cheese, drank a few sips of wine.

Gareth piled more wood on the fire, as he had at Beckery, then kept watch. Her nerves were shattered, her body ached, and with every breath she was assaulted again by the fear that Gawain would return at any moment to take her again by force. She cringed and shuddered, loathing the thought. In between her terror and her desperate prayers, the hours passed slowly, and neither Gareth nor Gwenhyfar slept. Sometime after midnight, Gwenhyfar could not stop the tears that rolled from her eyes. As Gareth watched, his face grew more agonized. Finally, he began to talk to her quietly of many things—of his childhood in Orkney, of his first love, of his dreams of chivalry, and then of his fear and shame. Gwenhyfar listened, saying very little.

Truth and Consequence

The sun rose, and with its golden light, unexpected courage flooded into Gwenhyfar's heart. Gareth pulled back the heavy woolen drape from the open window to let in a stream of dawn's light and chilled, fresh air. Gwenhyfar squinted and shivered, but she was grateful for the healing power of the sun and the cool air to breath. Gareth implored her to eat, pouring a cup of water for her. She drank thirstily and nibbled at a piece of bread. They sat in silence for another hour until, finally, a knock came at the door. It was Gaheris, who told Gareth to get the queen ready. They were going to the king's great hall.

Her gown badly ripped, face stained with tears and smudges of dirt from the road, her braid disheveled and hanging half undone and her thick black hair drifting wildly about her head, the queen walked into the great hall as she had on countless occasions. As always, she walked with grace, head held high, back straight, her gaze open and unflinching. This time she was flanked by Gawain and Agravaine, followed by Gaheris, Gareth, and the rest of

Gawain's knights. Even at the early hour, the hall was packed with all kinds of people who flooded in from village and countryside to watch the spectacle.

Once again, as if she had dreamt this before, she saw the inhabitants of the castle and court, the faces of concerned loved ones, some wet with tears, standing alongside those whose idle curiosity had brought them to watch the royal spectacle that would unfold on this day. Gossip, intrigue, innuendo, and heaving passions flew through the room on fleet wings as she passed. Some called out her name, yelling, "Courage!" and "Long live our queen!" or "Gwenhyfar, Queen of the Summer Country!" In response to these cheers, Gawain glowered and snorted, one hand on his sword as if he would draw it at any moment to dash off heads and make the blood flow.

As Gwenhyfar proceeded through the gauntlet of the writhing, the true beauty of her countenance shone through the hazard disarray of her appearance, beyond the bruises and dried blood that bespoke the violent abuse she had suffered at the hands of Gawain. Finally she came to a halt before Arthur, who sat upon his dais surrounded by Sir Cai and the senior knights—Bors, Peredur, and Bedevere—and many other knights and courtiers and ladies of the court, as well as the local magistrates who administered village law in Camelot.

Cai stood with clenched hands, the muscles in his jaw a rigid band of fury. The day before Cai had personally delivered the message from Gawain that he held the queen prisoner, and any attempt to see or speak to her would end not only in her death but in a battle to the death between the knights. It was an inescapable insurrection, an effective coup d-etat in which Gawain had, by far, the upper hand.

Cai glanced at the king and saw that his eyes were locked on Gwenhyfar, his face livid with wrath. Arthur gnashed his teeth, but he was beyond tears. For the first time in his life, the king realized his own powerlessness. Now, he was shocked at the sight of his queen. His eyes could not deny her ravaged face, and his heart contracted. He glanced at Gawain and could only surmise, by the arrogant victory written across his smug features, what may have transpired during the night.

Gwenhyfar would not meet her husband's eyes. Her heart was plunged into a cold rage, but beneath the rage was the pain of abject betrayal. Rather than look at him, she looked around at her people. So many faces, well known and unknown, swarmed before her eyes. In the faces of the knights she knew so well, Peredur, Bedevere, and Bors, she glimpsed horror and grave sorrow. Mordred stood nearby, a sneer of scorn and triumph on his face. The stricken faces of Lady Garwen and Lady Carys came into view; Garwen held a weeping Ghleanna in her arms. She saw Cynan the cook standing beside Farquar and Dafydd, both looking miserable, and a host of other friends who looked on helplessly. It's strange, she thought, that Bloedwyn is not here.

The shouting of Gwenhyfar's name grew in volume until it became overwhelming, like a chant at Imbolc. Then, back in the surging crowd, she saw Brother Paulinus. Catching her eye, he held one finger surreptitiously to his mouth and glanced around. Next to him was Caedmon, and beside them, a tall man of dignified bearing oddly dressed in the ragged robes of a beggar. His face was smudged with soot and he wore a wide-brimmed hat low over his face. Behind him, she saw another tall and rather burley beggar. Lancelot and Accolon.

Her face remained impassive but her heart soared. Just as quickly as she registered their presence, she sobered, knowing that all of their lives hung by a slender thread. The lines were clearly drawn between two sides of factions. This time Gawain would not let them go alive. Death rode the air, a palpable spectre waiting to drink the blood that would be spilled. Yes, death would take its toll before this day was over. She uttered a prayer to Ceridwen and Morrigan, begging for their help, knowing all the while that their fate was already written in the stars. But surely, her prayers might make a difference!

With a deep inhale, she looked up at her husband, finally meeting blue eyes, bloodshot and rimmed with shadows so deep it appeared he had spent the night wrestling all the demons of hell. His face was a mask of agony that looked as if it would crumple at any moment.

As madness swirled around them, Gwenhyfar's mind became calm and clear as the scrying pools of Avalon. Her heart opened, and love spilled out as she gazed upon Arthur. Compassion coursed through her veins, a prayer emerged from her heart as she beseeched the Goddess to care for the king. Seeing her love, Arthur's lips parted, his breath ragged as he staggered one step forward, reaching a tremulous hand out toward her. Cai pounded the floor with his seneschal's staff, four, five and six times, yelling over the din.

"Quiet! Quiet! Quiet in the hall!" The deafening sound of the huge bell tolling at the entrance to the hall finally brought a semblance of order, though chaos careened a drunken course just below the surface, threatening to take over again at any moment. People were restless, disturbed, hungry for blood.

Arthur spoke, turning his eyes toward the knights that held his wife in bondage. "How dare you, Gawain. This grudge should have been settled the last time you brought charges against the queen. Release her!"

Gawain threw his head back with a loud derisive laugh and took a pace forward. "We were unsatisfied with the last time this prisoner was brought to trial. In fact, the trial was circumvented by the witch of Avalon!" The susurrus of the crowd grew louder at this insult to the Lady of the Lake, while others nodded vigorously in agreement, fingering the wooden crosses that hung about their necks. Gwenhyfar could hear their jeers and curses interspersed among the utterances of outrage and support.

"We aim to have justice," Gawain continued. "The queen has plotted treason with your knight, Sir Lancelot. They intend to take over the throne and depose you, the Pendragon. The traitor Lancelot has run for his life—a coward as well, it turns out, leaving his woman here to face the lawful punishment! The penalty for treason is death, and we demand death for Gwenhyfar and Lancelot."

A loud gasp resounded through the hall. Some murmured, some yelled, "It's a travesty of justice!" and "Kill Gawain instead." Other shouted, "Death, death, death!" And "Hang the whore!" Behind her, Gareth shuffled uneasily. Terror scrolled across Arthur's face. He stood rooted, as if frozen in place, until Cai nudged him, leaned in to whisper, again pounding the floor with his staff and demanding order. Finally, the king shouted over the low rumble of the crowd.

"Queen Gwenhyfar is not guilty of treason. By the old laws, she has the right to have a champion. I have given permission for this…" his voice trailed off as a deafening crescendo of noise from the people drowned out his words. Cai stepped forward once more with a futile attempt to bring order, but it was too late.

"The king has spoken. Let it be heard that the queen is innocent!" Cai shouted and pounded his staff for order, but his words were also lost in the wild cacophony and mayhem that was breaking loose.

Raising an arm to punch the air with his fist, Gawain yelled over the noise, "Our king has gone mad! He is besotted with this witch. If the king is not able to mete justice, we will take it into our own hands. Hang her!" He grabbed Gwenhyfar by the hair at her neck, braid swinging wildly as she struggled, and dragged her backward toward the doors as the crowd closed in around them. The crushing swell of the mob dragged Gwenhyfar, Gawain, and the knights toward the entrance.

The beggar in rags struggled to get through the melee, throwing off his tattered robe and drawing a sword. "To the queen!" Lancelot shouted over the din. Hearing his familiar battle call, knights rallied to his side—Bedevere and Peredur leapt into action along with Blane, Gweir and several of the younger knights who shouldered their way through the maddening crowd to get to the queen. Arthur and Cai lurched into motion, jumping down from the dais, but they were caught in the crush of lunatic passion as people scrambled, pushed, shoved, fell down, and fights broke out within the crowd itself.

With a fierce grip on Gwenhyfar, Gawain burst through the door and into the morning sunlight that shone down in bright shafts in the courtyard of the castle. A hanging post had been erected overnight, and he dragged Gwenhyfar toward it, still pulling her by the neck and hair. As they crossed the yard, a new commotion broke out behind them and suddenly Gaheris, Agravaine, and Mordred were in combat, sword to sword, with Lancelot, Peredur, and Accolon.

Gwenhyfar blinked back stinging tears of pain as Gawain stopped in mid-stride, allowing her a glimpse of the combat. The loud clang of metal on metal interspersed with shouts and grunts as the knights fought, and within seconds Gweir and Bedevere arrived to throw themselves into the broil next to Accolon, swords drawn and facing off Agravaine and Gaheris and two of the toughest young knights.

"Hold on to her," Gawain ordered Gareth, shoving the queen into his younger brother's arms. He charged toward Lancelot, yelling for his company of knights to draw their swords and follow. Gareth took Gwenhyfar by the arm and restrained her, but as her eyes were desperately fastened to Lancelot's every move as he parried Agravaine stroke for stroke, sweat flying as he lunged and missed, spinning to parry yet another brutal blow. Gawain charged into the fight, attaching Lancelot and making it two against one, when Accolon stepped in, holding off Gawain with adroit blows and parries while Lancelot fought for his life against Agravaine's furious attack.

Gwenhyfar stood twenty feet away, held firm in the strong grip of Gareth in a swarming ring of bystanders who yelled encouragements or stood gaping as the knights fought to the death. Where was Arthur? What could have happened to him? With relief she saw the king breach the door and stride toward the battling knights, but just then a woman shrieked and Gawain screamed. She looked, dreading what she would find, and saw that Lancelot's sword had pierced through the belly, just below Agravaine's heart. The knight fell to the ground, his mouth gasping for air as he lay dying. Lancelot pulled the sword out and blood gushed into the dirt, pooling viscous and dark red as Agravaine's substance flowed from his body. His eyes were already glossing in death as Gawain knelt beside him with an agonized cry. Lancelot backed away slowly, dripping sword in hand, then turned to move toward Gwenhyfar.

Arthur shoved his way into the circle of people who backed off, recognizing the king. He stopped and stared down at Agravaine, who lay in a congealing lake of blood with Gaheris and Gawain at his side. Suddenly Gawain rose and lunged with a scream, but Lancelot turned and parried the thrust that would have killed him, then with one furious sword slash after another, he beat Gawain back toward Bedevere and a host of knights until he was held their captive at knife and sword point. The crowd gasped at Lancelot's astonishing speed and agile moves, the deadly focus of his intention. Through it all Gaheris knelt, weeping, at the side of his slain brother.

"You will die for this, Lancelot," Gawain shrieked, restrained by the knights. "I will hunt you down. There is nowhere you can go where you and that whore will be safe. Mark my words, Avalon's dog! You will pay for this!"

Face mottled with passion, breath heaving in his chest, Lancelot stared at Gawain for a fleeting moment. Without a word, he turned his back and moved toward Gwenhyfar. Sword drawn and still dripping with blood, he measured a determined course through a thick clot of people that stepped back before the raw visage of the knight's terrible face. Lancelot's eyes briefly scanned the crowd to locate Blane and Accolon, who had positioned themselves near the queen. The monks had their horses ready at the gate of the hill fort; they had only to push through the stunned and anxious crowd to escape Camelot.

Gawain screamed, "Gareth, kill him! Revenge for Agravaine's death!" The younger man hesitated, holding tightly to Gwenhyfar. Looking around in desperation, he saw Lancelot's deadly advance and Accolon and Blane standing nearby, swords drawn, their chests heaving. Gawain's voice pierced his ears, cracking with the strain of his scream, "Kill him... Kill Lancelot! Take the queen!"

Twenty feet away, Arthur shoved through the frothing crowd trying to reach Gwenhyfar and Gareth, but his progress was sabotaged by knots of people who wept or shouted or stood waiting anxiously, yet eager to witness the next death.

Holding the queen with a shaking hand, Gareth's fingers dug into her flesh as he pulled his sword, his face dark and suffused with suffering and confusion. "Goddess help us, he's not more than sixteen years," Gwenhyfar whispered to herself as Lancelot approached, his face wreathed in rage.

Surging forward through the throng, Arthur yelled. "Stop it! I command you! Enough death, enough blood!"

For the first time in his life, Lancelot ignored his king's order. He advanced, his face ghastly. When he was three strides away, he paused and leveled a steady gaze at Gareth. "Put down the sword. Give her to me, and you will live," he counseled, his voice even and deadly.

The courtyard fell silent, the crowd now immersed in the great drama in which fate decided who would live and who would die. From the corner of his eye, Lancelot noticed that the young knight named Griflet stood not far away from Accolon. Would he be a problem as well? Which side was he on now? He glanced at Accolon and Blane. They nodded, ready for whatever would happen next. He could hear Arthur, yelling a command, and knew that the king was trying desperately to reach him. All this he recognized with a ruthless clarity and calm honed in countless battles. But not even his king would gainsay his purpose now.

"Once more," Lancelot said, his voice steady, "give the queen to me, and you will go free. I will not hurt you."

Gareth's face contorted in fear. He swung Gwenhyfar around until he held her against his chest, his sword at her neck. Lancelot's face grew livid, but he held out a hand and asked again with a voice as hard as the blade in his hand. "This is your last chance. Give her to me, and the bloodshed ends. Harm her, and I will kill you."

Arthur's shout colluded with Gawain's screams that rent the air as he wrestled violently against the hands that held him fast. The tension grew unbearable until, with a garbled cry, Gareth squeezed the sword handle in his sweaty hand and Gwenhyfar felt the blade bite at her throat. In the split-second flash of that moment, she knew Gareth would die. A thin line of blood blossomed red along her neck and Lancelot lunged, in one swift motion grabbing and spinning her toward Blane, who pulled her to safety. Within seconds, Gareth lay bleeding to death, his hands clutched upon a mortal wound to his heart.

Gwenhyfar cried out, and pulling free of Blane, she knelt beside Lancelot, who was already at the side of the dying knight. Gareth's eyes were fastened upon Lancelot's as the dying lad whispered, "All will soon be well. The light of the Otherworld is upon me." A sob broke from Gwenhyfar's lips as the young man's eyes went blank and his head fell to the side. Time stood still for a split second, until Accolon spoke urgently at their side, "We must go!"

Grabbing the queen and pulling her up with him, Lancelot pounded toward the gate with Blane and Accolon, where the monks waited astride their horses with Bloedwyn on her palfry and the rest of their horses. Blinded by tears, Gwenhyfar was lifted by Lancelot onto his mount, then he jumped up behind her and spurred his mount to action. He saw that Accolon galloped ahead to insure the way was clear, then frowned when he saw that Griflet was close on their heels. There was no time to stop and ask questions; holding Gwenhyfar tight against him, Lancelot careened through the obstacle course of the village and down the road that led to the main gate, Blane and Blodwyn, Paulinus and Caedmon bringing up the rear.

When they breached the gate, Lancelot turned his horse in a circle to face Griflet. He charged, "What do you want?"

"I want to go with you," the young knight exclaimed, breathing hard. "I was on the wrong side, Sir. I realized it, almost too late."

"Not too late to let me escape at Beckery," Lancelot replied in haste, spurring his horse to gallop as he gestured to Griflet to fall in behind Blane.

A Healing by the Pool

They moved swiftly along the road going north toward the Tor in silence for two hours without stop. Now and then, when her shoulders shook with silent sobs, Lancelot leaned forward to press closer to Gwenhyfar, or gently circled her with his arms in a wordless embrace, attempting to offer comfort. He did not know what had happened in her hours of captivity at Gawain's mercy, but he swore under his breath. His heart ached not only for Gwenhyfar but for Gareth. He would gladly have killed Gawain, given half a chance, instead of his younger brother.

When they came to a crossroad, Accolon took the lead, looking toward the Tor to locate one of the intersecting secret paths toward Avalon. He guided them down a timbered path through pooling tidal waters and spongy marsh moss, through overgrown thickets and ash trees, with the shallow lake all around, until they came again to solid ground where an oak grove grew tall and thick.

Entering the grove, Accolon stopped, lifted a hand to his mouth and made the call of the hawk. A response came, quick and sure, and he took the faint evidence of a trail to the east. Within minutes they saw Morgan, Iona, and Andras, sitting beneath a venerable oak on a mossy mound, their horses tethered nearby. With one look at their faces, Morgan knew her priestess intuition—and her gut—had told her true. Something terrible had happened. Before anyone spoke, she gestured toward Griflet.

"Who is he?"

"He helped me escape two nights ago," Lancelot answered tersely. "When we were captured by Gawain, I lay bound and tied in the stable at Beckery, my sword and knives taken away. The monks came to my rescue and he pretended to sleep after leaving my sword free at his side. His name is Griflet. He risked his life for us."

Somewhat mollified, Morgan nodded. They dismounted and sat together under the tree while Accolon relayed the events of the king's court, the battle among the knights, and the deaths that followed. All the while Gwenhyfar sat unmoving while Bloedwyn fussed over her in silence, combing the knots from the queen's long hair and gently braiding it. Morgan listened carefully, glancing at Lancelot then looking steadily at the queen. Her eyes took in the blue bruise on Gwenhyfar's cheekbone, the shadows under her eyes, and the crusted line of dried blood on her throat.

After she had heard all that Accolon had to report, Morgan turned to Gwenhyfar and said, "I know where they spent the night last night. Where were you, once they took you inside the castle?"

"In Gawain's apartments." Gwenhyfar lifted her chin and took a deep breath, avoiding Morgan's eyes.

Lancelot looked sharply at her, concern moving like night shadows in his eyes. Before he could speak, Morgan stood and gestured to Gwenhyfar.

"Come with me."

Taking the younger woman by the hand, Morgan led the way to a clear, spring fed pool where she sat down unceremoniously and patted the ground beside her. Gwenhyfar hesitated, looking away in misery, causing Morgan to snap out a command.

"Sit down. We have no time to waste."

When Gwenhyfar was seated, Morgan probed. "Now, tell me what happened to you." Unable to restrain the overflow of tears, Gwenhyfar's mouth trembled as she uttered an inchoate sound of grief. This time Morgan spoke with infinite patience.

"It may seem that it was too horrible to tell me or maybe even to bear, but you must speak of it now. You are strong, Gwenhyfar. You are truly a queen, both temporal and spiritual. The Goddess is strong in you. You can regain your sovereignty. You can heal from this. I will help you begin. You and Laëllon will do the rest. For, have you forgotten," she smiled, "that he has the healing gift?"

At those words, Gwenhyfar took a deep breath, and the story of her moments alone with Gawain rushed out. Morgan listened in careworn silence, her eyes anchored on Gwenhyfar's face, her hand warm upon the younger woman's. When Gwenhyfar had finished with shedding tears and her eyes were dry, Morgan embraced her, whispering, "We do not have much time, sister, or I would use the light of the moon and stars, the sound of Taliesin's harp and Iona's songs. But because we cannot wait, or return to Avalon—for we know it is not safe for you—we will use the elements of the sun and water, the air and earth, to remove the poison of Gawain's assault."

Holding Gwenhyfar at arm's length, she instructed. "Look into the pool and see your reflection. Connect to your inmost self, relax, let go, and feel into the spirit of the pool. Know that this water is connected to all waters—the streams and rivers and oceans, the deep lakes of the north, the clouds and rain and mists. Let it all go into the sacred waters, the waters that mingle with the air you breathe, the light of the sun, the solid earth beneath you.

"Breathe in the essence of water, earth, fire and air. These are the substances of life. They are purifying you. Breathe, Gwenhyfar. Breathe in the healing power of water and air, and breathe out the darkness that was put into your body. Let the earth take that darkness, for she can purify it in the turning of the seasons, in the falling of rain and the decay of leaves, in the heat of the sun and the cooling rays of the moon. Keep breathing, sister."

They remained quiet for some time, breathing together. Morgan uttered what seemed to Gwenhyfar a prayer, spoken in an unknown language, and in that moment the clouds parted revealing a brilliant stretch of turquoise sky. The sun shone down in golden shafts to spangle with light the mosses and ferns and delicate grasses that grew about the pool in the grotto where she lay.

"Now, lay your burden upon the earth, turn your face up to the sun and let your skin take in its purifying rays. Breath in the healing power of the sun, breathe out any poison that lingers. Feel the solid earth beneath you, how she absorbs these poisons and consumes them. Keep breathing in this way... and if your mind intrudes, remember to breathe."

The priestess placed her hands upon Gwenhyfar's belly. They breathed together, and as the breath came and went, the coiled tension in her muscles and organs began to melt away. It seemed to Gwenhyfar that a graceful power suffused her body with light. After some moments, Morgan gently lifted her hands and placed them over Gwenhyfar's heart, and then finally, on her forehead and eyes. In every place she touched, the flow began again, bringing streams of energy and warmth into the deep interstices of her cells.

Their breath mingled, and Gwenhyfar began to drift and then soar until she flew far above the earth and clouds and, like a falcon on the wing, she saw far across the land. Rising up on windy drafts, then lilting upon the air, she was immersed in light, awash in waves and sheets and coruscations of light. All around her the carillon of the Goddess, the ringing and singing of infinite bells and voices raised in song reverberated, resounding in and through her on a vast ephemeral plane that danced with transparent colors. The configuration of a temple coalesced in the radiance, and although mysterious and veiled, she was certain that she felt and saw a feminine presence, a Lady of Light, emerge from the temple's arches of light.

"Ceridwen!" Gwenhyfar whispered, eyes still closed.

How long Gwenhyfar was suspended in the interlude of light, she did not know, for she disappeared in the blazing beauty of that place, losing all sense of herself. After a timeless time, her awareness re-emerged, and she felt herself effortlessly soaring and then floating, slowly descending the air currents to dip and glide down to the solid ground upon which her body lay. She saw that her heart was tethered by a silver thread to Lancelot, who awaited the return of his lady. He sat silently under an oak tree, along with the rest of their company. All of his being was focused on her, with infinite care and concern. Love surged within her, and she fell into a peaceful quietude in which she wandered in the sacred groves of her innermost heart, breathing deep the fragrances of the flowers that blossomed there.

The Lady of the Lake had been still as deep water, sitting in vigil beside the queen whose spirit wandered for that brief time in the Otherworld. She lifted a hand to wipe away one glistening tear that hovered on the curve of her own cheek as she watched and listened, and as the queen sailed free, Morgan prayed inwardly for the forces of love and light to fill the vessel that had been so desecrated by Gawain. And in her prayer, she asked also for help for Gawain, that he might find remorse and clarity in his rage and grief. She begged for help for the souls of the fallen knights, that they might be guided by the Lady of Light, by all the blessed powers of the Otherworld, to make their way in peace to whatever their destiny might be in the next turning of the wheel.

She prayed for Lancelot, for the journey ahead, for the young people and for the good monks who would accompany them. And last but not least, she prayed for Arthur, her brother, the only man she knew who could have prevented this tragedy. And yet, try as she might, she could not fathom how he might have been able to change the course of events, once they were set in motion. She bowed her head in humility. Some things can be changed; some things cannot. There are inexorable fates that we must face within our human sojourn, and she pondered this truth with a somber heart as she gazed at Gwenhyfar, who had returned from her inner journey. Her face was more relaxed and her smile was wan but steady, though her blue eyes were still shadowed with the swarm of her sorrows.

When the women returned, Gwenhyfar glanced once at Lancelot, and he saw that her spirit was tender and delicate. He was relieved to see that her face was brighter, and it seemed she had shed some of the heavy weight she bore.

"It is time for us to part," Morgan spoke simply, turning to her horse.

Their horses had grazed and drunk from the pools around the oak copse; they flicked their ears, whinneyed and stamped, ready to go. When all were mounted upon their steeds, with Gwenhyfar astride a fresh mount of her own, the Lady of the Lake wasted no time on sentiment but looked around, her eyes resting for a moment on each of them—Paulinus, Caedmon, Griflet, Blane, Bloedwen, then Gwenhyfar and Lancelot. With Accolon at her side, she took them in, one by one, then raised her hand in blessing.

"My friends, we will not meet again in this life, except perhaps in vision or dream. My blessing, and the blessing of Avalon, goes with you. Goddess keep you safe and well, and may your lives prosper and be fruitful. May you all know the joy and harmony of the One Spirit that guides all."

The companions bowed their heads to receive the Lady's blessings, then watched as Morgan and Accolon,

Iona and Andras reined their horses toward Avalon and within seconds disappeared into the dense foliage of the copse.

With a wordless press of his knees to his horse's side, Lancelot turned and steered through the forest back to the trail. Following him, their hearts were heavy and strangely light—the losses they had endured and the separation from all they had known and held dear was a palpable ache in the air between them. Agravaine and Gareth lay dead, Camelot was in the throes of chaos—indeed, it was covered by a pall of darkness that would not recede in their lifetime, nor in any time to come. Gwenhyfar dreaded the farewell she must say as they passed through Caerleon in Cymry on their way north. Inwardly, she felt herself teetering on the edge of a high cliff, with the forces of inexorable change swirling and blowing about them.

The Hand of Fate

Merging onto the road, Lancelot picked up their speed. As they moved at a trot down the trail, freedom beckoned to them, a beacon of light that called them to an unknown shore. Anticipating a request from the monks, Lancelot slowed down to ride beside them.

"There is no time to stop at the monastery to see Father Donnan."

Caedmon said nothing but moved on in silence, while Paulinus responded, "We do not need to see Father Donnan—our path is clear. We will accompany you to Alba and on, to Eilean Arrain."

"And then?" Lancelot asked.

Paulinus shrugged. "Who knows? We are free to follow our destiny as we are moved. We will see how the spirit moves us. If we have learned nothing else in our years at Ynis Witrin with Father Donnan, we have learned how to pray and how to listen." He smiled warmly, then clicked and pushed his heels into his horse's flanks to catch up with Caedmon, who was speeding to a gallop.

When they reached the Meare Pool—a vast pool of fresh water teeming with life, where the lake villagers often had their fishing boats—they saw two riders on horses waiting for something or someone on the trail that circled the Meare Pool. Lancelot halted their party and cautioned them to hide behind a thick stand of water willows. He motioned to Blane and Griflet.

"We will wait here while you go to the pool and talk to those two—find out what they are doing and let us know if it is safe to come ahead."

Lancelot watched, his eyes narrowed, then seeing the look of joy on Blane's face as he drew near the two riders, he looked at Gwenhyfar, a grim half-smile on his face. "Tis your lady in waiting, Ghleanna, and Farquar. I don't know if we should be happy or worried."

They galloped to the Meare Pool and, with no time to linger, they sat astride their horses by the water's edge and heard the story of how the two young lovers, Farquar and Ghleanna, had fled from Camelot in the wild grief and confusion after the bloodshed was over. They left in the desperate hope that they might somehow find Lancelot and Gwenhyfar. With an instinct that Lancelot might choose the back trail around the Meare Pool on his way north, Farquar had decided to go there first.

"I could not stay in Camelot after what happened to you, my Queen," Ghleanna admitted. Farquar gave a fierce nod of his head, then stared at Gwenhyfar, the agony of his conflict written across his young features.

"It is the same for me," he said haltingly, "As much as I have been, and still am, the loyal squire of the king, I could not stay after what I saw. The only thing I knew was that I could go home, to Dyfed, but more than that, I hoped I might have a chance to be with you," he stammered, "my queen, and...and with you, Sir Lancelot. Will you accept us? We don't know where you are going, but if you will allow us, we will come with you. We thought perhaps you would stop in Caerleon, so the queen can say goodbye..."

"We are not going to Caerleon," Lancelot replied, his words clipped and firm. Gwenhyfar looked at him in surprise.

"It is not safe," he continued. "My instinct tells me that Gawain will go there first to look for us." Lancelot looked away toward the northern Mendip Hills. His brow was stern but noble—even in the extremity of their circumstance, his face was a wordless poem of beauty. As Gwenhyfar watched him, her heart contracted with fear of losing him again, even as the memory of Gawain's assault surged up in a fresh wave of horror and revulsion. Thunder rumbled across the land, and Lancelot's horse stamped uneasily, ready to be on the way down the road. The summer was over, and they could taste the first hint of autumn's chill winds in the air.

Lancelot met her eyes with a nod of assent. The queen in Gwenhyfar spurred to action, reaching a hand to Farquar across the span of their horses as she spoke.

"Yes, you may come with us. You were right—we are headed north."

Lancelot stopped her with a gentle hand upon hers. "Say no more of our plans, my Lady. Yes," he glanced at the two young people, "you may join us, but you must do as I say. If I tell you to turn back at some point, or to leave us if the risks are too high, then you must agree to do it, with no argument. Are you agreed?"

Hand on his heart, Farquar pledged his obedience, then he glanced at Blane, who flashed a smile, overjoyed to have his closest friend and companion on the journey. Ghleanna and Bloedwyn had already drawn their horses side by side for an embrace.

"Now, let us be on our way," Gwenhyfar commanded. "I know that Lancelot is eager to leave." Spurring their horses with their heels, they galloped away, Lancelot and Gwenhyfar in the lead, their traveling party now increased by two.

As the sun moved across the western sky, they traveled through the rolling hills of the Mendips, dense with tall oak, ash, and beech groves and thickets of hawthorne or willow along the river's edge. Knowing that Gawain was likely to be on their heels, Lancelot set a fast pace going north. He said very little but turned now and then to look for Gwenhyfar, who did not ride beside him but kept pace with Bloedwyn and Ghleanna. His eyes were often shaded with concern as he looked upon her, every fiber of him beseeching her, but she would meet his eyes only when necessary. The blood on her neck had dried to a thin, crusted laceration, and he could see by the deepening purple and yellow bruise along her cheekbone and the drawn lines of her face that something terrible had befallen her in Gawain's hands.

By nightfall they reached the old Roman town of Aquae Sulis. Paulinus moved his horse up beside Lancelot with a question on his sun-browned face.

"Sir Lancelot, what do you say? There are brothers of Ynis Witrin who live here in their hermit's huts. Do you wish to stay and rest for some hours? They will feed us well, and they are able to keep their mouths closed."

Lancelot looked around at the companions, loathe to stop but knowing they must rest. "Yes, let us eat and sleep for a few hours. We leave when the Bear is high in the sky, travel by starlight since it is still moon dark these nights."

Paulinus and Caedmon took the lead, and soon they trotted into an enclave of several round, thatched-roof huts constructed of wattle and daub, sequestered deep in the forest outside Aquae Sulis. Several monks wearing coarsely-woven dark gray robes came out to greet them. Paulinus quickly drew them aside to confer, saying no more than that they were traveling under grave travail and sent by Father Donnan of Ynis Witrin, seeking shelter for one night. The monks glanced at the knights and ladies, then directed the newcomers into the biggest of the huts, where a large iron pot hung over a low fire. The steamy aroma of its contents wafted toward the travelers, and their mouths watered at the thought of hot food. Griflet took their horses to be fed and watered and bedded down in the small stable, while bowls of thick stew were ladled and passed around.

The monks were kind and unobtrusive—they made a point of asking no questions and soon left their unusual guests to fall into an exhausted slumber while Lancelot and the men took turns keeping watch. Now and then

Gwenhyfar woke to see Lancelot putting wood on the fire. At one point, she woke chilled, and moments later, he covered her with his cloak.

Long before dawn he woke them and they were on their way, taking the road north from Aquae Sulis toward the Severn Sea, where Lancelot called a halt to allow the horses to graze and drink from a streamlet. She stood beside her mount, one hand stroking the velvet length of the mare's neck as she grazed, pulling patches of green grass from the turf and munching with contentment. Gwenhyfar gazed at the white dunes and blue-green water to the west.

"My people call this water Môr Hafren," she mused, speaking the name in Cymraeg as she turned toward Brother Paulinus. "As a child I came here with my mother to collect seaweed and the marvelous branching sponges, the sea fans and corals. She loved them especially for their beauty." Lancelot listened, saying nothing, but his eyes lingered upon her.

Picking up speed, Lancelot skirted around the estuaries and mudflats, heading east to cross the River Severn by ferry at an ancient jetty built of stone left behind by the Romans who, four hundred years before, had taken Aquae Sulis—a place of springs and thermal waters sacred to the Britons—from the Dumnonii people who once lived there. As they approached the jetty, the sound of hooves beating upon the hard dirt of the road stopped them. Lancelot wheeled his horse around, drawing his sword and calling on the men to move the women to shelter.

"Gwenhyfar, take cover in the trees. Men, swords at the ready!" He ordered sharply, his horse dancing with excitement. The muscles in Lancelot's jaw flexed with tension as he strained, hand shielding his eyes, to see the identity of the two riders. Within moments it became clear as the golden hair of one tall and imposing rider came into unmistakable view. Gwenhyfar sat very still upon her horse, half hidden in a copse of beech trees behind Blane and Griflet.

"It is Arthur and Cai. They are alone." Lancelot determined, goading his horse to a trot and riding out to meet them. Watching the men as Lancelot drew up to parley with them, Gwenhyfar gathered her cloak about her, covering her head with its hood to watch with shadowed eyes from beneath its folds.

The three men galloped toward the waiting group, and as they grew closer, Gwenhyfar stiffened, squaring her shoulders and firming her resolve to meet whatever would come next. Before she could speak or move, Arthur was down from his horse and at her side, reaching a tentative hand up to her. She did not move but looked down at him as if across a chasm of fire. Within seconds Lancelot leapt from his horse to stand beside her, and as he faced Arthur, despite all that had transpired between them, an empty place in his heart ached at the sight of a man who suffered in abject misery.

"Gwenhyfar, have mercy upon me," Arthur pleaded. "I beg you, give me a moment before you leave." Lancelot stood rigid, clasping the bridle of her horse, his eyes hard and relentless upon Arthur. The queen remained still and quiet for some heartbeats, while the wind lifted the leaves of the beech trees in a gentle play of early autumn air, gainsaying the coming of the cold. Arthur hung in the balance, desperately wondering which way his wife's heart would go—to the cold of winter, or to the compromise of autumn, for surely their summer was gone forever.

"Alright." She roused herself to respond. Lancelot moved forward to proffer a strong hand as she climbed down from her horse. With some relief that she took the offer of his hand, he tossed the reins of their horses to Blane. Arthur stepped back, his breath coming heavy through lips distorted by the anguish of his pounding heart. Cai waited solemnly, dismounting to stand with Farquar and Griflet.

Gwenhyar walked into the copse with Lancelot, Arthur a few steps behind her, until the three were hidden from view. Releasing Lancelot's hand, she turned and faced Arthur, her hands hanging at her sides. Orielled within the hood of her cloak, her blue eyes burned bright against the pallid plains of her cheeks. There were no tears and she did not speak but waited, staring at her husband. The unadorned truth, the sheer finality of the moment shocked them, as Lancelot moved into the apex, completing the triangle they had known so well.

Swiping a large hand across his forehead, Arthur smoothed back his hair until he cupped the back of his neck, mouth turned down. He heaved a breath of such utter desolation that it would rend the heart of one less betrayed. Seeing his suffering, Gwenhyfar only watched and waited.

"Say what you have to say, Arthur." Lancelot interjected, not unkindly but with urgency. "We must leave. You of all people know that it is not safe for Gwenhyfar to linger here."

The king reached out to touch her hand, but she moved back, folding her arms and wrapping them across her body. As she did, the hood of her cloak fell back. Arthur gasped at the sight of the purple bruise, the thin wound across her neck, and the strained set of her gaunt face. With a long steady inhale, she looked up at a patch of blue sky that peeked through the canopy of green-gold beech leaves that fell down upon them, one at a time, like the first drops of rain. All hope fled as the certainty that she had gone beyond his reach sank into his heart, and he fell to his knees with a cry.

"For the sake of all that we have known to be holy, that we have shared together, Gwenhyfar, I beg your forgiveness!" Arthur's words rushed out, his cheeks burning with shame. She turned her gaze upon him with solemn reflection, considering the man who knelt before her, someone she had once known intimately but who was now separated from her by a gulf so wide it was unbreachable. But it was her silence that scorched his heart.

"Gwenhyfar, how will I bear to live without you?" His voice cracked with the strain of emotion. "I have destroyed everything we worked and fought for. I do not deserve your forgiveness, but I beg you for it." Seeing that she had gone beyond his reach, he buried his head in his hands and wept, his shoulders heaving with the gall of grief and regret that wracked his soul.

Lancelot saw the battle that waged within her heart. Her face, which had remained impassive, crumbled first with a quivering of lips that had been pressed into a fierce line. Her brow furrowed as she gazed down upon the man whose knees pressed into soft dirt and leaves on the forest floor. Then, images of Gawain took her breath away with cruel force, thrusting into her with a violence that shocked her body and mind. She saw Gareth stricken, the light ebbing from his eyes as his blood flowed out upon the ground.

Shaking her head to free her mind, she could not deny the evil that had been allowed to proliferate by Arthur's denial, his refusal to use his power and authority to stop Gawain. Gathering her resolve, she began to speak, and as the words came, the color seeped slowly back into her face though her voice shook with passion and her breast rose and fell with ragged breaths.

"Arthur, how could you stand mute and allow them to besmirch and accost me? To accuse me of treason? To thrust me into prison? Would you have also stood by passively and watched me die?" He stood transfixed by the power of her eyes as she stared at him, pausing, then uttered in a fierce whisper, "How could you let Gawain take me?"

Abruptly, she reached out a hand to shake his shoulder. Somehow she was aware that Lancelot watched her intently. His face reflected the throes of a passion she could not read, nor did she want to in that moment—her attention was on the king who looked up at her, his face stained and mottled with tears.

Arthur choked, his words faltering as he confessed the truth. "My soul was lost the night of Imbolc, when I watched you through a hidden grillwork of my own design."

Gwenhyfar's gasp of disbelief lingered sibilant upon the chill air. Recoiling, she took one step back to lay her hand upon the bole of tree.

"Yes, I watched you in my bedroom. And I saw you as I had never seen you before. The joy, the abandon, the love

I witnessed upon your face, Gwenhyfar, which matched so perfectly his own. I knew then that you shared something with Lancelot that you had never shared with me. I could not bear it." Tears welled in his eyes and he swallowed hard, as if he sought to dislodge the bone of the truth from his throat.

"In my madness, I was eaten from within by jealousy and pride and, yes, revenge. In these past days of death and loss, since you escaped, I have begun to face that I will suffer my betrayal of you until the end of my life."

He stared at her, his face brutally revealed, all masks of composure and kingly power stripped away. He bent over with a groan, catching himself with hands pressed flat upon the earthen carpet of fallen leaves. For passing moments in the beech copse, the only sound was the broken sobs of the man who had been her husband. Gwenhyfar and Lancelot did not look at one another, but kept their eyes upon the man they had each loved more than their own lives. An invisible wound bled from the recesses of Gwenhyfar's heart, seeping into her body to stain her soul. Her heart softened, and, with a fleeting glance at Lancelot, she placed a hand upon the king's bowed head that shook with tremors of remorse.

"I cannot help but say that I warned you, Arthur. Now your selfish pride and overweening ambition have ruined us," she whispered. "You have destroyed even more than you know. There was far more at stake than you and me." A single tear broke through her lashes to trace a slow passage down her cheek. She brushed it away as she raised Arthur up from his knees, exhorting him to stand. Looking up the height of him, her eyes were moist as they burned into his.

"I forgive you, Arthur, as best I can in this moment, with my own wounds still fresh. Perhaps in time, I will forgive you more." Her words were limpid and bare as she spoke. "But can you forgive yourself? Lancelot and I both came very close to death. Others died because of us. It is enough sorrow that we three, who shared a rare love, a noble vision of what could be, are now rent asunder in this life. It is enough sorrow that Camelot—our time of glorious deeds and noble causes—ends in betrayal, death, and terrible loss."

She pondered the man before her, weighing carefully her next words.

"Perhaps by the grace of the Goddess, and even by the grace of the Christian God, a full forgiveness will come, as their Lord Jesus taught. By the grace of Ceridwen, I will forgive you. We are all duty bound to forgive, ourselves and each other. Perhaps it will in some small way relieve the consequences of our actions.

"Even so, the Goddess will have her way with us, Arthur. Our actions will have reverberations in the world for generations to come. We must live with the truth as a coal that burns within our hearts, for that fire purifiy us."

She paused to take his measure and, seeing that he heard her, she pushed him, very gently, toward Lancelot.

"But there is another whom you must ask for forgiveness, Arthur. Do it now, before we are gone from you."

Arthur turned toward Lancelot, who looked back at him with grave and stern eyes. Even so, the knight's face was etched with pity, and the light in his eyes was a balm upon the king who took one step toward him, reaching out a careful hand that Lancelot grasped in his own. Arthur's mouth moved in a soundless agony, then he whispered.

"Forgive me, brother."

Lancelot looked long into the king's eyes then dropped his hand, his pity staunched. They stared at each other, for no words could suffice the aching breach between them, until Lancelot spoke with quiet force.

"Arthur, I will defend my queen until my dying breath. I can forgive your betrayal of me, but Gwenhyfar has been harmed, and badly, not only by you but because of you, by Gawain and his brothers."

Arthur winced but listened as Lancelot's words struck as fierce and true in their aim as the blade of his sword.

"Fate deals out inexorable and perfect punishment, my king," Lancelot laughed bitterly. "As my lady has said, perhaps it is enough sorrow that you must live with yourself without the company of your queen or your first knight. As for forgiveness, if the gods will it, it will come in time. One thing is sure—we will meet again, and it is in that world to come that we will reckon with one another once again."

A solemn regard passed between the two men who took the measure of one another without hope of any respite or refuge from the truth. Gwenhyfar did not look upon them but gazed into the greengold depths of the forest.

"You have always been the best of my knights, Lancelot," Arthur breathed with a heavy sigh. "I owe you my life, many times over." Resignation weighed upon his words and hung in the air like a mourning cloak. Lancelot said nothing but glanced toward their waiting companions. The sounds of the horses, their whickering and the stamping of hooves as they anticipated the road ahead, floated upon the air.

"We must go now, Gwenhyfar." Breaking the spell of the moment, Lancelot reached toward her, taking her hand and drawing her to him.

"There is another reason I rode to find you," Arthur delayed, this time with a different urgency. "Gawain has ridden north on the Roman road with Gaheris and several others. They are making way toward Caerleon as we speak. I knew you would not take the Fosseway but would come to this crossing of the River Severn, and because of that, I told him you would take the ferry further east, at Cockscomb. I am here to warn you, do not go to Caerleon."

Arthur cast a look to Gwenhyfar, his eyes beseeching. "I know you will wish to say goodbye to your kinsmen, but it is not safe for you. I will ride with Cai to Caerleon to waylay Gawain, and I will rally the knights there. Do not fear. We will turn him back to Camelot."

Lancelot moved decisively, sheltering Gwenhyar within the circle of his arm to move swiftly through the trees toward the horses, Arthur following close behind. Taking the reins from Blane, Lancelot steadied her horse as Gwenhyfar jumped up, then held her eyes fleetingly before he mounted his own steed with the agile grace she knew so well.

Arthur moved close to take the bridle of her horse in hand. "When you are settled, will you send word of where you are? Or at least that you are safe?"

Gwenhyfar looked away, her face troubled. It was Lancelot who answered. "No, Arthur. I do not deem it wise nor safe to send word of our location. As long as Gawain lives, he will come for us. You can be sure of one thing—as long as I am alive, I will guard Gwenhyfar with my life. Now, let us say goodbye." He reined in his horse with a lingering look at Cai and said, "Brother, may peace go with you."

Arthur walked to his horse and leapt into the saddle. With a click of his tongue, he dug his heels into the horse's side and moved off at a trot with Cai on his mount beside him, heading south. There was no backward glance—just the strong, broad shoulders of the king and his seneschal, growing smaller as they spurred their horses to a gallop and disappeared down the road.

Lancelot shielded his eyes as he looked to the west, where the sun would set within an hour. The companions watched him, waiting, as he sucked in his cheeks, as if chewing on a difficult decision. He looked at Gwenhyfar.

"I do not want to cross here, now that we know Gawain is east of here on the River Severn, and on his way to intercept us in Caerleon. We must go farther west and then north, bypass Caerleon altogether. There is a ferryman some leagues west of here, on the channel. He has a seaworthy boat with three sails and can take us across, but we may have to leave some of our horses."

His horse danced, eager to be off. "Tomorrow we will cross the Severn Sea and proceed north and then head back east toward Gwent, where Sir Caradoc rules. As for tonight, we can sleep in the forest."

Blane nodded, easily following Lancelot's train of thought. "I remember, sir, when you and I traveled together that way a few years ago, with my brother Llew, on our way from Gwent to Camelot."

Noticing the crestfallen faces of the two maidens, Gwenhyfar mustered a faint smile. "None of you are obliged to make this trip with me—it is a journey from which we will never return. I will understand, truly, if any of you decide to go home to Caerleon."

Ghleanna's face registered alarm and Bloedwyn, always quick to speak up, quickly protested. "Not at all, Lady!" She tossed her head, interjecting with a gulp. "We may be a bit sad, but we are with you. Whatever Sir Lancelot says, we will do. Tis only that we hoped to say goodbye to our mothers and fathers."

Taking pity, Lancelot relented. "Perhaps we can send a message to your mothers and fathers through Sir Caradoc, whose castle we will stay in, to say that you are safe. We will reach his castle, if we are lucky, tomorrow night or the next. He is Cymry by blood and by soul, and he will support his queen to the death if need be."

With a smile at Gwenhyfar, he recalled, "Sir Caradoc did not side with Arthur as battle leader until you married him."

Gwenhyfar said only, "I remember well."

Blane had brightened visibly at the mention of his own father and the possibility that he would soon see his lady mother as well. They turned their horses to the west, falling into line behind Lancelot, who rode vanguard, alone into the setting sun.

Exile
529 C.E.

Caradog and Tegau

They were lucky crossing the Severn Sea—the ferryman had a fine barque with three sails, and the wind was in their favor. Their party split to make two trips across, bringing all of their horses with them. Two days later they trotted into the tilting yard at Castle Morgannwg. They were greeted by Caradoc's squire, Gwynon, who helped Griflet and Farquar with the horses. Blane walked beside Lancelot and Gwenhyfar to greet his father.

A boy was sent to fetch Caradoc, and within minutes a strong, stout man with shaggy grey hair and bristling white brows appeared, striding through the castle door and out into the yard. Several dogs ran to lick his hands and trot along beside him as he approached with one hand upon his heart.

"Queen Gwenhyfar! What pleasure to see you again!" His smile was broad and genuine and creased his apple red cheeks with joy.

"Sir Caradog Vreichvras!" Using the full form of his Cymraeg name, she returned the smile, inclining her head graciously in response to his bow from the waist. "Indeed, it makes my heart glad to meet you again." His eyes sparkled at the sight of her, then a frown came upon his face as he saw the torn, muddy and bedraggled gown she wore, the pale cheeks and dusky shadows beneath her eyes. His eyes lingered on the bruise and scabbed line along her neck.

"By the Goddess, what calamity has befallen you, my queen? And where, I might ask, is the Pendragon?" Without waiting for an answer, he called for his page and a serving maid.

"We must remedy this situation at once." He murmured thoughtfully, looking at Lancelot's disheveled condition and taking in the expression on his son's face.

"Clearly it is a story that must be told, which I am eager to hear. But first, Olwen will show you to your rooms for a bath. I see you are traveling light. Fresh clothes will be delivered to you before supper. When we dine tonight, Lady Tegau will join us, and there will be good, hot food and ale, and wine from Bretonnia, and then you will tell your tale."

Gratefully, they followed Olwen. The queen was given an apartment where she would stay with Bloedwyn and Ghleanna. Blane would stay with Lancelot in a room next to the queen, while the monks would bed down in the dry haylofts of the stable with Griflet and Farquar. When Gwenhyfar had finished her bath, a knock came at the door. Ghleanna opened it and in swept Tegau, mother of Blane and wife of Caradoc, with Olwen and another serving maid, heavily laden with clothes for the queen and her maidens. There were gowns, silken underclothes, hosiery and soft leather boots that laced up to the knee, as well as warm shawls, practical heavy wool gowns for travel, and a fine woolen gown in hues of sunset and rose for Gwenhyfar.

After they had embraced and greeted one another, Gwenhyfar remarked, "Lady Tegau, it has been five years since I saw you last, and your beauty is greater than ever. Your generosity is deeply appreciated by all of my traveling party. It is no wonder the people of Gwent call you Eurfron, 'Golden Breast,' because your heart is as comely as your face!"

Tegau smiled and inclined her head at the compliment, but her piercing eyes swept over Gwenhyfar with some concern. "And you, Gwenhyfar, are also as beautiful as ever, but you have grown thin. Your mother would have worried to see you so—may the Goddess guide her soul's journey in Annwyn! You must stay at Morgannwg long enough for my cooks to lavish you with food, and for my weavers to fashion another cloak for you, my Lady. But, do not fret, we will decide everything later, after you have rested and eaten, and we have had a chance to hear why you are traveling through Gwent, as Caradoc told me, going north."

She soon left discreetly, giving the women time to dress before supper would be served. After a meal of duck roasted with apples from the harvest and a fine barley bread, they sat around the fire. The men and maids drank honey mead and ale, while the queen and Lancelot shared the promised golden wine with the lord and lady. They heard that Caradoc's eldest son, Llew, was away in Caerleon, and would return in a fortnight. It seemed that all was well in Caradoc's kingdom, and the harvest this year had been bounteous and satisfying.

Caradoc was shocked when he heard all that transpired in Camelot. Tegau's black eyes glanced at Gwenhyfar with anxious looks more than once. When the story had been told, Paulinus and Caedmon politely took their leave with Griflet and Farquar, while Bloedwyn and Ghleanna went upstairs to bed, leaving their elders to talk among themselves.

"Where will you go from here, Sir Lancelot?" Caradoc leaned in close, one hand winnowing his white beard.

"As much as I would like to go northwest to Emrys Dinas and take to the sea from the most northern port of Demetia, I think we must travel by land. I fear a long sea voyage—for what reason, I am not sure. Perhaps it is only an intuition of danger there. I do not believe the queen will be safe from Gawain until we are in Caledonia."

Caradoc nodded in agreement. "Aye, it is a long road between here and there, but if the weather holds fairly well, with winter coming, you can be in Caledonia by October quite easily. If the women are willing to travel hard, that is."

Gwenyfar bowed her head to hide a smile. "We are all excellent riders and quite capable, Sir Caradoc. We have no need to hold back our progress."

"Yes, my lady, I remember well your affinity for horses as a child. You were riding like a seasoned knight by the time you were twelve!" He chuckled at the memory.

Tegau's eyes sparkled as she recalled, "Yes, your mother had quite a time, getting you back from the hunt, or from one of your all day rides, in time for her feasts at the Round Table. In fact, the day you first met Arthur, you had been out riding all morning and came in, cheeks aflame and eyes bright, your midnight hair tangled and windblown. You were only sixteen, then."

Gwenhyfar's eyes crinkled briefly at the memory, then the smile faded. Her eyes roved to the flames in the fireplace and stayed there, her face growing pensive. Tegau reached over to gently squeeze her hand. Seeing that Lancelot watched her with a worried frown, Caradoc broached his question with care.

"And once you are in Caledonia?"

Lancelot hesitated, glancing at the older knight. "Arthur asked me where we would go, and I did not tell him."

Caradoc wheezed and blew his nose on a piece of linen cloth that he pulled from his damask jerkin. "I deem that wise. Do not feel you need to tell me either, Sir Lancelot, because I asked. But if you wish to have an ally here in the south, you can count on me and mine." He nodded toward Tegau.

"Sir Caradog and Lady Tegau are trustworthy, Lancelot." Gwenhyfar reproved gently. "Tegau is a kinswoman of my mother Tarian, and Caradog Vreichvras is known throughout Cymru for his loyalty to the sovereign queens of this land."

Lancelot smiled in response as he reached out to touch her, but she abruptly stood and walked to the fire where she warmed her hands. Seeing that she deftly avoided him, Lancelot let his hand drop and returned his gaze to the older man, whose keen eyes had missed nothing.

"Sir Caradoc, forgive me. My queen's safety is my first and only concern. I know very well how trustworthy you are, which is why I have brought us here, to take refuge in your haven. You and I have fought side by side in more than one battle. If you are willing to be our ally in the south, as you say, I would be most grateful."

Caradoc inclined his head. "That is all well understood and as it should be, sir. If you have need, you can call upon me."

As Gwenhyfar walked back to her seat, Lancelot paused until she was settled near Tegau. With a sigh, he began.

"I have spoken with the queen many times of an island, which I remember well, on the western coast of Caledonia. I lived there for some time as a young man. It is called Eilean Arainn. I came there by currach from Erin, the home of my grandmother. It was there, long ago, that I met Myrrdin and lived in a sea cave with him for some moons. Now that place calls to me."

He swirled the wine in his cup and lifted it to his mouth to down the dregs. Caradoc leaned over to pour another libation, but Lancelot declined the offer graciously. His brown eyes gleamed luminous in the firelight as he continued.

"There are Picts and other tribes—the Epidii and Caledones, ancient tribes—as well as Gaels of Erin living there. I remember the people as friendly, if you come in peace. The island is fair, with soft warm winds that come in from the sea, especially on its southern tip. There are sweeping moors and many standing stones and cairns of the Old Ones, and the people grow oats and barley. The forests are full of red deer, and seals and otters play on the shores. It is a beautiful and abundant land. I think perhaps we can start over there, build our shelters, grow food. Eventually, over time, we will build a stone dún, as the forts of Caledonia are called."

Sir Caradoc grinned. "It sounds a most inviting and auspicious land, Sir Lancelot. I thank you for giving me your confidence, as it makes the parting less painful for my lady and me. It is not easy to see my younger son Blane go into exile, but he goes to protect our queen—it could not be a more worthy cause that takes him to a new life. Perhaps, the years ahead, when you are settled and safe, you will send Blane on a quest to the south, and we will see our son again and hear news of you."

Lady Tegau listened quietly, then cautioned. "We do not know what the road ahead holds for any of us. If the Goddess wills it, it will happen. In our Cymraeg language, we have a word—cynefin—that means the place where we feel right with the universe. It is the special place where nature conspires to let you know your spirit is welcome to dwell. You will find this place for yourselves, I am certain. And now, I can see that the queen must have sleep."

Gwenhyfar stifled a yawn with one hand. "Despite such wonderful company, I am tired beyond exhaustion. Thank you, Lady Tegau, for all you have given."

Tegau fussed over her for a moment, calling for Olwen to bring an oil lamp to light the way for the queen. "Is there anything at all we can provide for you, Gwenhyfar?"

"No, Tegau, you have been most gracious in every way. My maidens, Bloedwyn and Ghleanna, will see to all my needs."

Lancelot stood up and bowed, as did Caradoc, as the queen rose from her seat to leave the room. At the door she turned, with a nod to Caradoc and a glance toward her champion. Lancelot's eyes followed her as she walked away, her departure leaving a chill ache in the gloaming of his heart. Tegau and Caradoc shared a knowing glance.

"She will heal." Tegau commented quietly, placing a warm hand upon Lancelot's arm. "Whatever it is that has happened, beyond that which we have heard tonight, it will take time."

"Pray be it soon," Lancelot muttered, "for she is suffering and will not let me help her." He glanced at his hosts. "I thank you for such good company, and for the generosity of your castle. I will retire now, and see you upon the morning light."

They stayed at Morgannwg for three days while Caradoc outfitted them for the road ahead. Food, a wagon, bedrolls with quilts and furs, new clothes, weapons, tools, and iron pots for cooking were pressed upon them by Caradoc and his lady. Caradoc himself gifted the queen's champion with fine, well-wrought knives, their handles inlaid with silver, gold, amethyst and quartz, replacing Lancelot's precious knives, taken from him at Beckery by Agravaine. He had guarded his sword with care since that night, when he retrieved it only with the help of Griflet, who had pretended sleep during his escape.

Blane, Griflet, and Farquar received crossbows and knives, and Gwenhyfar and the maidens were given small bronze daggers. The monks had their own weapons concealed beneath their robes—a fact that Caradoc found most amusing. Caedmon did accept with joy the gift of the lute that he had played with dexterity during their stay at Morgannwg. Tegau had insisted, pressing it on him with pleasure.

"Our bard, who returns soon with our son Lleu, is a fine maker of instruments; he will make another. The queen will need music in the moons to come."

After three days, Tegau came to Gwenhyfar's room as Bloedwyn dressed and plaited her hair before the evening meal. Pulling up a chair, she sat beside and watched as the long tresses were carefully untangled by the maid's deft comb.

"I hope you have found comfort here, Queen Gwenhyfar," Tegau began with a smile. "It gives me great honor—and a true pleasure—to offer our home to you."

Gwenhyfar returned the smile, though her own was worn and thin.

"Would it help to speak of what troubles you?" Lady Tegau reached out a warm hand and placed it upon the queen's arm. Gwenhyfar glanced up at Bloedwyn, meeting her eyes.

With a start, Bloedwyn bowed. "I must go to the kitchen for hot water, my lady, to set your braids. With your leave, I will return shortly."

When the door was closed behind the maid, Gwenhyfar looked at Tegau with a sigh. Her voice was low and steady as she spoke, but her eyes were filled with sorrow and something deeper that weighed heavy upon her heart.

"Lady Tegau, you are my mother's cousin and dearest friend. Even now, years after her death, I can feel the bond between you."

Tegau inclined her head, acknowledging the truth of Gwenhyfar's words as she responded. "The veil between this world and Annwyn is thin indeed. As we grow older this becomes more apparent, my dear. I see that you have paid a great price for the wisdom that grows within you."

Gwenhyfar looked down at her hands. "Tegau, it is not only the outrage that has been done to me personally, of which I shall not speak. There is much to mourn, beside the loss of my dignity. Arthur's folly and the evil of Gawain and those who follow him are the undoing of our way of life. I have seen it in my dreams."

Tegau listened carefully, saying nothing. Gwenhyfar stood and walked to the window, laying one hand upon the casement. "The truth of this is as clear to me as the sun on yonder garden, where the last of the autumn flowers bloom. I am like them... the last of my kind, as the life we have known withers and dies until Cymry is no more."

She stood silent and still, looking out at the purple asters and golden chrysanthemums that bloomed along the walls of the cloister. Turning back to Tegau, she sat down.

"There will be no more sovereign queens of our line, Tegau, who live and breathe as the land herself, who insure the continuity of life. I can feel the geasa that has rested upon me all my life ebbing away. Sovereignty will no longer be passed from mother to daughter. The sovereign right of the queens of Cymry will now pass to the kings, and—like Gawain and Arthur—they will not honor the mysteries of the goddess, rooted in earth and air and fire and water. They will not seek a tanaiste to marry a queen of royal blood but will sire sons to rule after them, as the Romans do. Just as Morgan has said that Avalon will recede into the Otherworld, so does the geasa of our royal line disappear from this world."

Tegau touched Gwenhyfar's shoulder. "We live in an era of great change, my queen—for that is what you will always be for me and for Caradog and many others. But do not lose heart, my dear. The ways of destiny and time are strange indeed. Seeds planted may lay dormant for many seasons, then suddenly the sun breaks through the clouds, or lightning strikes the ground as a storm blows in, or a butterfly opens and closes its wings as it trembles upon the milkweed at full moonrise—who knows what force of the Goddess causes a seed to sprout?"

Squeezing Gwenhyfar's hand with her own, she shrugged. "We do not know what the future holds, or how the wisdom of which you speak will resurge in some distant time and place that we cannot see."

The door opened and Bloedwyn returned, carrying a bowl of steaming water. Tegau stood and straightened the long embroidered vest that she wore over the bodice of her gown.

"We carry on as best we can, somehow trusting. Have faith, Gwenhyfar. The Christians have a saying from their master, Jesus. 'Place your treasures in heaven, not on earth where moth and dust doth corrupt.' This is wise, and when the times are hard, perhaps it is all we have."

Gwenhyfar smiled at Bloedwyn. "I know it well."

Tegau rose up from her seat. "I will look forward to seeing you at supper, within the hour, my dear."

As she swept out, closing the door behind her, Bloedwyn set the steaming water down and rummaged in the deep pocket of her skirt. Hefting a bag of soft leather in her hands, she sat down beside Gwenhyfar.

"Look, my lady. I have not had a moment to give these to you, but tonight seems a good time for you to wear them."

She handed the bag to Gwenhyfar, who gingerly opened the drawstring and pulled out a bundle in silken wrappings, within which gleamed her circlet of gold set with moonstones, three strands of sea pearls, and two wrist bands of copper, gold, and silver currents intertwined with snow quartz, sea pearls, and sgòthan na mara—the 'the light of the sea,' as the rare blue crystals were called.

She gasped in surprise, wonder spreading across her face. "How did you...?"

"On that terrible day when Gawain rode into the citadel with you as his captive, Blane came to me and told me to prepare to leave. I ran to your quarters and took these. I could not leave without them." A bright smile transformed her face as she took the circlet from Gwenhyfar's hand and placed it about the queen's brow.

The next morning they departed with a sturdy horse pulling the wagon and Caedmon at the reins. Again, Lancelot rode in the lead with Blane at his side. Behind him were Gwenhyfar and Bloedwyn, then Farquar and Ghleanna. Griflet and Paulinus rode rear guard, keeping a watchful eye at their backs. As they rolled and trotted out of sight, Caradoc turned to Tegau with a meaningful look.

"It is a tragic tale they have told us, my lady."

She nodded thoughtfully. "And it is not over yet, my lord. Our queen suffers a wound..."

Caradog bristled with concern, but she laid a warm hand upon his arm. "Aye, but it is not a wound that can be seen. It is lodged in her soul. Do you know what is the source of it?"

"We spoke of many things," Tegau responded, threading her arm through his, "but she would not tell me what happened with Gawain. I saw it clearly enough, though, as plain as day. It was in the air all around her. Well, let us pray for her, and for Sir Lancelot as well. And for Arthur. They are in the hands of the Goddess."

The Mending of Hearts

They had traveled for two weeks, slowed down by the wagon but glad for its contents, which made their campfires more enjoyable with the oats and barley flour, the crock of pig fat, the onions and bags of lentils sent by Tegau and Caradoc, all of which Paulinus—a fine cook, as it turned out—blended well with the rewards of the men's hunting and the women's gathering of green herbs along the way. At night Caedmon often pulled out his lute and Paulinus his reed flute and they joined in song. They tried to coax a song from Lancelot, whose voice was renowned, but after a few days he declined, his eyes straying toward the queen.

    Proceeding north, they were in need of warmer clothes and food supplies, and Lancelot made the decision to enter the city called Luguvalium by the Romans to seek for these. As they approached the busy town, Lancelot and Paulinus explained that the estuaries of two great rivers opened into a long inland saltwater body, which Lancelot remembered as the Tràchd Romhra. Luguvalium had been a sacred place of the Celtic tribes, called Caer Luguvalos—the stronghold or fort of the god of light, Lugh.

Caedmon, Griflet, and Farquar stayed with the younger women while Lancelot and Gwenhyfar, accompanied by Blane and Paulinus, went into the market with one of the horses to carry back the goods they sought to buy. Entering the honeycomb of the thriving stronghold, Lancelot recalled memories of his youth.

"I came here many years ago with Myrrdin. We stayed at the temple of Lugh, deep in the heart of this city. It was unforgettable. The temple was ablaze with the light of a hundred oil lamps. There were people of all kinds, Romans and Britons and people of the tribes—Selgovia, Novantae, and Damnonii—as well as Gaels from Erin. There are many more people here now, I wager."

Paulinus wiped the grime from his forehead as he trudged along beside the tall knight. "I too remember the Temple of Lugh. When I was last here, the merchant ships docked daily north of the city in the cold waters of Tràchd Romhra, flooding Luguvalium with people."

Gwenhyfar listened, taking in their experience as she looked in wonder at the scene that unfolded before her eyes. The market stretched out through the fortified town in a meandering spread of vendors, carts, shops, and people hawking or buying a wide variety of goods, vegetables, piled rounds of fresh bread, fruits, chickens, goats and cows, timber, crockery, wooden spoons, bolts of linen and wool, furs, cups, bowls and pots made of tin, clay, or bronze. As they winded their way through the noisy crowds, she saw people with hair, eyes, and skin of all colors.

Paulinus continued, "Those who arrive by ship come from as far away as Gaul, Rome, Greece, Palestine and Egypt, Macedonia, Byzantium. They come to trade spices, fruit, oil, and grains for tin, furs, gold."

Passing an oil vendor, Lancelot eyed an amphorae of olive oil, and the man called out, "Come back, sir knight... taste my oil. It is the best in Luguvalium!"

He stopped to buy the oil, passing the amphorae on to Paulinus, who tucked it into the large linen bag he wore over one shoulder. Keeping stride, they passed on toward a vegetable vendor, where Gwenhyfar picked out leeks, turnips, and a large bunch of fresh watercress. At another stall they found thick seal fur wraps. These Lancelot procured with a gold denarii, buying one for each of their party and heaping the bundle over his horse.

A beggar approached limping on his one leg, empty hands splayed before Gwenhyfar, his face creased with sorrow. He spoke a language she understood only a little, but Lancelot scolded in the Gaelic tongue of his grandmother.

"Here," he thrust a copper denarii into the man's hand. "Take this and go." Turning to Blane and Gwenhyfar, his face was lined with care. "I have had enough of this city. We have what we need. Let us go."

An hour later they were out the gates of Luguvalium and proceeding north on the road into Alba. They would have to take a boat to cross the salty waters of Tràchd Romhra, after which they would be in the lands of the Selgovia and then the Damnonii people, whom Lancelot remembered well.

Days of weary travel passed, rains came and went, but they often basked in warm days when bright rays of sun interplayed with the constant theatre of moving clouds. As they traveled north the hills became small mountains, and the waters of rivers and meandering streamlets—called burns as they learned from fellow travelers encountered along the way—ran dark but crystal clear. Lancelot and Paulinus were the only ones of their company who had traveled in Caledonia before, and their senses were dazzled by the sight of sweeping green moors that mingled with the yellow and red leaves of the autumn forest beneath black craggy peaks clothed in white mists that roved over a backdrop of dark blue thunderheads.

Passing an occasional dún, or along the roads or wagon trails, they sometimes gathered with people of the tribes. These encounters often began rife with tensions but resolved into peaceful exchanges, as Lancelot and Paulinus spoke many languages and could make themselves easily understood. Soon they came to the unfathomable depths of Loch Ken, along which they traveled for some days. There Paulinus told stories of the great lochs to the north in the highlands, and the painted people, the Pictish tribes, that ruled in the north and east of Alba.

The Romans had fought these wild tribes of Alba for years, finally building the wall decreed by their emperor, Hadrian, to keep the Picts out of the lowlands and Briton. That was before the Romans retreated, pulling out of Briton and Alba altogether, and returned to defend their homeland from the onslaught of so-called barbarians from the north of their continent. The painted people had many different names among their tribes, but all tattooed their skin with blue woad and decorated themselves with torcs and armbands of gold and bronze.

Despite idyllic moments when they sensed the hand of the Goddess upon them, the companions shared worried glances at the tension and brooding sorrow that hovered between the queen and her champion. All along the way Gwenhyfar kept her maidens close about her; they were a comfort to her, though try as she might to heal herself as Morgan had shown her, the poison of Gawain's assault still made her shudder and ache inside. Though she was kind and polite, she avoided Lancelot's eyes and his touch with skill and determination. It seemed to the others that she refused to see the worry that suffused his face, nor would she allow herself to feel the tangible pain of longing that they felt gnawing at his heart. When she retired, he often left the campfire, not to return until the stars had wheeled overhead and it was his turn to keep watch.

When finally they had passed into the highlands of Caledonia, in a region called Earra Ghàidheal, the brine of the sea excited their senses, bringing with it the knowledge that they were drawing near the place where they would seek a boat for passage to Eilean Arainn. Their eager enthusiasm was dampened by a storm that drove them to seek a better shelter than the oiled hides they had brought from Gwent. On a craggy hillside overlooking the sea, Lancelot brought them to a halt to watch the advance of a storm that swelled and raged over the waters. They could see Arainn, a vague mountainous shape swathed in mists and clouds across the choppy, wind-whipped water of the firth.

"Mannawydan is angry. He churns the water and makes crossing in a boat impossible." Lancelot frowned as they gathered around him on their horses. He scanned the turbulent sky. "It is as if Morrigan herself was riding in those black clouds! And at any rate," he added, "it is almost sunset. We must find a good shelter—the storm will be upon us soon."

Blane stirred in his saddle. "Perhaps the old Roman fort you once mentioned—a dún where you stayed with Myrrdin years ago on your journey south?"

"Yes, it should not be far from where we are now. I hope we can stay there until this storm passes and we can sail across the firth to Arainn." With a deft shift of the rein and a click of his tongue, he turned his horse easily, speeding up as the wagon rumbled down the hill. As they reached the valley they were buffeted by a cold wind that billowed, blowing their cloaks with a force that even their sturdy horses faltered to push against. Within minutes the clouds burst and they rode holding the oil-tanned hides over their heads as they trotted down the road as fast as the wagon could roll toward the gates of the inn.

Once inside the walled yard, Gwenhyfar sat astride her horse and peered through the waning light from under the dripping hide as Lancelot jumped down to meet the stable boy. They spoke briefly, then Lancelot shouted orders to the young knights and the monks. Making his way toward the three women who sat waiting upon their horses, she saw the determined set of his shoulders against the wind that blew in a steady, merciless gale. Within minutes he had gathered them together and hustled them into the inn, where they huddled, dripping, before an immense hearth with its roaring fire. Griflet and Farquar stood nearby while Lancelot spoke with the innkeeper, Blane at his side. Gwenhyar's eyes rested upon Lancelot's back, and she realized with an inward shock that he was suffering as much as she. Inwardly she writhed with pangs of conscience, for she knew that she had been concerned only with herself these past weeks.

The old Roman hillfort and outpost, now converted to a traveler's inn, had plenty of room for their rather large traveling party, which appeared rich and ostentatious to the eyes of the rough, churlish men who sat at tables over flagons of ale. They were weather-beaten and gnarled by life, and they fingered their knives and crossbows that rested upon the oak table as they stared boldly, curious about the knights and ladies who had arrived like phantoms out of the storm. They watched, eyes unblinking, as Lancelot pulled a gold coin from a pouch he withdrew from a deep pocket of the wool tunic he wore beneath his leather jerkin. It gleamed in the candlelight as he handed it to the innkeeper to secure three rooms, and when the deal was done, he walked to the fire and spoke in a low voice.

"My lady, we have three rooms—one for you, one for the women, and one for the knights." When she tried to protest that she did not need a room of her own, the ferocity in his glance made her uneasy. To quell further objections he added, "Paulinus and Caedmon insisted on staying in the stables with the horses and wagons. When I urged them to take a room, they said, 'Simplicity brings joy to a monk.' The rooms are on the second floor, up the stairs you see yonder. Blane and Farquar will see you settled and I will arrange for food—we will eat here, in the inn, after I have gone to the stables to see to our friends."

Blane escorted Gwenhyfar to her room and made a fire in the hearth, while Farquar and Griflet attended to the needs of the younger women. Returning to the main room of the inn and taking a seat at a long rectangle of table, they waited for supper. The knights drank cups of ale while Lancelot's eyes scanned the room, his hand resting on the long knife sheathed at his thigh as he watched the men who sat hunched at nearby tables. A spare but adequate hot meal of fish stew and seaweed was soon served, along with a dish made of oats and the mysterious parts of the sheep, abundantly flavored with fat and aromatic herbs and salt from the sea.

When they had eaten, Griflet took food to the monks in the stable while Lancelot, Farquar, and Blane escorted the women upstairs. The narrowed eyes of the men, who had ordered yet another flagon of ale, followed them as they climbed the stone steps and disappeared. When they arrived at the queen's room, she turned to bid goodnight to her ladies as Lancelot opened the door. She looked at him in surprise when he walked in behind her, closed the door and shoved a heavy iron bar in place to lock it from within.

"With or without your permission, my lady, I will sleep here this night. Though I doubt there will be much sleep in it, as the vermin downstairs look to be up to no good."

Glancing uneasily at the bed—a decent straw mattress with blankets and somewhat tattered seal furs spread upon it—she walked to the fire, holding her hands over the flames, her shoulders visibly tense. He followed her, stooping to pick up two logs and place them carefully upon the flames, then light two tapers on a table near the bed. Lancelot straightened his back as he stood beside her at the fireplace. The air was thick with the agitation between them, now heightened by their shared solitude. When he could bare it no longer, he turned to her, his face taut with the raw feeling that finally broke through his natural reserve. All politesse dropped as he grabbed her shoulders and turned her toward him.

"My love, can you not see what you are doing?"

She said nothing but averted her face to stare at the fire.

"Look at me, Gwenhyfar! The gods themselves are suffering your unwillingness to turn to me! You must let me share the burden of what happened to you, cariad."

Try as she might to elude his grasp, he stood before her, blocking her way. Her eyes blurred with tears as she looked anxiously from one side to another, pushing a shoulder against him in an attempt to shove past. In one swift move he spun her toward him and took her into his arms, where she struggled for a moment until, effortlessly, he held her in the firm grip of his embrace. A strangled sound came from her throat, but the circle of his arms only tightened, making her breath come in shallow pants.

She felt the muscles of his arms flex and suddenly he scooped her up and carried her to the bed and laid her upon it. Holding her firm, Lancelot pressed against her, pushing her down with his weight into the seal fur blanket. His pungent, familiar smell of sweat, leather, and rain overwhelmed her senses and again she cried out.

"Gwenhyfar," he breathed, his voice low and hoarse in her ear, "we cannot go on like this. If our love is not free to live, then this has all been for nothing. You must release the horror of what happened. You must face it and let it go."

She fell utterly still in his arms. Her inner world went blank and she wandered, aimless and desolate, in a cold void while time stretched out, the moments beating in sync with the thudding of their hearts. She hung suspended in that darkness as the tendrils of a forbidden anguish twined within her, even as she yearned for the warmth and goodness that called to her from an unknown place. After some time, a pale glimmer of light shone in the recesses of her mind and grew to radiate the emptiness. It flowed over and around her, through her, and with it came a sound that beckoned to her, vibrant with a great loving power.

Slowly she became aware that Lancelot rocked her body with his own and hummed—a remnant of remembered healing power, which he had learned from his grandmother Lacine, long ago and far away in the Connemarra Mountains. When he felt her muscles soften and her breathing deepen, he lowered the pitch to sing a wordless melody—three notes that flowed and twined back and forth, in and out—as he rocked her to the cadence of the song. His voice carried them along, and they drifted for a time. After awhile, he spoke again and his words penetrated through the haze of her inward journey.

"Gwenhyfar, you are safe. You can tell the story and then let it go." He waited in the backwash of silence. "Gwenhyfar," he called to her, "you are safe. You can let go."

From deep within her throat a soft keening began, growing to a delicate wail. Then the sobs came, wrenching and endless so it seemed, but infinite patience was the measure of his love as he held her, and together they rose and fell on the stormy sea of remembering. Her mind released the terrible images that had been locked within her, and a breath as deep as the sky filled her lungs. With the force of her exhale, she surrendered herself into his arms.

Holding her close to his heart, Lancelot waited, knowing she would soon begin to talk. And when she did, she spoke into his ear the truth of those moments alone with Gawain, her desperate attempt to fight him off, the blows he struck, the brutal rapacious attack, his contemptuous face, and finally her retreat to a place deep within herself to endure the assault.

When no more words came, she wept again, her tears pure and free as the springs of Ynis Witrin. She shed the tears of an endless grief, the loss of her homeland, her people, her sovereign right to rule as queen, and perhaps worst of all, of Arthur Pendragon. This was a sorrow of such subtle complexity that she could not yet speak of it, but she knew with certainty that there was only one person in the world who could fully understand the desolation of her heart, and she lay within the circle of his arms.

A warm wave enveloped her body, emanating from Lancelot and flooding her blood and belly and bones, reconciling and restoring the holy innocence she knew to be her deepest self. Leaning back into the bed pillows, she looked into his brown eyes. He reached up to wipe away her tears with one finger, then traced the line her cheek where the bruise had been.

As suddenly as the slithering thread of fear had wound itself into her gut and lodged there that fated night in

Gawain's chambers, so now her eyes absorbed the glow of Lancelot's eyes and love burst within her heart. Love streamed through her like light through a cloud, opening her from within to shine in brilliant coruscations. In that moment the strain of the past years dissolved and there was no leering, hateful Gawain threatening her body and soul, no Arthur with his compromised, convoluted love and betrayal, and no court of Camelot, divided in its loyalties and quick to look aside when condemnation and even death loomed near.

There was no one there except her champion, the one who knew and understood all she had lived, endured, suffered. The radiance in her eyes as she smiled into his was the elixir for which he had longed over their journey into exile, for Lancelot too had lost everything he held dear—Avalon, his king and dearest friend, the company of the knighthood, all the icons of chivalry and nobility that he held sacred. His voice broke with emotion as he whispered, "Gwenhyfar, cariad...I thought I had lost you. Goddess help me, for my soul has great need of you."

He held her until they slept peacefully in each other's arms. An hour passed, then Lancelot disentangled from her and rose to stir the coals and feed the fire. When the flames crackled into a blaze, he drank from his water skin, then brought it to Gwenhyfar and bade her to drink before he settled back under the blankets. She reached for him with such fervor that he looked at her in surprise. Desire surged in him when he saw that her eyes were clear and her smile inviting, and he wrapped her in his arms.

"Dawn is hours away," he breathed, his voice husky.

His body lay lean and bold against the length of her, and the magnetic allure of him overwhelmed her senses, coursing in the blood that beat hard in her veins. Her breath quickened as she molded against him, her eyes seeking his face. Incandescent brown eyes burned into hers, as urgent and direct as his whisper.

"My need for you is great, Gwenhyfar ..."

She silenced him with a kiss, then held him hard and fast in her arms.

"Then come to me, cariad," she entreated, lips against his ear. She pressed against him to receive the warmth of his hands that tugged away her gown and undergarments. Finding the soft flesh there, one warm hand swept down the length of her back then rested firm, palm flat upon the base of her spine, while the other hand moved to her breasts, seeking and finding a nipple. With a sigh, she reveled in his touch as pleasure streamed through her body like comets across a night sky.

He sat up to pull at the laces of his leather trews and peel them away from his hips and legs. When finally he was free, she pulled him against her and arched to meet him. His mouth came down upon hers and in their kiss, they opened and soared free as they wrestled beneath the blankets, clutching and grasping in their need to merge. Within seconds his fingers found melting silken flesh.

"I cannot wait, love, my need is too great," he gasped.

"Please," she begged, "take all I have to give, my Laëllon."

He hefted his weight above her, poised on one arm, then moans of pleasure and whispered words of love gilded their world as they rode the waves of passion, their labor urgent and holy. When she pleaded for more, he furrowed deep to meet the hidden springs that gushed. The muscles of his arms flexed as he held himself up to look down upon her, his glance sweeping over tumescent breasts, the curve of her belly and the dark mound of her sex. Then his eyes sought hers, and they locked together gaze to gaze until he was overcome by the bliss in her eyes as she crested the peak, calling out his name, and the hot pearls of his seed exploded.

It was an hour before dawn when Lancelot opened his eyes and lay still, listening for sounds of the storm. All was quiet but an owl that hooted nearby. His arms tightened around Gwenyfar's body and he breathed deep, relishing the scent of her. Now he had to take her safely to Eilean Arainn, and after that, they would begin to build a new life. After many hopeless days, the fires of inspiration dawned within him. He stroked her hair away from her face and watched as she opened her eyes, diamonds glittering in the dim light of the dying fire.

"You have healed me, Laëllon." Her whispered words were hoarse and tender.

His fingers lingered along the lines of her face. "It is our love that has healed you, Gwenhyfar. Beyond the gods and goddesses is the Great Spirit, which the Christians say is the one God. I know it is that Supreme Intelligence guiding our lives, though God's ways are impossible to fathom."

He stroked her back as he reflected softly. "Myrrdin once told me that the Creator longs for our love to unfold like the petals of a rose in summer. When full blown, our love is returned to its Maker. I believe that the love we share, Gwenhyfar, pleases God." He touched her face again. "My queen, I pledge to you, again and again, the strength and blood of my body, my mind, my heart, my soul."

They lay together in tranquil respite, washed in the ebb and flow of the inner fires they had ignited, until Lancelot stirred, sat and pulled her up with him.

"It is time, cariad."

Caledonia

It was with great relief that the travelers saw Gwenhyfar and Lancelot emerge that morning with shining eyes, their hands entwined. Lancelot soon learned from the innkeeper that a flat-bottomed merchant scow, which sailed a regular trade route from Bretonnia to Alba, would arrive in two days' time. Its captain was a good man and a fine sailor; he could get them across the seawater to the island. When the day dawned bright with sun and the waters were calm, even serene, Lancelot muttered, half to himself.

"Mannywydan and Ceridwen are with us, thanks be to the Goddess."

By midday they saw the large, sturdy scow—with three sails and men at the oars as well—sailing in toward Inbhir Air, where they had lodged at the inn. When she was docked at the rock jetty, the captain looked them over with a scrutinizing eye, knowing he and his crew would earn more than one gold piece for the service requested by the tall, imposing knight who stood before him.

"Aye, it will take two trips to cross the channel of Linne

Chluaidh," he shrugged with a glance at their nine horses and the small wagon. "If we are favored by the winds, it can be done in one day. If not, it will take two. But we will not go to the southern tip of the isle, as you ask. There are far too many hidden reefs and rocks there. Nay, we will take you to the cove on her eastern shore. There you can land and travel with your horses and wagon up over the mountain, south, to the place you seek. There is an old trail that runs that way. You may be surprised by the inhabitants of that isle. They are fierce but amiable if you come in peace."

Fingering the rope that he repaired, he grunted. "I do not know what you are running from, but you look to be in need of shelter and a safe place. There is a great, protected dún further north along the shores of Alba, at Dunadd, where the horse people, the Epidii, still live—now with a good many folk of Erin scattered among them."

Griflet had been looking out over the water toward Arrain. Turning to the captain, he asked, "Erin? What place is that?"

"Tis the name for the land also known as Irlandis. Across the water to the west from Alba. You will hear of it often here. The king in Dunadd is a good man, of Dalriada in Erin, indeed. I know him well, and I believe he would welcome you, knights and ladies. Why do you not sail there?"

Lancelot listened, looking out toward the island. "Yes, I know Dunadd. I stayed there for a few nights once, and it is a fine dún indeed. But I lived for many moons on Eilean Arainn, and my heart draws me back again."

The captain nodded thoughtfully. "Aye, tis a beautiful isle indeed. Not so easy to get to, mind you. But there are a good many people living in Machrie, the high moors of the western reaches of the isle, where the old standing stones are. There is a dún with many round houses that are sturdy enough, and they grow oats and barley. Hunting is good there. If you don't mind a currach, there is plenty of fishing to be had. You will do well enough, with all these strong lads with you." He chuckled, looking at the young knights who waited nearby sharpening their knives, and the monks who were busy brushing the coats of the horses.

Lancelot called to them. "Let us load the wagon."

Unhitching the horses, they pulled the wagon aboard the scow. When it was safely tied down on deck with its wooden wheels well blocked, the captain gave a nod of satisfaction.

"Alright then, be here at first light. With the wagon, we will take six of you and four horses on the first trip. Then the three others, with the remaining horses."

The next day they sailed before the sun had peaked above the eastern horizon, making the first crossing that carried the three women, Lancelot, Blane and Farquar, while Griflet stayed with the monks and would, hopefully, make it by nightfall to the shore of Arainn. As the scow scudded easily over glistening wavelets, the captain talked about an islet just north of the shore where they would land. He called it Inis Shroin.

"What does it mean?" Ghleanna asked as she watched the little island come into view.

"It means, Isle of the Water Spirit," the captain replied, "because of a place—a cave with a spring—held sacred by the people who live on Arrain. They say a goodly fairy lives there. She is known to heal people who come in faith." The salt water of the firth was gently whipped by a balmy wind that moved the ever-shifting clouds fast and low, opening the sky at times for glimpses of blue and shafts of sunlight that peaked through and made the sea a luminous pattern of waves.

"The place where you will disembark," the captain continued, "is known to seamen as Eas á Chrannaig, because of the two waterfalls near there. You will find it amenable. Near the strand there are few huts and a small stronghold with a stable where travelers sometimes lodge, I believe. You would be surprised how many travel from Erin to Alba and back again these days. Perhaps you can stay there for a night or two."

As the weather changed and a blustering sky predicted imminent rain, they unloaded the wagon and coaxed the horses, now quite skittish from their voyage, off the scow and down the rock jetty to shore. Lancelot handed a gold coin to the captain, who pocketed it quickly in the folds of his leather vest. Jumping off the scow, Lancelot made his way down the jetty. The captain called out, "We will return to Ayr, before the weather hits. It will be tomorrow, or as soon as we can sail, that we arrive with your friends."

Farquar had already hitched one of the horses to the wagon and seated the women upon it. Lancelot rode along beside the wagon, where Gwenhyfar sat upon the bench beside Farquar, who held the reins as they trundled over the rocky shore. They headed toward a small cluster of thatched roof round houses set around one larger house built of stone, which were sheltered by stone walls and trees at the edge of a forest that grew down the hillside and up to the rocks and sand of the beach. As they approached, they saw a young man with red hair chopping firewood outside and another leading a horse toward the stable. A few mud-besmudged children played in the yard, and the people stopped their tasks or talking to watch as the strangers arrived.

"Greetings," the red-haired one called. "I see you've just landed from yon scow. Are you needing a place to sleep tonight?" He spoke a Gaelic language, familiar enough that the knights were relieved to understand his words, at least well enough to catch the gist of the meaning.

"Aye," Blane answered, striding forward with Farquar. Grasping forearms with the red-haired man in the customary greeting, they could see they were of a similar age, and the islander quickly introduced himself.

"My name is Angaidh, and that is my woman, Ciaran." He gestured toward the young woman with a baby strapped across her back, who had just walked out of the nearest hut. "Ye are welcome to our home. We do not have much, but we will share what we have with you."

His voice was friendly, but he looked at Lancelot with some hesitation.

He had never seen such a man—tall, lithe, well-muscled, the seasoned knight wore his long sword sheathed in a jeweled scabbard. Dark brown hair fell in damp waves that rested upon the shoulders of his weather-worn leather jerkin. His heavy woolen cloak was thrown back over one shoulder to reveal a dagger at his thigh and shorter blade at his ankle. His face was lined with care and stamped with the unmistakable weight of authority. Angaidh's instincts prickled as he sensed the danger and power that emanated from the man, who clearly had the skill to wield his weapons with ease and moved with fluid confidence as he jumped down from his steed to take the hand of his lady.

Angaidh's eyes roved to the weapons that his other new acquaintances bore as well, then he looked again at the women who were climbing down from the wagon, his eyes riveting upon the older of the three. There was an aura of nobility around her, though she wore no special sign of royalty or jewels, except the golden stag brooch that pinned the cloak upon her chest. Her hair was plaited into two long black braids that hung below her waist. She said very little, but when the tall knight helped her down from the wagon, her face was wreathed in a smile of such radiance that she shone with light.

The maidens with her were weary but smiling as well, as Farquar helped them descend and they looked around at their new surroundings. Ciaran came forward and invited the women inside, pointing to the coming squall and leading them into the stone house. The sun would set within a few hours, as this was the dark time of the year when the hours of light were few, and supper would be served soon.

When their horses were bedded down for the night in the stable and the rain had begun to fall, they shared the evening meal of mussel stew cooked by Ciaran's mother, Vevila. Two or three large families seemed to live there, and they milled about, lively and busy with food or small tasks that could be accomplished by the dull light of tallow candles. They soon discovered that the men of the clan, except for Angaidh and one gray-haired elder, were gone hunting and would return in some days.

Vevila seemed to be the headwoman; they heard that her husband, Rogan, was away with the hunting party of their small dún. She had a lovely voice, and she sang songs for the visitors and told stories of the amazing healing powers of the blessed fairy who lived in a cave on the small island, Inis Shroin, just across the water from their enclave. Bloedwen and Ghleanna were soon learning words in the language of their hosts, who shared eagerly, answering the questions of Farquar and Blane about weather, the island, hunting, and the customs of Eilean Arrain.

As the evening wore on, the young knights and maidens were enjoying a gay exchange with Ciaran and Angaidh when the latter asked where they had traveled from and what their purpose was in coming to their remote island. A teeming silence ensued.

Angaidh pressed, "By the sound of your speech, you must be from the south. Do you have news of the battle leader, Arthur Pendragon, and the wars against the Saxons? Or of his lady queen, Gwenhyfar? Or perhaps of his first knight, Sir Lancelot? We relish the tales of Bedevere, Bors, Peredur, Sir Gawain or any of the knights of the Round Table! We are eager for such stories of the great war against the Saxons. News from the outer world helps us through the long winter nights here on Arainn."

Blane glanced at Lancelot, who merely raised his brows, gesturing for the younger man to respond.

"You do well to ask our purpose, which has brought us to this rare place," Blane began diplomatically. "We wish to settle here, friend. Sir Laëllon," he nodded toward Lancelot, "is my lord, and I am his squire, but we are weary from the southern wars, now that Arthur has indeed vanquished the Saxons. Once we are settled here on Arainn, we promise to share stories. For now, we want to know everything you have to tell us about this blessed place, where we wish to enter a quiet life of farming, of seasons and hunting." He reached out to lay a gentle hand upon Bloedwyn's as he admitted with a bashful grin, "And children, at some point."

Angaidh smiled at Ciaran, who held a babe to her own breast to suckle while Vevila stoked the fire then passed around a platter with a knife and a large lump of cheese, made from the milk of the furry sheep they had seen grazing past the shore earlier in the day. Vevila glanced now and then at the striking older woman and the man—the knight and his lady. He had stayed at her side throughout the evening, often holding her hand. She wondered what their story might be. As surely as the stars moved across the sky, all her instincts told her that these two had royal blood in their veins. Her instincts told her they were running from a terrible plight.

Taking a clay pot of ale around to fill their cups after the meal, she stopped before Gwenhyfar and asked, "And you, my lady, what is your name?"

The queen smiled graciously, taking the proffered ale in her cup. "My name is Wynlolaigh, and I thank you most gratefully for the hospitality you have shared with us this night." Vevila smiled broadly in return, bowing slightly then hesitating before she moved on to pour the next cup.

"It is a good life we have here," Angaidh offered. "But tis a hard one." His warning was friendly but straightforward. "The place you have said you wish to go is uninhabited, except for a few druids and some wild women, healers and priestesses of the old ways. They live there in small round houses made of stone, not far from the sea. I have been there a few times, but mostly we go across the hills to the moors west of here. That is the place where the Caledonii and Epidii, the people of Arainn live, near the standing stones."

Farquar blinked. "I am most interested in these standing stones. They must be as ancient as the tall sarcen stones we call the Elders, far to the south."

Lancelot shifted in his seat, joining the conversation at last.

"First we must build shelters and learn to exist here ourselves, Farquar. Now it is time for my lady to rest." The young knights stood up as the queen rose to leave. Seeing this, Angaidh and Ciaran looked from one to another, their brows raised.

Vevila lead Gwenhyfar and Lancelot outside along a stone pathway and into a small hut. Its thatched roof dripped with rain and she lifted the oiled hide that served as a door and pointed within, motioning to wood piled by the hearth and the shelves where woolen blankets were folded. Wishing them a good night's rest, she disappeared into the darkness, following the path back to the stone house.

Griflet and the monks arrived by midday the next day with their horses, and the travelers set out straightaway on the road over the mountains. They moved slowly on their horses alongside the bumbling of the wagon over stones and deep ruts, catching endless vistas of water along the way.

As they crested the hill, a pleasing spread of sandy beach and endless blue-green water welcomed them. It was beautiful and remote, and a far distance from Camelot and the Summer Country. The word Tegau had spoken, cynfyn—the place where one's spirit is at home—came unbidden to Gwenhyfar's mind. She turned to Lancelot, who rode quietly beside her on his horse.

With a smile, she whispered, "Laëllon, tis our place, my love," and their spirits lifted and soared.

Eilean Arainn
529-530 C.E.

A New Life

The first weeks and months on Eilean Arainn were not easy. With none of the courtly amenities to which they were accustomed in Camelot and Caerleon, the women encountered challenges and hardships that the men had known only in their warrior days. Despite deprivations and hard work with the winter coming on, they were eager and enthusiastic as their new life emerged in the weeks that rolled by. Working from sunrise to sunset, it was not the best season to build, with frequent squalls that blew in from the sea, but build they did. Within three months they had five timbered, wattle and daub huts, built under the careful instruction of Paulinus and Caedmon.

Gwenhyfar and the young women took the first of these, until two more were available and the queen and Lancelot moved in together. At the winter solstice the two young couples were handfasted, and the next finished hut was taken by Blane and Bloedwyn and the third by Ghleanna and Farquar. The fourth hut was taken by the remaining men, though the monks were often gone for days at a time with their horses on pilgrimage to the holy isle, Inis Shroin. The fifth hut was the biggest, built to serve as their communal kitchen and gathering place. They traded gold or silver coins with the local people for oiled skins, copper and bronze pots, rendered fat, grain, dried meat and fish, and woolen cloth to get them through the winter and spring.

As Angaidh had said, there were two druids living nearby, as well as women who were honored as priestesses and healers. It was the druids who connected the Britons with the Caledonii and Epidii tribes who lived in the moors. At first these tribal people were wary and challenging, but Lancelot, who understood and spoke fluidly their Gaelic language, quickly assuaged their fears and befriended them. When the people saw that the newcomers meant no harm but were honorable warriors and worthy hunters skilled at the crossbow, knife, and sword, they were welcomed and then included in the progress of day-to-day life.

Word spread among the villagers of Machrie Moor that the two eldest of the Britons were high born royals from Cymru or Dumnonia in the south, which resulted in some awe and avid curiosity, soon becoming a source of pleasant gossip and speculation. When they saw the huts built by the Britons, the island people were fascinated by the construction. And so it was that Paulinus and Caedmon were soon busy, teaching them how to build in the peculiar method of the monks at Ynis Witrin—round timbered huts made with clay, mud, straw, and stone, with thick thatched roofs.

As they mingled, the Britons discovered that the islanders worshipped the sun and the moon, the earth and sky and the sea, and the powers and spirits of the otherworld. They too revered Mannawydan, god of the sea, Ceridwen, Brigid, and the feared Morrigan. At the heart of their mysteries was the Creideamh Sídhe that had seeped across the channel from Erin over centuries of time—the fairy faith, those beings of light who were known to Avalon and the Summer Country as the Old Ones.

For the Caledonians and people of Erin, these Aes Sídhe took form as their gods and goddesses who were celebrated and worshipped in the raw elements, in the cycles of the seasons at solstice and equinox, in secret rituals amidst the standing stones of the moors. They celebrated as well the holy festivals of Samhain, Imbolc, Beltane, and Lughnasadh, and in all this the Britons recognized the threads, with nuances of difference, shared in common with their own customs, gods, and goddesses.

But unlike the Britons and Celts of the south, the islanders knew very little of the Christian god. Some had heard of the renowned missionary from Erin, Father Padrig, who had traveled all over Alba and Briton and had lived with the monks of Ynis Witrin for some time. The Britons were not surprised to discover that there was mixed sentiment and a wariness among the people when his name came up. Indeed, Father Padrig had done much to cause ill feeling between the Christians and the native Britons.

The druids and priestesses were curious about Paulinus and Caedmon, and as the monks learned the nuances of language in their new home, tensions relaxed. Many discussions between the Christians and the druids were plied deep into the night, usually over ale or the potent fermented spirit made from the barley cultivated in the rolling hills of the moors. They spoke of the purifying powers of Imbolc, known to the monks as Candlemas or Saint Brigit's Day—the coming celebration in which every person on Eilean Arainn would worship Brighid and the renewal of life.

As the spring rite drew near, Griflet and Farquar were fishing one clear afternoon in late January around the skerry called Pladda, not far from their growing enclave, when they saw three people walking over the hills toward their huts. They had with them a small herd of sheep and a shaggy dog. They were greeted by Lancelot and Gwenhyfar, and when the fishermen came in for supper, they learned that the visitors were three Gaels from Erin. As it turned out, they had come to share the Imbolc festival with the Britons, bringing with them a gift of six sheep, five of them milking ewes. The young men's names were Lulach and Máel, and their sister was Galena—a maid as tender and lovely as the dawn, with rosy cheeks, nut brown hair and blue eyes.

As they crowded together around the kitchen fire over supper, Lulach regaled them with a touch of the Erin propensity for a prophetic tone, as he explained how they came to be on Eilean Arainn.

"We made our way in a currach across the narrow sea, braving storms and fairy fogs. Aye, we have wandered across land and water to arrive here in Alba, on this fair isle. We have lived this past year with the Caledonians in their village at the standing stones to the east—it is from them that we heard of you. They say you are a queen," he looked at Gwenhyfar, dipping his head respectfully, "maybe even Gwenhyfar herself. But now you are known as Lady Wynlolaigh, who has come here to live in exile. Is it so?"

Galena chirped, "They say that you come from the great battle leader in the south, in Briton, Arthur Pendragon—we have heard about him since we were babes at our mother's knee. And you, sir," she looked at Lancelot, "the people say you are a knight of the Round Table. Could it be you are really Lancelot and Gwenhyfar? It is for this reason we have come."

Lancelot listened, caution mixing easily with humor upon his features. They had heard these rumours before, as the druids had shared the villagers' gossip with Paulinus and Caedmon, and it had spurred many speculations as to how they had learned such things. But then, the Caledonians were known to have special powers of insight and dreams.

He glanced at Gwenhyfar, then molded the truth to his own purpose. "I do know many a story about the fabled Round Table of Arthur Pendragon, but we have come from Demetia, in the far north of Cymru. I grew up in Erin, as you did—in the mountains of Connemarra."

Looking around at his young knights, Laëllon continued. "We fought in the Saxon wars of the south under our liege lord, who swore fealty to Arthur, but now we have come to live a simple life here, to be fishermen and hunt amongst the seabirds and dolphins." He glanced at Griflet, who was watching Galena with great interest.

Right away Galena taught Bloedwyn and Ghleanna how to milk the ewes, and cheese-making began in earnest. They were preparing for the coming of Imbolc, and they discovered that Galena was also proficient in gathering seeds and edible plants that grew year round on the isle. Lulach and Máel negotiated a trade with the villagers—a catch of salmon for a yearling calf—that would be slaughtered, its blood offered in the Imbolc fire along with ewe's milk, and its roasted flesh eaten in the feast that would be served later that night.

When the day of celebration came, a huge pile of wood was set upon the beach, along with a smaller fire where the meat was roasted on a spit and bread baked upon hot stones at the fires' edge. The ritual was much simpler than the complex rites of Dyfed and Gwent, but the raw power of the elements—the licking hot flames, the cold salty air and the rhythmic whoosh and swish of the tide upon the sand—piqued their senses, and the excitement and anticipation was thick in the air as they gathered around the fire in the late afternoon. When the sun reached the western horizon, the first oblations to Brighid began, and they watched with avid faces as the druids and priestesses made the milk and blood offering.

As twilight descended upon sea and land, Laëllon and Gwenhyfar sat upon woven reed mats placed upon the sand before the unfolding ritual. The moment came when, in Caerleon, the queen would have been asked to give her blessing as sovereign of the land, and Laëllon looked at her, a question in his eyes.

Reaching a hand to hers, he queried, "Do you miss it?"

"Only a little," she answered with a faint smile.

Bloedwyn whispered to Galena, who walked boldly to the priestess. Gwenhyfar watched as the young Gael pointed toward her, and the priestess, an old woman named Ewa, looked in her direction, long white braids swinging. She reached out a withered arm and crooked her fingers, not asking but demanding that Gwenhyfar come.

Standing to straighten her woolen tunic and pull her heavy cloak about her, Gwenhyfar proceeded to the fire and stood before Ewa. The old priestess looked her up and down with penetrating black eyes, then reached out a hand to clasp her arm.

"Lady, this girl says you are a queen among your people in the south. Is it so?"

Gwenhyfar nodded once.

"Then you must give a blessing on this night. Come, Wynlolaigh." She clamped her mouth shut, jaw jutting, when she had spoken, and Gwenhyfar could see that the woman was missing several teeth. She made a mental note to see to it that Ewa received some of their soft ewe cheese after Imbolc, then she bowed her head, accepting the command of the ancient one who stood before her.

Turning around to face their group, now joined by a few islanders of Arrain and a score of people she had never seen before, Gwenhyfar raised her arms and looked up to the dark, encumbered sky. For so many years she had spoken the words of blessing at this rite, but on this night the words of another prayer, spoken only by the queens of Cymry, sprang to her mind unbidden.

Knower of the Hidden
Light in Darkness,
I call You, Brighid!
Knower of destiny and fate,
Keeper of the Cauldron of Plenty,
I call You, Ceridwen!
Arianrhod, Bloeduedd, and

Morrigan, mistress of death and birth,
I call You! Goddess, in all your forms,
Hear me! For I am poetry in motion,
I am the smile in Your Heart.
I am Brighid's child,
I am Ceridwen's daughter.

Lowering her arms, Gwenhyfar's clear, strong voice carried over the song of the ocean, the wind, the snapping of the fire.

"Hear me, oh people of Cill Cynfyn, this beautiful place where the Goddess has brought us, wanderers in exile, who have traveled far from our homes. We give thanks for this new beginning, this place, these people, this food, and this land. May Brighid be honored and gladdened to give us new life, to enrich our fields and make fertile our ewes and cows, bring rain and sun to ripen the grain and make the flowers blossom and bear fruit. May Brighid bring us many babes to grow healthy, happy, and wise in the year to come!"

She breathed the salt air in through her nose, looking around at the people whose faces glowed in the flickering light of the bonfire flames. She saw a glitter of tears in the eyes of Blane and Bloedwyn, Farquar and Ghleanna, and she knew what it meant to them to receive her blessing on this night. Paulinus and Caedmon were wiping their eyes as well, and Griflet stood beside Galena, a soft smile upon his face as he reached an arm around her waist. With the soft sigh of her out breath, Gwenhyfar's eyes rested upon Laëllon as she gathered her cloak about her and returned to his side.

The whoosh of waves upon the shore measured their silence until Paulinus strummed the strings of his lute, humming a haunting melody, and Caedmon pulled out his pipes. A drum appeared in the hands of Lulach, and the strong spirit of the highlands began to flow, warming their blood against the cold. While music and song took over the night, and the young people danced with abandon upon the sandy shore, Gwenhyfar and Laëllon rose to make their way over the low dunes along the path to their hut.

Laëllon set himself straightaway to lighting a tallow candle, which dimly illuminated the room of their round hut, and then a fire in the modest stone hearth. Shedding their cloaks, they settled upon the bed—a woolen pallet with a heavy linen mattress, stuffed with dried heather and moss, softened with duck and swan feathers, supplied by the men's hunts. Wrapping his arms around her solid warmth, Laëllon pulled Gwenhyfar down on the bed and kissed her hair. His breath plumed in a faint white mist as he spoke, watching the flames of the hearth licking up.

"It will be warm soon. I am happy to see that you have regained your health, cariad. You were so thin when we first arrived. And now there is some flesh upon your lovely bones. The gift of the ewes and their milk will help in more ways than one," he chuckled. "It is good that Griflet is not alone now among the young couples. Galena is a fine match for him."

"Hmm," she responded dreamily. "Yes, it is so."

"And thanks to the lass, who was brave to ask the ferocious Ewa, we were blessed by you tonight, our queen." He put his fingers beneath her chin and tipped her face to look into her eyes. "It touched my heart, Gwenhyfar, to see you like that once again."

She smiled in response but remained quiet and inward.

"What is it, cariad? Is there something on your mind?"

Faint sounds of lute and drum and pipe drifted on the night air, and they could hear the echoes of ancient songs and shouts of joy. He waited, knowing that she would speak when she was ready.

"My blood flows every month, near the full of the moon," she began. He listened, his head cocked attentively toward her.

"It has not come since we were together at Samhain." Black lashes fringed her cheeks as she looked down, then raised her eyes to meet his. "That was three months ago, Laëllon."

He leaned forward, taking her shoulders in his hands. "What do mean, Gwenhyfar? Are you ill?"

A sweet sound escaped her lips, somewhere between a gasp and a sweet laugh. "No, cariad, I am not sick. I am with child. The Goddess has rendered a miracle in this once-barren body."

Astonishment and joy flared in Laëllon's eyes and he held her to his chest in a wordless embrace, their hearts and minds mingling in wonder.

"By the light of the Goddess and all that we hold sacred! What sweet irony, the mysterious workings of destiny! It is a miracle, Gwenhyfar. Our child ... cariad, our child."

That night Laëllon slumbered, but his sleep was light and burned with an inner fire. Suddenly, he discovered himself traveling alone in a currach across the sea. He was heading west into the sun when a brood of ominous clouds amassed on the horizon and wind began to blow. The sea was whipped and churned into mountainous waves that threatened to inundate his small craft that heaved and bucked in the maelstrom.

Despite the threat of elemental powers unleashed, his spirit was calm and emboldened by an intuition that led him onward, eager and searching, into the mist. Then, just as suddenly as the storm had appeared, the sea became calm and glassy, and a thick haze of fog obscured his sight. He floated in a sea of silver mist that drifted across his vision and finally cleared to reveal a green island, more beautiful than any he had seen in his life, with high mountains and forests that grew tall and serene to the edges of a white sandy shore.

His boat floated effortlessly to lodge where the waves purled upon the beach, and jumping out, he splashed through the water toward the trees. Breaking through a thick copse, he emerged upon the wide sweep of a grassy hillside covered with blossoming apple trees. Ascending the hill, he noticed that the apple trees both bloomed and bore fruit, rosy gold from the sun that spangled the dew upon emerald grass and verdant forest. Looking around in amazement, he saw that the natural world all around him shone with an unearthly radiance, and in that moment, his mind became lucid and free in the certainty that he had journeyed to the Otherworld. At the top of the hill rose a castle, built with a cunning design and intricacy that charmed his mind. An inexorable force pulled him forward, and, as he approached, a wooden drawbridge creaked heavily as it descended. Fascinated, drawn as if by an invisible lure, he walked through the gates.

The courtyard was full of flowers, its walls covered with climbing rose, laden with blossoms of all colors, the stones concealed by a glossy overgrowth of leafy vines. His senses reeled at the impact of sheer beauty, and yet his mind remained steady and clear as he moved through the throng. There were many noble people there, some singing and playing instruments, others picking bouquets or engaged in gladdened conversation. An overwhelming longing pierced Laëllon's heart as he drank in with a great thirst the sweet flow of harmony, the glad air of virtue, chivalry and happiness.

A gallant young knight stepped forward, opening his arms warmly, as if he had know Laëllon for years, nay lifetimes. Beckoning him to follow, the knight ushered him to the open doors of the castle, wherein he was entreated by noble ladies to enter inside the walls and wind his way up wide stone steps that landed at the entrance to a vast hall. On one end was an immense hearth, and beside it stood two people, whose radiance flooded the hall with light. With a jolt of joyous recognition, Laëllon hurried toward them.

"Nimuë," he breathed softly, smiling into the woman's eyes, his heart soaring with joy. "Myrrdin! Much has transpired since last we met."

Nimuë stood tall and regal, her long golden hair twining gently to the floor and flowing all about her. Her eyes shone with a supernal light, and she gazed at Laëllon with a love that suffused his mind and soul. Her voice cascaded like music in his ears.

"You did well, Laëllon, to take Gwenhyfar away. It has cost you both a great deal, and at times you felt alone. But we have been with you all along, watching from this place where we dwell. Though you could not perceive our forms, we have been near you often, helping wherever we could."

A flow of dazzling energy swept through and around them, and suddenly the castle, apple trees, gentle shore, and ocean had fallen away, and they were transported to a vast plane of light—an unknown place of brilliant shining beyond form. Myrrdin spoke, his eyes emitting traces of that light, and it seemed to Laëllon that Myrrdin held him somehow close to his heart.

"Laëllon, this is the last time you will see us in your earthly life, but we will meet again in the realms beyond time. Now we have a message to deliver. You must know that your time on the island is a temporary idyll. Soon the Christians will come, a man of faith called Donnan, who will establish a monastery on Inis Shroin, and your monks will follow him. Many more people of Erin will come, and they will establish a great kingdom in Alba. Soon after the Vikings will come in their long boats, seeking to dominate, bringing war and bloodshed. There will be many test and trials for Briton and Alba and Erin, land of the Old Ones.

"Through all this you will be guided from within. Be ready to start over again, in another place. Watch for the signs, and you will know when to move and where to go. Your child will be born, and he will grow strong and wise to lead you all… "

Their forms became translucent then flickered in and out of his sight. Knowing they were soon to disappear, Laëllon cried out, "What of Arthur?"

It was Nimuë who answered. "Do not worry for Arthur Pendragon. He is also guided by us. In the end, he will be well, though the remainder of his days will be humbled and surcharged by grief and sorrow. It is the price he pays for the many lessons he has learned. But Laëllon, all this is only a fleeting dream. Arthur will return to the Otherworld, as will you and Gwenhyfar. Then you will know that you three have never been separate in truth, but only by the appearance of things. You each had a part to play."

His vision blurred, blinded by light, as they disappeared. He heard only Nimuë's voice. "Until we meet again, remember..."

Laëllon woke with a start, beads of sweat dampening his brow. Wiping away the moisture, he breathed in the salty air then rose from their bed, sliding out carefully from beneath the furs. Gwenhyfar slept peacefully. He did not want wake her but sat beside the flames, stirring and feeding the banked embers as he mulled over the dream. It was alive and vivid, and his heart soared as he remembered. He sat for a long time, listening to the wind that wailed outside their hut.

After a time, the rustling among the furs told him that his queen stirred. She sat up, brushing a strand of hair from her face. She rose, pulling a shawl about her shoulders, and moved beside him at the fire. Warming her hands, she glanced at him. Laëllon saw that her blue eyes smiled and shone silver in the firelight.

"I dreamt of Myrrdin," she whispered, "and Nimuë..."

Glastonbury
(Ynis Witrin)
698 C.E.

Epilogue

Tammas Pender dipped the quill into a pot of ink and continued his painstaking work, squinting in the dim light of a candle that burned on the oaken desk of his hut. In the stone hearth a fire sputtered uneasily against the searing drafts of midwinter. He could hear the rhythmic ping of sleet against the wattle and daub walls of his hermit's hut and upon the fallen leaves that covered the ground outside. A broken cough racked the monk's thin frame, and the linen cloth he pressed to his lips came away bloody. He knew he should sleep before the first call to prayer in the morning, which would come long before dawn, but he was driven to finish his task. His time on earth was soon to end, and he raced to finish before he could write no more. Standing to stretch his aching bones, Tammas heaped dry wood upon the waning fire and sat back at his desk.

Thirty years has passed since he left his father's house at the age of fourteen to enter the monastery of Ynis Witrin. Sir Morgan Pender was not happy to lose his only son to the monastery; he was known to those few who remembered as the fifth generation grandson of Arthur Pendragon and Lady Garwen, the first of the king's three mistresses. The Pender family had been the guardians of a great story, which began with a time before Arthur's marriage to Gwenhyfar, when he had courted a maiden named Garwen and their union produced a son named Rowland. After Arthur's marriage, their love affair waned; it was Queen Gwenhyfar who made Garwen a lady of the court at Camelot and saw to it that her son was tutored and well cared for.

His thoughts ranging far, Tammas began to drouse as the fire roared to life, and soon the feather pen fell from his hand, staining the vellum with ink as he wandered in vivid memory. As a very young monk, he had begun writing down his family's story in secret, working by candlelight late into the nights. Then Father Bregoret arrived as the new head of the monastery at Ynis Witrin. Noticing the monk's cell illumined by candles, Father Bregoret—a Celt by blood—caught Tammas by surprise late one night with pen in hand. It was his discovery of the Pender family secrets that inspired the abbot to take a keen interest in the monk's work as the years passed. Bregoret believed the story was of great importance to their Celtic heritage, sorely eroded by time and circumstance. As abbot of the monastery, he gave Tammas Pender the time he needed to finish scribing the most important work of his lifetime, titled, The Queen's Tale: A Histoire of Arthur Pendragon, Queen Gwenhyfar, and Sir Lancelot.

And so the story unfolded: how the foremothers of Garwen had once served Nimuë, the Lady of the Lake, and her family worshipped in the old way. Garwen's loyalty to

Avalon and to the Cymry queen ran deep and true, and she was greatly troubled by the events of Gwenhyfar's arrest and her bare escape with Lancelot. When Gwenhyfar disappeared, gossip swirled across the countryside, fast and biting as a winter wind. People were eager to believe or pretend that they knew what had happened in the royal court. Some said that Gwenhyfar was so ashamed of her infidelity to Arthur that she took vows of celibacy, shearing off her long black hair to join the nuns at Beckery. They nodded among themselves with satisfaction: indeed, the convent of Mary Magdalene was a fitting place for such a one to atone for her sins. Eventually this became the story, actively encouraged by a growing wave of Christians who promoted their version of the story of Jesus, as it was told by the Roman papal church, now over four hundred years old.

A few others were certain that the queen had been killed by Gawain or gone into hiding in Gwynedd, in the northern parts of Cymru. It was said that Lancelot, who was suspected to have the faery blood of Avalon in his veins, had been expelled from the court at Camelot, driven away to become a wandering mystic, forever questing for relief from the pain of his unrequited love for Gwenhyfar. But Garwin had watched as the king cloaked the truth of the queen's exile with his first knight. Arthur himself told the story time and again, as he struggled to protect his own power and throw Gawain off the trail of Gwenhyfar and Lancelot—for the fierce knight of Orkney thundered across the land enraged after Agravaine and Gareth were slain.

After Arthur's death the Angles and Saxons and Jutes had returned to swarm in force upon Briton, conquering and subduing her ancient people, their small kingdoms and villages, striking as well at the heart of Briton's spiritual heritage. The new order, ruled by Saxons, did not want the memory of the great king, Arthur Pendragon, inciting rebellion and fanning the flames of the original inhabitants of Briton, who remembered how the renowned battle leader had staved off the invaders for decades, united the tribes, and brought a time of peace to the people. Even the monk Gildas, who had written a widely-circulated histoire during Arthur's lifetime, had omitted the hallowed name of Arthur Pendragon—though he mentioned the battles in which Arthur lead the Britons to victory against the Saxon invaders. And so, as the generations came and went, Arthur's name was forbidden, stricken from records and histories.

Camelot and its story belonged to the era of ancient Briton, and its time was gone. The lives of Arthur, Gwenhyfar, and Lancelot quickly became legends, and within a hundred years the truth was passed on by word of mouth, embellished and re-written many times over by the religious imagination of a people under siege by invasion, war, political and cultural suppression. As time passed the vanquishers merged with the Britons—with their strong underpinnings of Roman influence—and the new religion of Jesus Christ to generate the wave of the future—a nation that would emerge to be called England.

Now, almost two hundred years later, there were only a rare few elders who dimly recalled that the blood of Arthur Pendragon ran in the veins of his descendants. The proliferation of vague and fantastic legends troubled the Pender family, whose maternal ancestor, Garwen, had told her son Rowland the full story of what occurred, as she heard it from Bloedwyn and Ghleanna, the handmaidens of Gwenhyfar, and from Bloedwyn's husband Blane.

As if waking from a dream, Tammas started and struggled to sit up. His thoughts wandered back to his ancient grandmother, Garwen. He whispered a prayer for her spirit, hoping that she was happy in the Otherworld. He was grateful to the far-sighted Father Bregoret, to whom he had confessed his family's secrets so many years ago. He could go to his death knowing that his chronicle would be preserved by the monks of Ynis Witrin.

Crossing himself, Tammas said a second prayer, this time to Mary, Mother of God, and to Mary Magdalene, Lady of Light. Tammas bowed his head to the task, dipped the feather pen into the inkwell and scratched careful letters upon the vellum, inscribing the last chapter of the story.

And so it was that Gwenhyfar and Sir Lancelot went into exile, in the month of October, in 529 the year of our Lord, with a small and loyal group of companions. While they journeyed into the northern parts of Caledonia and settled there— as eventually told by Caradog Vraichvas, who learned their story from his son, Blane—Arthur eventually made an uneasy peace with Sir Gawain and his faction, who knew nothing of Arthur's complicity with the queen and her champion. Nor did they know of the king's impotence—it was a well-kept secret carefully guarded by Sir Cai, Lady Carys, Lady Garwen and a few trusted servants. Life at court continued, with the days and weeks dragging into months, until a year had passed since Gwenhyfar and Lancelot had disappeared into the mists.

After a lifetime of abundance and plenty, Camelot and the Summer Country entered an era of scourge and privation. Crops withered, producing only small caches of grain to store for the winter months. Vegetable gardens yielded sparse harvests, and the land was mired in gloom. Even red deer, fox, pheasant and wild boar, once plentiful, melted into the deep forest and the hunters too often came back with empty hands. The fishermens' nets sagged half full, and the mothers and cooks lamented their stew pots, which yielded only thin gruels and watery soups.

The power and glory of Arthur's reign and court began to dwindle like a waning moon. Steeped in grief and longing for his queen and his first knight, Arthur remained at court in Camelot surrounded by his loyal knights, who were dismayed when their leader ranted, holding his ale flagon aloft and wiping tears from his eyes as he raved, speaking in riddles of a "grail," a sacred vessel that was lost or hidden somewhere. As the seasons brought on relentless cycles of cold and heat and driving rains that scorched or drowned or froze crops and gardens, Arthur grew desperate in his yearning for that grail.

Decay and dissolution gnawed at the heart of Camelot as their spirits sank deeper into despair. They no longer made the gay summer progress of their peaceful years to establish court in Caerleon, where the Round Table sat silent, empty, and unused. In the Summer Country, the seasonal feasts were dreary, with Arthur spewing nonsense like a madman or, more often, sunk into himself and his cups of mead. Sometimes he would rouse himself and yell out, "Lies! Lies!" when the bards sang about the glorious deeds of their king. Even the older songs, the *thrilling melodies of harp and lute, held no joy for the fading king. Instead of courtly revelry, Arthur sent his knights away on wild quests to recover the magical grail that had been lost, in hopes to restore the fecundity of the land. The knights did not know for what they searched, only that the Pendragon willed it so.*

The king had ordered that the queen's name never be spoken—nor that of her champion—but the people did not forget. In Camelot no one spoke of Gwenhyfar, but in Caerleon the people muttered or talked out right, wagging their heads in consternation as they grumbled, "Tis the loss of our queen that has brought these hard times upon us. The land itself is in sorrow." Indeed, the relationship between Camelot and Caerleon was severed, and the Cymry were ever suspicious and angry at the strange disappearance of their queen. Likewise across the narrow sea in Bretannia, all around Joyeuse Garde where Lancelot had grown up as boy, the story was passed on, and Lancelot's name was remembered.

One day, when the king was drunk on his favorite Breton wine and weeping in his cups, one of his vassals was announced in the great hall of the court. It was Gereint, king of Cornovia where Arthur was born, who had arrived with his wife Enid and their daughter, a maiden named Winifred. They were announced by Sir Cai, who had plotted with Gereint to marry Arthur to the maiden, in hopes that his spirits would be lifted along with the darkness that seemed to have fallen upon his rule and their land.

Arthur lifted his eyes and saw the young Winifred. She had long blonde hair braided and arranged in circlets around her head. She was tiny, fair, and pert with darting eyes the size and color of hazel nuts. She chattered with gay abandon, oblivious to all. It was clear to everyone in the court that she was nothing like Gwenhyfar, who had been tall and regal and elegant in her beauty. Nonetheless, this maiden was full of youthful vigor and potential fertility, and the court prayed that Arthur would be smitten and she might warm his bed, bring some happiness to assuage his sorrows, and produce a legitimate heir to bolster their king, who had aged so severely. And, as the daughter of Gereint, king of Cornovia, their union might bring fecundity back to the land.

The marriage took place at Imbolc, but a terrible storm passed through, rendering the ceremony bleak and dank with a woebegone mood that weighed like a sodden blanket upon the company. Though some of the older knights, like Cai, Blamore, Bedevere and Finbeus, stayed at Camelot with the king, many of the knights were away on quests, and the Lady of the Lake would not deign to come. Her absence, as Arthur's half-sister and as the symbol of the Old Ones and Avalon, was sorely felt by those at court like Cai and Lady Carys, who held to the old ways. The Christians were smug, satisfied and glad at this turn of events, as the pagan rites set them on edge and frightened them. Most of the common people walked away shaking their heads in dismay and fear, unsatisfied and worried for their future.

With Arthur's knights scattered about on quests, Mordred began to hover at the king's side, insinuating himself into daily affairs, acting on the king's behalf and in his name, much to the chagrin of Sir Cai, Sir Bedevere, and the older knights. Years passed in wanderings and uncertainty, and in this tedium Mordred began to make his power over the king known to all.

Winifred did not beget or bear a child. She spent her life riding, playing with her dogs, embroidering and gossiping with her women, spending much of her time with her father and mother in Cornovia. Still, she loved the king in her own way, and sat at his side at events of court, seemingly demur and patient but always eager to get back to her horses and dogs. As time moved on, Arthur and Winifred each went their own way.

Finally, Mordred's ambitious dreams and schemes to take the Pendragon throne came to a peak when he fomented rebellion among the younger knights. Surrounded by his supporters, Mordred went to Gwynedd in the northwestern part of Cymru with a plan to be crowned as tanaiste, the worthy successor, in the traditional way at Dinas Emrys. It was in that mythic place where Merlin had long ago seen the two dragons—one red and one white—beneath the pool, and prophesied the coming of a great king. From there Mordred sent a challenge to Arthur, in which the prince denounced his father's failing power and declared himself high king of Briton.

Arthur, Cai, Bedevere, Finbeus, Bors, Blamore and many of the knights of the original Round Table rode out to battle Sir Mordred and his host. The battle took place in Tregalen, in the Cymru region known as Snowdonia. Twenty-one years after the Battle of Mount Badon, in which Arthur and his forces had routed the Saxons, the king fought his own son. The battle was short and fierce, leaving the field awash in death and carnage. In hand-to-hand combat, Mordred was killed by Arthur, but the king was mortally wounded by his son. Arthur survived long enough to be transported to Avalon by Sir Bedevere, the only knight of the Round Table to live to tell the tale of the final brave actions of Arthur Pendragon in his last stand, at the Battle of Camlann, in the year of 539 Anno Domini.

It was Morgan, the Lady of the Lake, who received her brother's body from the last living knight, Sir Bedevere, who brought his king to be buried near Avalon, not far from the foot of the Tor. Only one year later, seeing in her mirror pool that their time had come to an end, Morgan sent the inhabitants of Avalon away, and with the help of Taliesin, she burned the halls and dwellings of Avalon to the ground. Nothing but the Tor remained.

Asking Father Donnan and the monks of Ynis Witrin to protect and preserve the remains of Arthur Pendragon, her last words to them were, "Guard these bones and preserve all that you have known of Avalon, as our world recedes into the Otherworld. The day will come when the king will rise again, and he will not be broken but whole. His vision of unity for the people of Briton and all those who love this fair land will live eternal." Morgan disappeared with Taliesin and her circle of closest apprentices. Some said she disappeared into the mists, following Nimuë and Myrrdin into the Otherworld.

The monks of Ynis Witrin became the guardians and caretakers of the knowledge of Avalon and its secrets. Twas a great irony that the Christians, who played a role in the disappearance of the tradition of the Old Ones, would be the ones who became the guardians of the relics of Avalon.

When Winifred died many years later, with the old ways of the Summer Country dissolving more each year, the monks exhumed Arthur's bones and placed her small body at the feet of the king. They were buried together deep in the grounds *of the monastery, beneath a stone pyramid that marked the sight. Avalon and Camelot were gone, scattered by the winds of change. The Knights of the Round Table had perished or disappeared to live simple lives as farmers and gentry.*

And so, this chronicle is written by Tammas Pender, two hundred years later. Even today, the hearts of the people still long for the golden days when Arthur and Gwenhyfar ruled the land with their first knight, Sir Lancelot.

Tammas paused, his work almost finished. He stared into the fire, pondering the strange sense that plagued him—not of completion but of a living stream that flowed from the past through the present and into the future, a continuous thread of shining light that was woven through the narration of the histoire. Dipping the quill again into the pot of ink, he gathered his strength to write the last prophetic words of his tale.

Some say that Arthur's mission failed, but this chronicler looks with an open heart and a discerning eye. Life after life the great warrior king seeks to be reunited with his queen and her champion—the true knight, his best knight—as the wise of Avalon say that these three companions of the soul travel together through time. At the very least, they may somehow represent, symbolically, a part of every person who quests for the sacred grail that shines within the human heart. Despite their foibles as human beings, they were uplifted, even exalted, by a time of chivalry, beauty, and honor, when great deeds were accomplished. Although Briton could not hold against the invaders, and England was destined to be born from the merging of many peoples, during the time of Camelot a noble sentiment flourished—an unsurpassed mood that championed the ardour of love. Truly, the Camelot of Arthur and Gwenhyfar and Lancelot appeared in the world and then disappeared, a brief flame, leaving behind an unforgettable legacy for all times—the vision of a golden age of noble ideals, of gentle, strong, and wise women, and of knightly virtue among gallant men. It was an age of chivalry.

With the blessings of my spiritual benefactor, Father Bregoret, this chronicle has been compiled by Brother Tammas Pender, monk of Glastonbury in 698, a scion of Arthur by Lady Garwen and their son, Rowland Pender. As their direct descendant, within these pages I impart the secret knowledge passed down to me through my ancestral grandmother, the Lady Garwen of Camelot, my grandmother, Lady Gwyneth Pender, and through my father, Sir Morgan Pender of Ynis Witrin, known also as Glastonbury. I pray whoever reads this histoire may benefit from this tale, for those who know the truth will remain forever changed by the lives of Arthur and the true queen, Gwenhyfar, her champion Sir Lancelot, and by Camelot and the Knights of the Round Table of Caerleon.

The next day Tammas handed a thick stack of vellum, tied with leather thongs, to Father Bregoret, who took the manuscript to the monastery church and stored it carefully amongst the sacred relics and books and altars presided over by carven images of Mary, the Mother of Jesus, and Mary Magdalene, the Lady of Light. Less than a month later, Tammas took his last breaths, and the monks mourned his going, for he was the last of his line, and with him went a vast pool of memories.

The histoire remained hidden in the Old Church of Glastonbury until it was removed for safeguarding, at peril to their lives, during the fire of 1184 by those monks of Glastonbury who called themselves in secret the Company of Avalon. In 1539, at the time of the Dissolution of the Monasteries, the manuscript disappeared along with the bones of King Arthur and Winifred, his second queen.

www.ingramcontent.com/pod-product-compliance
Lightning Source LLC
Chambersburg PA
CBHW071952290426
44109CB00018B/2002